COCAINE WARS

FAT FREDDIE THOMPSON AND THE CRUMLIN/ DRIMNAGH FEUD

AUTHOR BIOGRAPHY

Mick McCaffrey is the author of the best-seller *The Irish Scissor Sisters*. He is news editor of the *Sunday Tribune*. As security editor at both the *Sunday Tribune* and *Evening Herald*, he has specialised in crime journalism for the last seven years.

Praise for *The Irish Scissor Sisters*

'This is a unique insight into the underbelly of a 'new' Ireland. Riveting.'
Joe Duffy, RTÉ

COCAINE WARS

FAT FREDDIE THOMPSON
AND THE CRUMLIN/
DRIMNAGH FEUD

Mick McCaffrey

MERLIN
PUBLISHING

MERLIN
PUBLISHING

First published in 2010 by
Merlin Publishing
Newmarket Hall, Cork Street
Dublin 8, Ireland
Tel: +353 1 453 5866
Fax: +353 1 453 5930
publishing@merlin.ie
www.merlinwolfhound.com

ISBN 978 1907162 084

A CIP catalogue record for this book is available from the
British Library.

10 9 8 7 6 5 4 3 2 1

Typeset by Artwerk Ltd
Cover design by Graham Thew Design
Front cover image courtesy of www.bigstockphoto.com
Printed and bound by CPI Cox & Wyman, Great Britain

For Jennifer Stevens

ACKNOWLEDGEMENTS

Thanks to the many Gardaí and members of the legal profession who gave up their time to speak to me. Their insight and knowledge was an invaluable help. This book would not have been possible without them.

Thanks to *Sunday Tribune* Editor, Noirín Hegarty, and Deputy Editor, Diarmuid Doyle, for giving me the time to write this. Maureen Gillespie and Mark Condren from the *Sunday Tribune* picture department were always happy to organise photos at short notice.

The advice given to me by journalists Ken Foy from the *Irish Daily Star Sunday* and Jim Cusack of the *Sunday Independent* was an enormous help, and was very much appreciated.

Gerry Curran from the Courts Service Press Office was always available to answer any queries; as was the staff of the Irish Prison Service Press Office.

Thanks to Chenile Keogh, Managing Director of Merlin Publishing, for all her help and support. Thanks also to Merlin's Robert Doran for copy-editing and proofreading. Thanks to solicitor Kieran Kelly for his help and suggestions.

Thanks to Kenneth Swan, Donal Galvin, Brian Hurl, Ronan Bent, Dave Dehora, Gareth Curley, Mark Hilliard and Brendan Cronin. Also, thanks to Tim Tuomey for giving me the encouragement to get into journalism. Thanks to Ian Mallon, Deputy Editor of the *Evening Herald*, for giving me my break.

Thanks also to my mother and father, sisters, brothers-in-law, and nieces and nephews.

Finally, to Jennifer Stevens, who encouraged me to write this book from the outset, even though it was a difficult topic. I wouldn't have been able to finish it without her support and advice.

CONTENTS

GANG MEMBERS
* = Deceased

Thompson/Gavin gang and associates

'Fat' Freddie Thompson
Declan Gavin*
Aidan Gavin
Paddy Doyle*
Gavin Byrne*
Darren Geoghegan*
David Byrne
Liam Brannigan
Karl Dempsey
Graham Whelan
Ritchie Thompson
Eoin O'Connor
Paul Warren*
Philip Griffiths
Albert Doyle
Christopher 'Git' McDonagh*

Freddie Thompson's gang is aligned to the McCarthy/Dundon gang in Limerick.

Rattigan gang and associates

Brian Rattigan
Shay O'Byrne*
Joey Rattigan*
Eddie Redmond
Eddie Rice
John Roche*
Noel Roche*
Wayne Zambra*
Mr X
Anthony Cannon*
Trevor Brunton
Gary Bryan*
Shane Maloney
Wayne McNally
Karl Kavanagh
Eric Wansboro

Brian Rattigan's gang is aligned to the Keane/Collopy faction in Limerick.

Other victims
Ian Kenny*, Eddie McCabe*, Terry Dunleavy*

INTRODUCTION

They started out as most criminals do – robbing cars, joyriding and getting involved in petty thieving. They were boyhood friends and neighbours. They had gone to the same primary school, and those that continued in education also ended up in the same secondary school. They were a tight group – around ten friends who were fiercely loyal and protective of each other. If you took on one, you took them all on. That was the way it was. Crumlin and Drimnagh towards the end of the 1990s was a tough place. Notorious criminals like 'The General', Martin Cahill; 'The Viper', Martin Foley; Seamus 'Shavo' Hogan and Dublin's original drug baron, Larry Dunne, all hailed from the area. Crumlin and Drimnagh are often referred to as the 'home of organised crime in Ireland'. Many in the local community treated these old-school gangsters like Robin Hood type figures. The gang looked up to these men, admired their lifestyles and made a vow that one day they would be like them and would have what they had – one way or another. Their chance came earlier than they anticipated. In 1996, *Sunday Independent* journalist Veronica Guerin was murdered at the behest of John Gilligan, the country's biggest drug importer. An unprecedented wave of public outrage followed, and the government made Gilligan its public enemy number one. A massive Garda investigation put Gilligan and his gang out of business, and almost overnight a major vacuum developed in Dublin's gangland. The gang had started working for John Gilligan a few years before his downfall and had started to move up the drug dealing ladder. With Gilligan permanently out of the way, the young and eager gang were perfectly posititoned to take over, and did so with gusto. The gang developed contacts with two Irish expatriates in Spain and then with contacts further afield. They built up a supply line and began importing millions of euro worth of cocaine, heroin and ecstasy into the capital. As sweeteners, and to show their appreciation to the gang for its business, the foreign suppliers threw in dozens of high-powered weapons with each shipment. The mob began to make tens of thousands of euro each week dealing drugs, and had soon conquered the market around Crumlin, Drimnagh and Dublin's south-inner city. The future seemed bright, but a petty squabble saw the gang permanently disintegrate – with deadly results.

Two separate groups formed, with Brian Rattigan leading one faction, and 'Fat' Freddie Thompson taking over the other. Over the next nine years 16, people would lose their lives as part of the feud, either directly or indirectly – the average victim being just 23 years old. The falling out of old friends quickly became the deadliest gangland feud in the history of the state. Gardaí struggled to keep on top of hostilities, with literally hundreds of tit-for-tat incidents being recorded. The Gardaí's dedication and hard work undoubtedly saved lives, but the accepted rule in the area of never cooperating with the police made the detectives' lives very difficult, and they were always fighting to keep a lid on the feud. The deep hatred that the two rival gangs had for each other made the frequent peace efforts futile. The feud did not just have an impact on the lives of the dead victims; dozens of other lives have been permanently destroyed. From the innocent residents caught up in attacks of mistaken identity to the relatives of feuding criminals becoming virtual prisoners in their own homes, unable to even drop their children to school because of the very real fear that they could be attacked and murdered. It is a feud that has driven a deep wedge between what was once a very close-knit community. Many of the criminals who have been central players also desperately tried to get out but found that they were in too far. One notorious hitman took to driving around Dublin dressed as a woman, so he wouldn't be recognised and shot. While the money man for one of the mobs managed to evade the law and invest hundreds of thousands of euro in property, he wasn't able to escape a bullet to the head from his own gang. For the first time, the story is told of how one gang leader orchestrated murders from the comfort of his prison cell, with only his beloved pet budgie for company. The Crumlin-Drimnagh feud has changed the political landscape in this country. It has resulted in one Justice Minister nearly having to fall on his sword because of an ill-conceived remark. It has directly led to a crack anti-gangland Garda unit being formed and the introduction of draconian legislation to allow Gardaí to permanently take feuding criminals off the street. Nearly a decade after the feud first began, it is more entrenched than ever, and there is little sign that it will ever end.

A new generation of feuding criminals have emerged and is taking the battle forward, even though most of the original gang members are either dead or serving lengthy jail sentences. This will surely mean that Gardaí will have their hands full over the next few years, and that even more young people will be sucked into this senseless feud. Towards the end of the 1980s, Larry Dunne spoke to Gardaí about the next generation of criminals. He said: 'If you think we're bad, wait until you see what's coming behind us.' This quote has never been more apt.

The Crumlin-Drimnagh feud will probably be the deadliest that the country will ever see. It has given the area an undeserved notoriety and divided what once was a close-knit community. Sixteen people have now lost their lives and there is little doubt that the murders will keep on happening, all because of a petty falling out between a group friends.

ONE

A feud is born

Declan Gavin was tired after spending more than a day bagging and tagging the two kilograms of cocaine and 49,000 ecstasy tablets. He had booked into the Holiday Inn hotel on Dublin's Pearse Street the day before, Thursday, 9 March 2000, and along with Graham Whelan and Philip Griffiths had worked through the night breaking up the drugs haul into individual deals. The drugs would be worth around €1.7m on the street, and 19-year-old Gavin and his gang expected to make a profit of nearly €1m on their investment. Things were going well for Deco Gavin of late. He was quickly becoming a very wealthy young man because of his burgeoning drug dealing business, which was supplying large amounts of cocaine in his native Drimnagh and Crumlin.

The three men had come to the Holiday Inn well equipped for their work. The two kilos of coke came in a solid block and they used hammers to break up the drugs into smaller blocks. They then put these into coffee grinders and blenders to crush them into a fine powder, which was mixed with glucose to make the finished product. The drugs were then packed into one gram deals – about three lines of cocaine – which would sell for up to €80 a bag. Once the individual bags were all sold on the streets, the gang would net around €750,000.

The e tablets would fetch at least €10 and possibly up to €15 each, depending on how pure they were. So although the trio were putting in the work, they would be rewarded handsomely.

Generally, drugs gangs can make a minimum of five times their investment on a shipment and possibly up to eight or nine times what they paid, if they break the drugs up in the most efficient way, so the job was a very important one.

Declan Gavin should really not have been in the Holiday Inn in the first place. Around Dublin there are three or four expert 'cutters' of cocaine who specialise in breaking the drugs up into individual deals. Gavin did this by mixing glucose, a white powder, with the pure cocaine, although the mixing agent of choice today is Lidocaine, which is a local anesthetic often used by dentists. Lidocaine numbs the sensors in the membrane of a drug user's nose and gives them a good buzz, leading them to believe that the cocaine is stronger than it actually is. Cocaine in Ireland is very weak, and masking agents like Lidocaine, Procaine and Xylocaine are vital in fooling users into thinking that their drugs are purer than they actually are.

A good cutter can make four diluted kilos out of one relatively pure kilo, which means that the profit margin is increased dramatically. However, Declan Gavin did not trust cutters because he believed that if they spent a day or two mixing cocaine, it was inevitable that they would steal some. This was a short-sighted attitude on his part, because neither he nor his two accomplices were skilled in mixing cocaine. It would prove to be a fatal error on his behalf.

In order to get repeat custom, you need to ensure that the cocaine you sell is always of good quality; otherwise the user will go elsewhere. It was all about the profit for Gavin though, and he wasn't prepared to pay an expert cutter the €35,000 fee that is standard for cutting down two kilos of cocaine. So he really shouldn't have been in the Holiday Inn with the drugs at all, because the first rule of being a successful drug dealer is never to touch the product. This is a principle that was adopted by Ireland's first major drug importers, the Dunne family, in the early 1980s. Larry Dunne was the leader of the family and the mastermind behind the smuggling racket. Foot soldiers who used to handle heroin on his behalf often joked, 'Larry doesn't carry', because Dunne knew that the Gardaí would have great difficulty linking him to any seizures if he wasn't in possession of the drugs.

Declan Gavin was one of the leaders of the drugs gang that controlled distribution in Dublin 12. There were about ten senior members of the gang. Whelan and Griffiths were only foot soldiers brought in to break up the coke under Gavin's watchful eye. The gang members had clubbed together to buy the batch of cocaine and ecstasy and would probably have paid about €170,000 upfront to buy the two kilos of cocaine. However, it is also possible that they were given a kilo on credit because they were such good customers of their Dutch supplier. Just a euro or two would have been paid up front for each ecstasy tablet. Gavin had probably personally invested €35,000 in the shipment, so it was in his interests to make sure that things went smoothly.

Organising drugs shipments is a logistical nightmare and is very costly, hence the temptation to dilute the finished product and make as much money as is possible. When a drug dealer organises a shipment with his Dutch or Spanish supplier, it is not just a case of popping over on a flight, packing the drugs into a suitcase and returning home the next day. Professional drug importers send at least two 'mules' to the Netherlands to pick up the drugs. They are supervised by a senior and trusted member of the drugs gang, who accompanies them and always watches from a distance to make sure that nothing goes wrong and that the mules do not cream drugs off the main stash. This necessitates booking hotel rooms and organising flights, often with false passports, so that the authorities don't find out the real identity of those travelling. This is a very expensive business. Then there is the matter of organising the drugs to be driven back to Ireland. A long-distance lorry driver is usually paid around €30,000 a trip to bring the drugs in through Dublin or Rosslare Ports. So before any drugs arrive in the country, up to €100,000 can be spent on the logistics. This is before unforeseen problems, such as a mule carrying cash through Dublin Airport on the outward journey being caught by Customs and having the money seized, or the Gardaí getting a tip-off and confiscating the cocaine as it comes into the country.

Even arriving at the hotel without getting caught had been something of a victory, but there was still serious work to do before the gang could cash in. Gavin, Whelan and Griffiths had rented two adjoining rooms in the hotel. They worked shifts, with two of the men breaking up the coke, while the third caught up on some sleep. The Holiday Inn traditionally attracts tourists eager to see the sights of the capital, and, usually, the vast majority of guests are out during the day and return to their rooms in the afternoon, leaving them vacant for most of the day. The three men told hotel staff that they did not want to be disturbed and turned away the cleaners when they came to change the bed linen. When this happened two days in a row, a vigilant member of staff became suspicious and wondered what three Dublin men in their late teens were doing in two hotel rooms for well over a day without coming out once. He reported his suspicions to hotel management, and Gardaí at nearby Pearse Street station were informed. Five uniformed officers came to the hotel to see what was going on. They knocked on the door, identified themselves as Gardaí and ordered the men to open it. There was no response, so the door had to be forcibly opened. Graham Whelan and Philip Griffiths were caught red-handed. Griffiths was observed running over to a window and throwing a blue holdall out onto the car park below. It was subsequently found to contain cocaine. The two men offered no resistance and were quickly cuffed while reinforcements were called. The Gardaí knew that they were dealing with a major drugs haul. In 2000, a €1.7m haul would have been the equivalent of finding €10m worth of drugs today because drugs were far more difficult to source at that time. The Gardaí burst into the adjoining room hopeful of finding more drugs. They found Declan Gavin lying dozing on a bed, but he was not physically holding any drugs, although there was cocaine in the room. Gavin was also arrested and taken to Pearse Street. Coffee grinders, weighing equipment and packages for bagging the drugs were also recovered, as well as other drug mixing paraphernalia. A major Garda investigation was launched under the command of Detective Inspector John Fitzpatrick. At the station none of the three men cooperated with the investigating detectives. They were all used to being quizzed by Gardaí and knew that the drill was to keep quiet and say absolutely nothing.

Declan Gavin was questioned for all of Friday evening and Saturday. However, because he was not actually in the process of handling the drugs, the Director of Public Prosecutions (DPP) decided that he should not be immediately charged, but that investigations should continue and a full file be forwarded for consideration in due course. On the Saturday evening, a disbelieving Declan Gavin was released from custody without charge. His two pals were not as lucky. On the Monday morning, 17-year-old Graham Whelan and 19-year-old Philip Griffiths appeared before Dublin District Court, where they were both charged with possession of drugs with intent to supply. The pair were given bail. Back in Crumlin the post-mortem immediately began over how the cops had found out that the drugs were being cut in the hotel room. Suspicion soon fell on Declan Gavin.

The main person pointing the finger was Gavin's friend and one of his main partners in crime, Brian Rattigan. Rattigan, a 20-year-old from Cooley Road in Drimnagh, and other members of the gang could not believe that he had been freed without being charged, and the word soon spread that he was a Garda informant. There was no evidence to prove this and it wasn't actually the case, but Gavin was labelled a tout and he and Brian Rattigan fell out spectacularly, with the gang splitting in two amid serious recriminations.

Rattigan wanted to be paid for the drugs that were seized, but Gavin put it down to an occupational hazard and laughed, declaring that he wouldn't pay Rattigan a penny of his €35,000 investment. Gavin also accused Rattigan of having touted to the police, and it was obvious that the two sides would not be able to reach any common ground. Both men were hot-headed and more than prepared to use violence and intimidation against any enemy or perceived enemy. A dispute that had been building had now escalated, and it was obvious that there would inevitably be bloodshed before a truce was declared.

The suspicions that Gavin was a 'rat' did not come out of thin air, and the fact was that he had history of avoiding charges for the possession of large quantities of illegal drugs. On 14 August 1999, Gavin fell into a trap set up by the Garda National Drugs Unit (GNDU) at Ballymount Cross in Dublin 12. The GNDU operation, which was led by Detective Inspector Brian Sutton, Detective Sergeant Pat Walsh and Detective Sergeant Christy Mangan, was set up after intelligence was received that a large number of ecstasy tablets were being moved by criminals from Crumlin. Gardaí had been watching a white van from 6.00am that morning, when it picked up a number of cardboard boxes in Balbriggan from another car. In the early afternoon, Gardaí stopped the van, which was being driven by 26-year-old Donal Keenan, from Galtymore Close in Drimnagh. The 30-year-old passenger, Thomas Delaney, was also from Galtymore Close. There were 100,000 ecstasy tablets, worth up to €1.5m, wrapped in plastic bags and packed in cardboard boxes in the back of the van. The M50 in Dublin was under construction at the time, and there was a large amount of traffic in the area after a major traffic jam had developed. Delaney and Keenan were cuffed and taken away by DS Pat Walsh, but DI Brian Sutton noticed that Delaney's mobile phone had been ringing incessantly while the arrests had been taking place. Sutton answered the phone, and there was a man with a thick Dublin accent at the other end who asked, 'Is everything ok?' DI Sutton said that he was a member of Dublin Fire Brigade and there had been an accident involving a white van, and that the two occupants had been injured and were being rushed to Tallaght Hospital by ambulance. At that moment, an ambulance happened to go by the arrest scene with its sirens on. The man at the other end of the phone seemed very panicked and quickly hung up. Gardaí were sitting in an unmarked car waiting for the van to be towed away, when a man approached it, slid open the door and attempted to take the drugs. He was quickly arrested and identification found in his wallet revealed him to be Declan Gavin. The GNDU officers didn't know who he was and were not expecting him to be there. He had been shadowing the drugs van in a car to make sure that the delivery went smoothly, but had become separated in the heavy traffic. The car was being driven by a notorious drug dealer from the north-inner city, Christopher 'Bouncer' Hutch, who had invested in the shipment. Hutch was not arrested. When Gavin lost site of his friends, he rang the phone and thought that Brian Sutton was really from the Fire Brigade because he had heard the ambulance siren with his own ears. Thinking that his two friends were injured, he rushed up to the van to get the drugs before Gardaí came to investigate the supposed traffic accident. Again, he was caught red-handed, but the DPP decided that he should not be charged. Because he was not driving the van, was not a passenger in it and had not touched the drugs, there was not sufficient proof that they belonged to him. While Gavin appeared to have the number of lives normally associated with cats, his friends were, once again, not so fortunate. In January 2001, Thomas Delaney was jailed for seven years after being found guilty of having the ecstasy with intent for sale and supply. In court Delaney said he was paid just £300 for ferrying the drugs and that he 'wasn't the main man' in the operation, but he refused to reveal Gavin's name. Two days before he was due in court, Delaney answered a call to his door at 3.30am and was shot at point blank range. He was lucky to survive. Gardaí believe that people who had been involved in importing the seized ecstasy wanted him dead so he wouldn't inform on them from the dock. The threat obviously worked, because Delaney wisely didn't say a word against them. Donal Keenan pleaded guilty to the offence and he was jailed for five years.

Declan Gavin was given the benefit of the doubt after the Ballymount arrest, but lightning doesn't strike twice, and when he was released after the Holiday Inn, the consensus was that he was a Garda agent, which can be a fatal thing to be accused of. Just a few months after he was freed, the Gardaí did send a completed file to the DPP, and orders came back to charge him. He was subsequently brought before the courts, and a trial date was scheduled for October 2001. But the tout label had stuck and there was no way that he and Rattigan could mend fences now.

In February 2001, Graham Whelan, who lived in Clonard Road in Drimnagh, pleaded guilty to possession of the drugs found at the Holiday Inn. Judge Elizabeth Dunne heard that Whelan was 17 years old at the time of the offence and was being influenced by older, more ruthless criminals. The mandatory sentence for possession of such a large quantity of drugs was ten years imprisonment. Sergeant Seamus Boland from Pearse Street gave evidence that Whelan had told detectives that he could 'do ten years on his head' and had failed to cooperate with them. Judge Dunne decided to waive the mandatory ten years because of Whelan's young age and the fact that he had pleaded guilty. He was handed a six-year jail sentence, which would not start until October 2001 because Whelan was already serving a sentence for assault, which he had committed while out on bail after the Holiday Inn seizure.

The previous week had seen Philip Griffiths, who was from Rafters Road in Drimnagh, appear before the same judge to face his punishment. Griffiths, who was then 20, also pleaded guilty. Senior Counsel Barry White, who was defending, said that Griffiths was not in charge of the operation and only ranked number two of the three men involved (the main figure being Declan Gavin). Griffiths told Judge Dunne that he was awarded £15,500 in compensation from his job in 1998, and then left employment and lived off the award. He then began using cocaine and quickly became addicted. The money was soon spent, and he fell into debt with Gavin, who was supplying him with his drugs. He told the court: 'When I ran out of money, he put it on the slate, and I was then approached by this person to bring drugs from one point to another as part payment for my debts and continuing addiction.' Judge Dunne said that because of the legislation that required a mandatory 10-year-term for quantities of drugs over £10,000, her hands were somewhat tied. She said she did not want to see Griffiths 'sacrificed as a lesson to others'. Taking into account his age and the fact that he had weaned himself off drugs, the judge sentenced Griffiths to seven years in jail, and said she would review the sentence in October 2004, saying: 'It makes me sad to see someone of his age come to court on such a serious matter.' Local TD, the late Tony Gregory, lashed the sentence as being 'crazy' and too lenient, saying: 'It's hard to take these sentences seriously. There's absolutely no consistency.'

* * *

Declan Gavin was born on 19 September 1980. He lived with his mother, Pauline, sister and brother, Aidan, on Mourne Road, Drimnagh. He was a single man and had no children. He was popular with women and always had plenty of female attention. He was unemployed and made money by selling vast quantities of illegal drugs. Despite the fact that he never had a job and never paid tax in his life, Gavin never had to sign on for unemployment assistance, because he was making so much money from dealing. Despite his youth, Declan Gavin was heavily involved in the large-scale sale and supply of heroin, cocaine and ecstasy in the Crumlin and Drimnagh area, and had built up a reputation with Gardaí across Dublin because of the sheer size of his burgeoning drug business. When he was in his teens, Gavin and some of his friends, including Brian Rattigan, began to realise the potential wealth that could be accumulated from drug importation.

They managed to get in touch with members of the infamous drug gang led by John Gilligan. They worked out a deal where they received regular shipments of ecstasy and cocaine, effectively working as wholesalers for 'Factory' John's gang. They received a commission, while the majority of the profit went back to Gilligan. The aspiring young drug dealers made a few quid for themselves but they were bringing drugs money back to Gilligan by the sack full – literally – and they were the ones who were taking all the risks. As they became more established, the Gilligan gang allowed them to go to Amsterdam and meet with the suppliers and organise the shipments of the drugs back to Ireland. It was a lot of risk for very little reward, and Brian Rattigan and Declan Gavin were getting sick of it. They were determined to cut out the middleman in order to make far bigger profits, and they got their chance after the Gilligan gang imploded. In the summer of 1996 John Gilligan arranged for the murder of crime journalist

Veronica Guerin, and the government and Gardaí launched an unprecedented blitz on him and his cronies. A special Garda unit, under Detective Inspector Tony Hickey, was set up in Lucan Garda Station to investigate the murder, and many senior members were either jailed or fled the jurisdiction. The Criminal Assets Bureau (CAB) was also established, and began to forensically examine the assets of major crime figures and seize all assets that could not be explained or that were bought with the proceeds of crime. Gilligan and the majority of his gang were convicted of drug dealing on a massive scale, and the gang was effectively broken up over night. The result was that a major vacuum developed in the distribution of drugs in and around Dublin's south inner-city, and a drugs drought occurred across the entire city. This resulted in a major increase in the number of robberies and burglaries on chemists and GP practices by desperate junkies needing to get high. Another initiative of the government and the Garda Commissioner in 1995 was perhaps more important than the establishment of CAB but is rarely mentioned. The Garda National Drugs Unit (GNDU) was set up under the leadership of experienced Chief Superintendent Kevin Carty, and its aim was to dismantle organised drugs networks involved in large scale importation and distribution. The GNDU also investigates international drug importation and cooperates with international agencies to ensure that intelligence is shared. Over the years, the 50 or so GNDU detectives would seize tens of millions of euro worth of drugs that led to dozens of successful prosecutions.

* * *

Deco Gavin and Brian Rattigan knew that they could easily fill the void. They had been dealing with the Amsterdam supplier for a couple of years by this stage and were trusted customers. As far as the supplier was concerned, they always

paid on time and were professional to deal with, so they were
hooked up with their own supply. Over the years, they would
extend their supply route to include Spain. As well as
sending over the cocaine and ecstasy, the Dutch contacts
would include free firearms with each shipment as a
sweetener. Up to 50 guns of every variety came with the
drugs. This meant that the group had access to lethal
firearms, such as Glock 9mm pistols, and assault rifles, such
as the infamous AK-47. For the first time in Ireland, lethal
fragmentation grenades were also imported with drugs and
Gardaí would later seize several of them. The gang would
show over the next few years that they were not afraid to use
the deadly arsenal.

The end of the 1990s was a boom time in Ireland. The
Celtic Tiger economy meant that many middle-class people
had unprecedented access to money. This rise in wealth also
saw a rise in drug use, especially the use of cocaine for leisure
purposes. It marked the beginning of the cocaine epidemic
that continues to this day. Besides the increase in drug use
amongst the middle classes, there was also a lot of drug use in
working-class Dublin. Many were hooked on heroin and
required their daily fix, whether or not they had the means
to afford it. Crumlin and Drimnagh, not far from the city
centre in the Garda 'G' District were prime examples.

In the early 1930s, Dublin Corporation began a large
building programme in the area. Families from Dublin's inner
city were moved from overcrowded conditions and were
relocated to Crumlin (*Croimghlinn* – 'Crooked Glen') and
Drimnagh (*Druimneach* – 'Ridged Lands'). Due to many
reasons, the area has had a long history of drug problems and
suffers high levels of unemployment and it has always had a
large number of drug addicts. It quickly became little more
than a ghetto, with the authorities failing to build any
infrastructure to support the growing population or give the
residents anything to do. Many of them inevitably drifted

into crime. Detectives who work in Dublin 12 say it is a unique area when it comes to policing. From the time the first house was built, there was always a suspicion about the Gardaí. An unwritten rule developed that you should never, ever talk to the police. Criminals in nearby Tallaght and the city centre will engage with Gardaí and talk to them, but almost without exception in Dublin 12, the suspects, keep their heads down and don't answer a single question, certainly not one that is on the record. In certain parts of Crumlin and Drimnagh, a Garda informant is regarded as being worse than a paedophile. This suspicion about Gardaí led to some of the country's most infamous criminals coming out of Crumlin. It was home to 'The General', Martin Cahill; 'The Viper', Martin Foley, and his ruthless henchman, Seamus 'Shavo' Hogan. One senior detective once called Crumlin 'the home of organised crime in Ireland'. Because of the poverty there, Crumlin and Drimnagh proved to be extremely lucrative drug dealing turf.

Most of the original members of the gang led by Brian Rattigan and Declan Gavin had grown up together around a small area in Drimnagh and Crumlin and were regarded as being extremely tight and close-knit. The original, founding members of the gang were Brian Rattigan, Declan Gavin and his brother, Aidan, brothers John and Noel Roche, Shay O'Byrne, Eddie Redmond, Darren Geoghegan, Gavin Byrne and another man who cannot be named for legal reasons and will be referred to as Mr X throughout this book. The boyhood friends all went to the same school in Drimnagh and had played for the same football team and been members of the same boxing club. The members were extremely violent and determined to make serious amounts of money. They were not about to allow anybody get in their way of their ambition. They started out as petty thieves and joyriders and many were users of drugs, especially cocaine, and often mixed them with bodybuilding steroids. A night out would start with ten or 12 pints of beer followed by two or three ecstasy tablets and four or five lines of cocaine. This made them extremely unstable and paranoid, meaning they would fly off the handle over the slightest thing and were often suspicious of each other's motives, thinking that other members were plotting against them. The first sign of tension in the gang appeared in early 1998, when a dispute arose between various members of the gang over some money that had apparently gone missing. There was a series of tit-for-tat assaults and criminal damage was done to cars and houses of the core gang members. These assaults and incidents of criminal damage eventually spread out to target friends, families and even unconnected relatives of the core gang members. This led to other individuals from outside the immediate gang becoming involved in the growing feud. People like 'Fat' Freddie Thompson from Maryland in Dublin 8, and Paddy Doyle from Portland Row, in the north-inner city, were dragged into the hostilities. This meant that what was essentially an internal gang feud warped into something far greater and extended far further than Drimnagh and Crumlin.

The best account of the origins of the dispute was given to Gardaí by Freddie Thompson when he was arrested on 25 March 1999, on suspicion of shooting at the house of Noel Roche. Roche was then 21 years old and was one of the main members of the gang. Thompson told detectives that the feud first kicked off in 1998, when Derek Lodge set Declan Gavin's motorbike alight. Lodge was 23 and lived in Kilworth Road in Drimnagh with his parents, his two brothers and sister. He was a mechanic and had the reputation of being a difficult individual who constantly harassed his neighbours and was generally a troublemaker. He worked in a small portacabin at the front of the family home and often sold bric-a-brac at various markets around Dublin. He was a violent hothead and had attacked two

Gardaí with a hatchet and threatened to 'cut them into f***ing pieces' after they searched his house in 1998. Lodge became part of the Gavin/Rattigan gang through his friendship with Noel and John Roche. Lodge and the Roche brothers had lived on the same street all their lives, although Lodge would not have been close to either Brian Rattigan or Declan Gavin. When Gavin's beloved motorbike was burnt out, he went ballistic and tried to petrol bomb the Lodge's family home. This led to Lodge retaliating and burning Declan Gavin's mother's car with acid, thereby worsening the dispute. Acid attacks on cars, or 'nitromortizing', as criminals in the area call it, is a tradition in Crumlin and is seen as sending an effective message because the acid burns deep into the car's bodywork, meaning that it has to be re-sprayed.

Over the next year or so, verbal arguments, fist fights and criminal damage to vehicles and houses were commonplace. Then more serious incidents occurred, such as shots being fired through doors and windows of houses in the early hours of the morning. In most cases Gardaí only learned of these incidents through informants, and when they were made aware that something criminal had occurred, their investigations were stymied by the fact that they usually received little or no cooperation from the injured parties. There was a feeling that 'This is Crumlin; Thanks, but we take care of our own problems.' The Gardaí were certainly not seen as being part of the solution.

Brian Rattigan took Derek Lodge's side in the argument over Declan Gavin's motorbike. This was because of his close friendship with John and Noel Roche. Mr X, Shay O'Byrne, the boyfriend of Rattigan's sister, Sharon and Eddie Redmond sided with Rattigan.

Because of Rattigan's dominant personality and bullying ways, he did not command loyalty from the whole gang, so others in the group were more than prepared to side with

Declan Gavin after the row with Lodge. Staying loyal to Gavin were his brother Aidan, Gavin Byrne, Darren Geoghegan, Freddie Thompson and Paddy Doyle.

Brian Rattigan and Declan Gavin rose to the top of the gang because they were regarded as being intelligent. Gavin was genuinely smart and had a gift for drug dealing. He had the brain of an accountant and everything was stored in his head – he did not need records. If the gang needed a couple of mules to travel to the Netherlands at short notice, Gavin would immediately know who to choose and would know their mobile phone numbers off the top of his head. If the gang gave half a kilo of coke to a subcontractor five weeks ago at €35,000 upfront with the rest due a month later, he always knew that an extra €800 in interest was due, because the balance of €15,000 was a week late. This might not sound like much of a gift, but many members of the gang were not considered very bright. Because of his smarts, the gang naturally gravitated towards him. Freddie Thompson in particular was a big Deco Gavin fan and spoke about him in reverential terms. Brian Rattigan was not considered as smart, but he had people who were close to him who were very intelligent and knew how to plan the deals and organise the cash. This meant that he was also popular. So, when the split occurred, it was natural that Gavin would lead his side, and that Brian Rattigan would be the boss of the other faction.

* * *

Rattigan was born on 20 July 1980, and lived at Cooley Road in Drimnagh with his mother, Christine, who was generally known as Dinah; his brother Joey and sister, Sharon. His other brother, Richard, split his time between the family home and his girlfriend's house. Brian's father, Ricky Rattigan, had a massive heart attack while asleep in bed in 1995, and died. It is believed that Sharon Rattigan went to wake up her father but could not rouse him. Then Brian went into the bedroom and realised his dad was dead. The pair are said to have been very close, and the death had a profound effect on the whole family.

Brian Rattigan is involved in a long-term relationship with Natasha McEnroe from Captains Road in Crumlin, the couple have one child. He previously worked with a builders' providers company and as a labourer on road building projects, but had been unemployed since he was released from serving a prison sentence for assault, in February 2001. In April 2001, he was convicted of two counts of assault causing harm at Trim Circuit Court, following an incident that occurred in Navan in June 1999, during which he beat two youths with a sewer rod and a bottle, causing both men serious head injuries. One of the victims required 24 stitches, and the other youth needed 30 stitches and even a blood transfusion, such was the extent of his injuries. Brian Rattigan had the reputation of being a very heavy drinker and a regular user of large amounts of cocaine and other illegal drugs. Gardaí regarded Rattigan as being particularly violent and dangerous, and at least two officers would be present at all times whenever they were dealing with him.

Although tension between the two factions was very high, they bizarrely continued to do business together. This was down to the fact that they were making so much money, so pragmatism prevailed. Although a shot might have been fired into a gang member's house on a Friday night, the following morning the victim and perpetrator would meet to break up a fresh drugs shipment.

It is estimated that at the time of the Holiday Inn seizure, the main members of the gang were making at least €6,000 cash in a good week, after all their expenses, Garda seizures, bad debts and everything else were taken into account. Teenagers making such serious money are often tempted by the finer things in life, and the Rattigan and Gavin gang members were no different. Despite the fact that the CAB could seize assets that could not be accounted for, the gang members made no attempt to hide their wealth and reveled in the fact that they were earning such vast amounts of money. Some bought top-of-the-range BMW jeeps that had come on the market in Ireland for the first time and cost over €70,000; others invested in buying or renting penthouse apartments across Dublin, in Spain and further afield. Taking four or five long-haul holidays a year was standard practice, and Declan Gavin never left his house without having at least €500 cash on him. The majority of the gang members did not have jobs but had lifestyles akin to the country's top bank executives.

The first documented feud incident occurred on 4 March 1999, when a shot was fired through the front window of Noel Roche's house on Kilworth Road around midnight. Noel Roche was extremely close to Brian Rattigan. Declan Gavin and Freddie Thompson had been the main suspects. Indeed, when the house was shot at, a neighbour heard a shout from the Roche's of: 'If anyone is interested, it was Deco Gavin.' On 13 March, two shots were discharged at Noel Roche's front door at around 1.00am. This was the incident that Freddie Thompson had been arrested for when he gave the first account of why the feud had begun. Declan Gavin was also arrested, but there was insufficient evidence to charge either man, and they were both released without charge. A fragile peace descended after this, and the two sides obviously made up and continued to work together, because there were no incidents – except Declan Gavin's drug-possession arrest in August 1999 – until the Holiday Inn seizure in March 2000.

Brian Rattigan and Declan Gavin had once been the best of friends. After the Holiday Inn seizure they were now the worst of enemies. It was clear that something had to give.

TWO

A night of drama

By the summer of 2001, the fragile truce between Declan Gavin's and Brian Rattigan's gangs had broken. On 5 June, shots were fired into Darren Geoghegan's home at Galtymore Drive in Crumlin during a drive-by shooting. Noel Roche and Brian Rattigan were suspected of being behind the attack, although Gardaí did not have enough evidence to arrest them. Shooting at Darren Geoghegan's home was a big deal.

Born on 3 November 1979, Geoghegan was fast developing into a key figure in the Gavin gang, and had started to take control of handling the gang's money, which was one of the most important and sought-after jobs. Geoghegan and 20-year-old 'Fat' Freddie Thompson were extremely close and usually travelled in the same car, plotting how they were going to grow their empire. In April 2001, three shotgun blasts were fired through the front door and a downstairs window of a house in Lucan at around 3.40am. Gardaí rushed to the scene, and the householder told them that the only reason he could think why his house had been shot-up was that he had been involved in a fight in a nightclub two weeks previously. He had thought no more about the incident, but when Gardaí heard the names of the two men he had fought with – Freddie Thompson and Darren Geoghegan – the incident made perfect sense to them. The gang members had long memories and would not just forget about the minor row. Shooting at Geoghegan's home was a no-no, especially as his grandfather had narrowly avoided injury, and Declan Gavin was furious when he heard. He swore revenge. That summer was shaping up to be a long and tense one.

*   *   *

It was a night that Joey Rattigan had been looking forward to for many months; 24 August 2001 was the day he turned 18 and became an adult in the eyes of the law, although his involvement in crime meant that he had lost his childhood innocence many years before. Brian Rattigan was determined that his younger brother would have a night that he would never forget, and the celebrations had been planned for weeks. The Rattigan family home at Cooley Road in Drimnagh was to be the venue. The three-bedroom corporation house was located in one of a number of cul-de-sacs that are known locally as keyholes. Joey turned 18 on a Friday and spent the day cleaning the house and buying slabs of beer for his guests, knowing that the party was likely to be fairly lively. Brian Rattigan had the drugs taken care of. Being a major dealer, he had no problem sourcing cocaine and he had plenty of white powder in his bedroom, if any of the partygoers got sick of alcohol. Dinah Rattigan, Brian and Joey's mother, had no problem with opening up the house for a good knees-up. The family home had the reputation of being a bit of an open house anyway. Dinah was planning to go into the city centre with her sister and other relations, and would head back to her house after the pubs had closed to celebrate with her youngest lad. Both Brian and Joey still lived at home, and 19-year-old Sharon had also yet to leave the nest. Brian's girlfriend, Natasha McEnroe, was a regular visitor to the Rattigan household. She usually spent at least a couple of nights a week there. Another regular house guest was Shay O'Byrne, Sharon's fella. The 19-year-old was very much a part of the family. Apart from his long-term relationship with Sharon, O'Byrne was also involved in Brian Rattigan's drug gang. The Rattigan family were tight and looked after each other. Ritchie Rattigan, who was exactly a year older than Brian, lived between the family home and another house on Cooley Road with his girlfriend. Although Brian was nearly three years older than Joey, the two were very close. Brian had been teaching Joey his trade – drug dealing and intimidation – and saw a bright future for his brother in his gang, which was growing bigger by the month. The two lads shared many of the same friends, and the group was loyal and fiercely protective of each other. From the early evening, a steady group of friends and associates began to converge on the house; the booze was flowing freely and the music playing loudly.

Mr X, one of the older members of the gang, arrived. He was a few years older than Joey Rattigan, but the two were good friends. He was also from Drimnagh. Mr X was a serious criminal with convictions for drug dealing. As the night went on, the music got louder, and several people at the party started snorting lines of cocaine, including Brian Rattigan. The banter was flowing and the crowd was in good spirits. The birthday boy was taken out into the front garden and given the bumps to celebrate him becoming a man.

Some time in the evening, Shane Maloney and John Roche arrived at the Rattigan's. They had spent the evening at the Kestral pub in Walkinstown, before going to Coco's nightclub in Tallaght. Shane Maloney, a 20-year-old from nearby Drimnagh Road, drove his silver Nissan Micra and parked it outside the Rattigan's. John Roche was a neighbour and good friend of Mr X's. Roche was 22 years old and lived with his parents and two brothers, one of whom, Noel, was also a key player in the Rattigan gang. Although he was jobless, John Roche led a lavish lifestyle and had come to the attention of Gardaí who suspected that he was making thousands of euro each week dealing drugs. Despite the attention of the law, Roche had only minor convictions for road traffic incidents and possession of an offensive weapon.

After 1.00am, Dinah Rattigan arrived back from town to join in the festivities. She was with one of her sisters, her sister's partner and her niece. They had a few drinks with the younger crowd. The night was shaping up to be a memorable one.

A few kilometres away, in Crumlin village, the night of Brian Rattigan's sworn enemy, Declan Gavin, was coming to an end. Gavin had begun the evening at a 21st birthday party in the Transport Club in Crumlin with his friend Eamon Daly and Daly's girlfriend, as well as a group of other people. After spending a few hours at the party, the group headed into town before going their separate ways. Gavin went to Club M nightclub in Blooms Hotel in the busy Temple Bar area. He left after 2.00am, and met back up with Eamon Daly. The pair decided to head to Abrakebabra at the Crumlin Shopping Centre and get some food to soak up the night's pints. They left Daly's girlfriend and her friends in town, and it was agreed that they would meet up again later. Gavin and Daly hailed a taxi and arrived in Crumlin just before 2.30am.

Although Crumlin and Drimnagh cover a large area, there are some traditions that are usually strictly observed among young people living there. At the end of a night out, they invariably head back towards home and get some food, before deciding whether to call it a night and go home or maybe head to a house party that somebody was throwing. Because the same people around the same age usually went to the same places, most people knew each other. Many of those going to Abrakebabra on the night of 24th into 25th of August 2001 would have been at school together, played football together or just bumped into one another in the chipper each week. Declan Gavin was an instantly recognisable figure to his peers hanging around the shopping centre that night. He was a month away from his 21st birthday and was planning a massive party that was bound to attract a couple of hundred people at least. People knew that Gavin was an up-and-coming drug dealer, and he was known to flash the cash and be generous, probably more out of showing off than actual kindness. If you were looking to score with a group of young ones, buying their grub at the end of the night wasn't a bad way to start. And Deco Gavin was certainly never short of cash. The little setback at the Holiday Inn in March 2000 hadn't dented his confidence and it was a case of business as usual for Gavin. He was still moving large amounts of cocaine and ecstasy around the Dublin 12 area and beyond. He was expecting to be charged over what happened that day with Graham Whelan and Philip Griffiths and his attitude was that if he was going to jail, he may as well make as much cash as possible before being sent down.

When the cab pulled up outside Abrakebabra, a row was developing between a group of lads who Gavin knew and some strangers who were in a parked car. There was a lot of shouting and a few golf clubs were produced. It looked like serious violence was about to occur. Gavin was in good form though, and went over and intervened. He spoke to the lads he knew and had a word with the strangers, telling them that nobody wanted to see any trouble. He managed to broker a peace deal, and the car drove off without any punches being thrown. Over the next half an hour, Declan Gavin met about a dozen people, all of whom were later tracked down by Gardaí. A group of three women later said that Gavin was in good form and was not injured or bleeding in any way. Some time before 3.00am, a few people saw Gavin kissing an unknown girl outside the restaurant, and it was clear that his night was ending on a high note. He was spending his time moving in and out of Abrakebabra and chatting casually to anyone he knew. Just before 3.00am, a group of friends saw

Gavin outside the chipper. Another group of five friends arrived at Abrakebabra at around 3.15am, having come across the city from Finglas, where they had spent the night in the Castle nightclub. John Malone, Justin Beatty, Andrew Murray, James Fullam and David Byrne bumped into Gavin outside Abrakebabra, and the group had a conversation before Gavin headed back into the restaurant to get some food. While queuing up for his burger, another group of women arrived in Abrakebabra and bumped into him. They all knew him and he was in good form that night, even generously paying for their food. When the four friends left the restaurant, Gavin was outside with a group of people and asked the girls if he could share a taxi with them. The boyfriend of one of the women was on the way to pick them up, so they declined Gavin's offer of a shared car.

Back at the house party in the Rattigans', some of the guests were getting hungry. Shane Maloney and John Roche suggested driving to Abrakebabra in Crumlin village to get some food. Abrakebabra on the Crumlin Road was around 50 metres from Sundrive Road Garda Station, on the junction of Crumlin Road and Sundrive Road. It was one of a terrace of shops fronting onto the Crumlin Road, adjacent to the main front entrance of the shopping centre. It had large plate-glass windows and a glass door, and seated around 20 people in an 'L' shape around a counter. To the rear of the chipper, behind the counter, was a small kitchen area. Behind the seating at the counter were ladies' and gents' toilets, and the front door was covered by a canopy. Outside was a little-used taxi rank, where cars usually parked.

Nobody else wanted to leave the party, so the two lads jumped in Maloney's 'D' registered silver Nissan Micra and drove the 1.8 kilometres to the restaurant. It was just after 3.05am at this stage. They parked the car and spotted Declan Gavin talking to a group of four girls outside the chipper. Roche and Gavin had been good friends for many years, but they were now in rival gangs after the seizure in the Holiday Inn, and tensions between the two groups were very high. Roche jumped out of the car and shouted over at Gavin that he was a 'rat' and had informed to the Gardaí on Graham Whelan and Philip Griffiths. Roche cursed him and said that Gavin was enjoying his chips, while Whelan and Griffiths were languishing behind bars. Gavin was no shrinking violet and gave as good as he got. He told Roche to 'f*** off' and said that he was no 'rat' and would be soon charged over the Holiday Inn seizure and would be joining the other two lads in prison for 'ten years'. Gavin told Roche that if anyone was a rat that it was him, although he didn't provide any specific details of when John Roche had been a police informant. The two men were screaming at each other from a distance of about four and a half metres and never actually physically confronted each other or threw any punches. John Roche was well able to look after himself, but he didn't want to take on Gavin without any reinforcements, especially with so many people who were friendly with Gavin hanging around the area at the time. Shane Maloney told Roche to calm down and forget the food, and they got into Maloney's Micra and headed back to the party. The incident between Declan Gavin and John Roche had only lasted a couple of minutes.

Back at Cooley Road, 19-year-old Karl Kavanagh invited a group who had been drinking in Brian Rattigan's house to go to his place. He lived just 30 metres away in a house on the same road. Karl Kavanagh lived with his mother and father, as well as his 20-year-old sister, Catherine, Ritchie Rattigan's girlfriend. His parents were away, so he had a free house. John Roche, Shane Maloney, Brian Rattigan, Mr X, Mark O'Reilly, Joey Rattigan, Greg Bourke and Alex Hooper all went up to Kavanagh's. Catherine Kavanagh was already in the house. Because she was going out with Ritchie Rattigan, there was always a great deal of movement between the two houses. As the group arrived at the Kavanaghs', John

Roche brought up the row with Declan Gavin outside Abrakebabra. He explained that the pair had a heated exchange and that Gavin even had the cheek to call him a rat, when the world and its mother knew that the only reason that Deco Gavin was a free man was that he had been a Garda informant for years. Brian Rattigan lost the plot and said that a few of the group should head back up to Abrakebabra and sort Gavin out. Rattigan had taken a lot of cocaine at this stage and he was wired and full of nervous energy. Rattigan then got a knife and balaclava and got back into the front seat of Shane Maloney's Micra, with Mr X and John Roche scrambling into the back. The car pulled up outside Abrakebabra shortly before 3.30am.

THREE

Cold-blooded murder

When Rattigan spotted someone he knew, 21-year-old trainee soldier John Malone, he rolled down the car window and had a brief conversation with him. Several witnesses saw this exchange take place, and later told Gardaí about it. While Rattigan was having the conversation with Malone, Declan Gavin was standing outside Abrakebabra chatting to a young woman. The woman heard someone shouting 'rats'. She looked and saw that they were shouting out the window of the parked car. Because she thought that the insults were levelled at her, she said: 'What are ye saying?' Then someone in the car replied: 'What are you looking at, slapper?' Other witnesses also described hearing the word 'rat' being shouted along with 'There he is.'

When Rattigan spotted Gavin, he pulled on a balaclava to cover his face and pulled a knife out of his pocket. Then he jumped out of the car and ran towards Gavin, who was taken by surprise. Gavin was standing in the middle of a fairly large group of people; many of them saw Rattigan run towards him and they quickly scattered. Brian Rattigan stabbed Gavin once in the middle of the chest. Although the knife attack had inflicted a very serious injury, Gavin was aware enough to realise that he had to get away from his attacker. Despite his injury, he managed to run into Abrakebabra. A security guard held the door closed behind him preventing Rattigan from getting inside.

Mr X, Shane Maloney and John Roche stayed in or around the Micra during the stabbing incident, which was over in less than two minutes. According to witness accounts, Rattigan spent a few seconds trying to pull the door open, but he was drawing attention to himself and was seen by at least a dozen witnesses. However, it wasn't obvious who he was to some onlookers, because he was wearing the balaclava. Rattigan gave up and ran. As he was on his way back to the car, Mark Skerritt got hold of a golf club from the back of his car and chased him. Witnesses differed on whether or not Skerritt managed to strike him with the golf club, but he certainly lashed out at him. When Rattigan got inside the car, Skerritt turned his attention to Maloney's Micra and smashed it over the bonnet, breaking the golf club in two. With that the Micra sped off into the night. A number of witnesses later described the voice of a female shouting, 'It's the Rattigans', as the car left the scene.

Back in Abrakebabra, Declan Gavin staggered from the front door and collapsed in the small kitchen area. Several people in the restaurant tried to help him. A woman who was in the restaurant ran to help; she applied pressure to Gavin's knife wound in a bid to stop the bleeding. She also performed mouth-to-mouth resuscitation, when it became clear that the injured man was on the brink of death. Darren Geoghegan and Patrick Doyle had arrived just after the stabbing; they were also in the kitchen trying to pull Gavin back from the brink. Somebody said that an ambulance had been called, so the group tried to keep Gavin alive until the medical experts arrived.

On the morning of 25 August 2001, Garda David Pidgeon was on duty at the public area of Sundrive Road Garda Station. A security guard from Abrakebabra ran into the station in a distressed state. He said that a man had just been stabbed in the chipper. Garda Pidgeon immediately circulated this information over the Garda radio system to all squad cars on duty in the area. Gardaí Thomas Lynch and Michael Redmond were in their patrol car when they heard the message and rushed to the scene. They were soon joined by Garda Pidgeon and Gardaí Sean O'Sullivan, Colm Quinn and Brian Clerkin. When the officers arrived at the premises, they noted that a man was lying in the back of the kitchen area. He was alive but unconscious and was bleeding from a large stab wound to the chest. Four people were around him administering first aid, including well-known criminals Patrick Doyle and Darren Geoghegan.

Shortly before 4.00am, an ambulance crew – Brendan Walsh and Mick O'Reilly – arrived at the scene and assessed the injured Declan Gavin. It was obvious that the injuries were severe, and it was decided that Gavin should be immediately transported to hospital. The ambulance rushed to St James's Hospital, which is less than a five-minute drive from Crumlin village. Gardaí Colm Quinn and David Pidgeon followed behind the ambulance in a patrol car, while the other officers at the scene preserved it for investigation, and identified and took the names of as many people at the scene as was possible. It was clear that witnesses would be needed for a possible future court case. Darren Geoghegan also followed the ambulance in his car to see what condition his friend was in.

At St James's Hospital the ambulance crew handed Declan Gavin over to the care of the hospital staff. Geoghegan had phoned Declan Gavin's mother, Pauline, while he was following the ambulance, so she knew what was happening almost immediately. Pauline Gavin soon arrived at the hospital with her other son, Aidan, and her daughter. The news was not good, and following surgery and attempted resuscitation in an operating theatre, the doctor pronounced Declan Gavin dead. Gavin had died from a single stab wound to the heart. That morning Pauline Gavin did what no parent ever expects to do – she formally identified her son's body.

Gavin's sister was present with her when she confirmed to
Garda Marion Keane that it was Declan Gavin's body.

State Pathologist Dr John Harbison conducted a post
mortem on Gavin's remains that afternoon. During the two-
hour examination, Dr Harbison found that the principal
injury, to an otherwise healthy body, was a stab wound on the
right side of the chest, around two and a half inches long.
The fatal injury was caused by a knife being thrust through
cartilage into the right atrial appendage of the heart, causing
bleeding, which caused the right lung to collapse and the left
lung to partially collapse. A second superficial injury was
observed on the radical side of the right index finger, which
Dr Harbison felt could be construed as a defensive wound,
while Gavin was trying to fend off his attacker. A toxicology
report showed a urinary alcohol level of 227 milligrams of
alcohol per 100 millilitres of blood, which meant that
Declan Gavin had drunk around ten pints. The report
showed no traces of drugs.

In the immediate aftermath of Declan Gavin's stabbing,
an incident room was set up in Sundrive Road Garda Station
under the leadership of Chief Superintendent Noel Smith.
Local Superintendents John Manley and Detective Superintendent Denis Donegan headed the investigation, and
Detective Inspector Dominic Hayes of the National Bureau
of Criminal Investigation was also a key figure. Detective
Inspector Tom Mulligan from Crumlin Garda Station was
the day-to-day officer in charge of the murder inquiry. Over
50 officers were assigned to the murder on a full-time basis.
Detective Gardaí John Doggett, Eamon O'Loughlin and
Garda Katherina Joyce manned the incident room.

At first light a major forensic investigation got underway
at Abrakebabra, conducted by a four-person team from the
Garda Technical Bureau at Garda Headquarters. Detective
Garda Seamus Quinn from the Ballistics Section examined
the scene, and found blood in various places. Detective Garda

Christopher O'Connor from the Fingerprints Section discovered a visible finger and palm mark in what appeared to be blood on the front window of the restaurant, two inches to the left of the door and 62 inches from the base of the window.

Detective Garda Caroline Hughes from the Photography Section took photos of what would later be a key piece of evidence. The palm mark taken from the window was compared to Brian Rattigan's palm and fingerprints, which were on record from when he had been previously arrested, and it was concluded that the palm mark was made from Rattigan's left palm. Later, DNA analysis of the blood next to Rattigan's finger mark was examined. It matched Declan Gavin's DNA. No blood was taken from the finger mark, as Bureau personnel decided not to distort the finger mark characteristics, so that adequate comparative features would remain intact. This turned out to be a pivotal development and would later prove to be a crucial decision.

It is believed that Brian Rattigan disposed of the murder weapon, his clothes and balaclava after leaving Abrakebabra. The movements of the four men in the Micra cannot be accounted for until they arrived back to the Kavanaghs' house, 90 or so minutes later. Karl Kavanagh, Catherine Kavanagh, Ritchie Rattigan, Joey Rattigan, Mark O'Reilly and Greg Bourke were still in the house when the four men returned. John Roche, Joey and Brian Rattigan discussed Declan Gavin's stabbing while they continued to drink. A radio bulletin came on the radio at 7.00am – broadcasting news of a stabbing at Abrakebabra in Crumlin. Some of those present laughed and cheered at the news. After a while, Brian Rattigan told Shane Maloney to 'get rid' of the car in order to eliminate any forensic evidence. According to a statement later given to Gardaí, Maloney drove the Micra to the Texaco garage at the Cranley Centre on the Naas Road with another man. The other man bought a bottle of orange, emptied it and filled it with petrol. The car was then driven to Cookstown Industrial Estate, where it was partially burnt out. Shane Maloney then received a phone call from Brian Rattigan warning him not to get a taxi back to Cooley Road.

The party at the Kavanaghs' broke up shortly afterwards, and the four men went into hiding anticipating that they would all be arrested. They were correct. They were all wanted men.

At around 8.30pm on the morning of Saturday, 25 August 2001, a woman was walking through the field at the back of Cookstown Industrial Estate in Tallaght. She noticed smoke and saw a car on fire. A call was made to the fire brigade. She didn't see anybody else around the car, which she described as a small, three-door vehicle. The car was on fire on the side of the road directly outside Paramount Freight. The Dublin Fire Brigade arrived and extinguished the blaze. When the flames were put out, it emerged that the car was a Nissan Micra, registration 93 D 38843. Gardaí arrived at the industrial estate at around 10.30am, and Detective Garda Tony Tighe and Garda Gavin Ross preserved the scene. They were sure that the burnt-out car had something to do with the murder the night before. The vehicle was taken to a secure storage facility at Santry Garda Station that afternoon. The remains of burnt clothing and footwear were found in the boot. Two unidentified palm prints were taken from the front wing of the driver's side of the car.

Just hours after the killing, Gardaí had interviewed several witnesses. They knew that four men had been at the scene when the murder occurred, and that the men had left in a car. Officers quickly learned from confidential informants and other sources that these men were Brian Rattigan, Shane Maloney, Mr X and John Roche. The main focus of the investigation switched to investigating the movements of the four men on the night of the murder. The fact that Shane Maloney's Nissan Micra had been burnt out was a further indication that the men had something to do with Declan Gavin's murder. After preliminary investigations, Gardaí learned of Joey Rattigan's 18th birthday party, and also knew about the gathering in Karl Kavanagh's house, after the party.

As the Garda investigation kicked into full gear, various detectives were assigned the jobs of interviewing witnesses and potential witnesses, who had seen Declan Gavin in and around the time of his murder. These witnesses included staff and customers at Abrakebabra and the nearby Texas Fried Chicken. A video recording of the front entrance to Abrakebabra was seized from a security camera, and although it did not cover the roadway where Shane Maloney's car pulled up, or the location of the actual stabbing, it was very useful in identifying people at the scene at the time. The camera footage had a second counter and did capture Declan Gavin staggering and being chased by another man, who is wearing a balaclava and appears to have a large object in his hand. Witnesses were shown stills of the footage, and several identified themselves and others from these stills. Some witnesses also confirmed that Declan Gavin was not injured or bleeding, prior to his encounter with the knife-man.

FOUR

What the witnesses did or did not see

Although some people were cooperating with Gardaí in giving statements about what they had seen, it soon became apparent that investigators were receiving less than full cooperation from some very important witnesses at the scene. Discrepancies in statements, off the record comments and recorded and unsigned memos indicated that several witnesses knew the identity of the culprits, but were not prepared to name them for fear of retribution. This lived up to the Crumlin and Drimnagh tradition of not cooperating with the law at any cost. Because of this reluctance to cooperate, 22 people were arrested during the course of the murder investigation, mainly for withholding information.

Gardaí knew there were several reasons why they were not receiving full cooperation. One of the main reasons was that many people had a lot of animosity towards the police and the criminal justice system in general, and as a result were openly hostile and uncooperative. Some individuals just did not want to cooperate with a force that they had been taught to despise. Certain other people who witnessed the stabbing were involved in criminality. These ranged from petty criminals to members of the Gavin gang, who were involved in the wholesale supply of illegal drugs. Witnesses Darren Geoghegan and Paddy Doyle certainly fitted into this category. Other, more innocent, witnesses understandably feared helping to identify men who were involved in a dispute between two violent rival criminal gangs. But Gardaí found that over the course of the investigation, the prevailing notion among many of the potential witnesses was that the naming of any individual to the Gardaí, regardless of the seriousness of the crime involved and the fact that a man had lost his life, would lead to the person being labelled a 'rat'. Gardaí eventually divided the witnesses to events before, during and after the murder into two distinct groups – 'independent' and 'other' witnesses.

The 'independent' witnesses were classed as normal witnesses to events leading to the death of Declan Gavin. They gave full and detailed statements with largely accurate descriptions, and were regarded by Gardaí as being without prejudice, malicious intent or fear of intimidation. Most of these people had no previous criminal convictions and were not involved in the feud. Unfortunately, this often meant that because of their nature of abiding by the law, they were often unable to identify the key players involved in the murder.

The 'other' witnesses were mostly friends and associates of Declan Gavin or other people who were aware of the identities of those involved in the murder, but for one reason or another did not fully cooperate with Gardaí. Many of these 'other' witnesses were regarded as unlikely to give evidence in any future court proceedings. Many of them eventually identified the culprits to Gardaí, but it was usually after they were arrested, or when they were speaking off the record. Often when they spoke to Gardaí, they refused to sign their interview notes – meaning the evidence gathered was not admissible in court and was severely compromised.

Of the independent witnesses present, many gave detailed statements that helped Gardaí to build up a picture of what happened. A security guard said he saw four men in a 'silver Nissan small two-door car' pull up outside the premises. He

then saw the front seat passenger put on a black balaclava
and get out of the car with a knife in his hand. 'Before he
[Declan Gavin] got a chance to do anything, the man with
the knife lashed out at him.' He then described how Gavin
initially struggled to get into Abrakebabra, and also
described how a man with a golf club chased the knife-man
after the stabbing occurred, while others threw missiles at the
escaping Nissan car.

None of the Abrakebabra staff were able to help Gardaí
to identify the killer, because he had been wearing a
balaclava. Another witness described how he saw the silver
Nissan pull up, and heard the front seat passenger shout 'rat'
at a man standing in a crowd. The passenger, who was
wearing a balaclava, then jumped out while carrying a knife
in his right hand. He stabbed the man he had called a 'rat'
seconds earlier, and the knife made contact with him
somewhere in the chest area. He saw the injured man run
into Abrakebabra, leaving a trail of blood behind him, while
the knife-man followed him. He then said that the knife-
man was unable to get into the restaurant. He also described
how a bystander attacked the Nissan with a golf club, and he
was of the opinion that several of the bystanders knew the
identity of the attacker, although he did not.

David Bryne, who was Declan Gavin's close friend and a
member of his gang, gave a statement to Gardaí in which he
detailed how he was in the area around Crumlin Shopping
Centre with four friends. The group arrived at Abrakebabra at
around 3.20am, and he had a short conversation with Declan
Gavin. Shortly after this, he turned and saw Gavin being
chased into Abrakebabra by a man with a balaclava who was
carrying a silver knife. When the knife-man was unable to get
into the chipper, he kicked the door and then turned and
went towards the parked Nissan. Byrne then ran into
Abrakebabra to see if Gavin was all right. He was later able
to identify himself from CCTV stills shown to him by Gardaí.

Mark Skerritt and three of his friends had spent the night of the murder in the Vatican nightclub in Harcourt Street. Then one of them drove the group of four to Abrakebabra at about 3.00am. Skerritt was involved on the periphery of the row that Declan Gavin broke up, although there were no cross words exchanged between the two men. Skerritt was around Abrakebabra when the Nissan Micra pulled up, and he heard the front seat passenger shout out: 'Deco, ye rat… You're dead.' He then saw the passenger pull on a balaclava and get out of the car with a 'big butchers knife' in his hand. Skerritt later told Gardaí that a passenger in the back of the Micra pointed out Declan Gavin to the knife-man, saying: 'There he is over there', before saying, 'Get the rat.' Skerritt remembered the knife-man approaching Gavin and saying: 'Deco, it's me', or, 'Deco, do you remember me?' before stabbing him in the chest. Mark Skerritt was close by his friend's car when the assault occurred; he went to the boot and got a golf club. He then chased the knife-man, who by now was running back to the Micra. Skerritt then swung at the knife-man, hitting him on the back. The knife-man managed to get into the getaway car, and Skerritt hit the car with the golf club, before the vehicle left the scene. Mark Skerritt stated that he knew who the knife-man was, but he was not prepared to identify him, for fear of a revenge attack being carried out on him.

Detectives interviewed Declan Gavin's friend Eamon Daly, and he told them about Gavin's movements on the night of the murder. After the 21st birthday party in the Transport Club, they headed into town but then separated, with each going to a different nightclub. They arranged to meet up again at Abrakebabra. Before the stabbing incident, Daly saw Gavin outside 'kissing a bird', but she had left the scene before the Nissan Micra arrived.

Daly remembered a car pulling up outside Abrakebabra with at least three people in it. He said that a man got out of the front passenger door wearing a balaclava and carrying a knife. 'He was roaring and shouting like he was psyching himself up', was how Daly described him. After the stabbing occurred, Andrew Murray gave Daly a lift to nearby Dolphin's Barn Fire Station to get an ambulance. While they were on the way to the station, they were pulled over by Gardaí. The Gardaí had heard about the murder and thought that the pair speeding down the road might have been escaping the murder scene. They soon discovered that Daly and Murray were simply trying to get help for their dying friend.

Gardaí eventually found out that the man who carried out the murder had been talking to John Malone before the incident, but they did not know this when they interviewed the 21-year-old in the hours after of the killing. Malone was undergoing basic training at Cathal Brugha army barracks. He was living in Saggart but was originally from Drimnagh. He made a statement describing how he and a group of friends arrived at Abrakebabra after 3.00am, where they saw Declan Gavin 'talking to a girl'. They were at the steps outside the Irish Permanent, which was next door to the restaurant. He said he saw a 'silvery coloured Micra', and that the driver of the car 'said something to me'. He then observed a man in the front passenger seat wearing a balaclava and carrying a knife, while there were 'two or three in the back. I didn't get a good look at them.' Malone then stated that the knife-man chased Declan Gavin to Abrakebabra, before pushing the door open enough to get his arm in and swing at Gavin with the knife.

On 29 August, Malone was interviewed again but was not detained. He elaborated on his first statement, saying he 'knew two or three people in the car', and said a number of those in the car were saying: '"Where is he? Where is he?" I knew these people were looking for Declan Gavin as they had been fighting with him for years.' He stated that he knew the knife-man, the driver and one of the rear-seat passengers, but he refused to name them and said, 'I am afraid for my family's lives, that they would be in danger.'

When interviewed by Gardaí on the morning after the murder, Justin Beatty, from Tallaght, said that he had taken ecstasy and three or four lines of cocaine at the Castle nightclub in Finglas, so he was 'off his head' when he arrived with his mates at Abrakebabra. He said he did not see the stabbing because he had been relieving himself at the time, but heard screaming and a woman saying: 'He has a knife', and saw people running. After that he saw the Nissan Micra speed away from the scene, and he ran into the restaurant to see what had happened. He could not get into the kitchen because the manager closed the door on him. He kicked in the door and saw Declan Gavin lying injured on the ground.

Andrew Murray, a soldier in the Irish Army, was at the Castle nightclub in Finglas with Justin Beatty and three other friends. He initially told Gardaí that he witnessed John Malone talking to the occupants of the Nissan Micra before the knife-man got out. 'I saw this guy stab Declan Gavin with the knife. This stabbing happened on the steps leading down to Abrekebabra.' He stated that he and John Malone discussed the stabbing on their way home, and the culprits mentioned were Mr X and Rattigan. He would not put this in his statement, as he was afraid of retribution. In a further statement, three days after the murder, he went on to say that when the Micra arrived, 'A tall fella who I think was Mr X got out of this Nissan Micra. I know Mr X to see and I know he is friendly with the Rattigans.' In two unsigned memorandums of interview, Andrew Murray said that he recognised three of the people involved in the stabbing, but did not want to name them because he was 'not a rat'. He then went on to name Brian Rattigan, Mr X and Shane Maloney. He said that Brian Rattigan stabbed Gavin, but he would not sign anything with the names of the three men on it because he was afraid.

Several witnesses described the girl who spoke to Gavin just seconds before the murder as having spoken to the occupants of the Micra just before the stabbing. In her original interview on the day after the murder, she recalled chatting to Declan Gavin at the restaurant. She described the Micra pulling up and a passenger shouting 'rats' out the window. 'I said: "What are ye saying?" as I walked by', she confirmed. She didn't see the actual stabbing but did see Mark Skerritt chase the knife-man with a golf club. She later said that Skerritt had given her the handle of the broken golf club, which she threw away.

Darren Geoghegan and Patrick Doyle were good friends and criminal associates of Declan Gavin. They both arrived at Abrakebabra just after the stabbing and did not witness anything at all. When they heard that their mate had been stabbed and was in a bad way, they rushed into the restaurant. They saw Gavin lying on the kitchen floor, surrounded by two women who were giving him first aid. Geoghegan initially refused to cooperate with Gardaí and give a statement. He was later interviewed in Cloverhill Prison after being sent there on remand for a road traffic offence, and then again at Sundrive Road Garda Station, after he was taken out of prison for questioning. He remembered arriving at the scene just before the Gardaí. He followed the ambulance in his car to St James's Hospital, and rang Gavin's mother, Pauline, to tell her what had happened. It was Pauline Gavin who later told Geoghegan that her son had passed away.

Patrick Doyle was interviewed at Ronanstown Garda Station after being arrested under Section 30 of the Offences Against the State Act for possession of a firearm. During his interview, Doyle confirmed that it was his belief that Brian Rattigan was behind the stabbing. He also volunteered to Gardaí that Shane Maloney was around when it happened. Doyle did point out that he was not there, though, and everything he had heard was second-hand from different people.

After interviewing the known witnesses at Abrakebabra, Gardaí had built up a detailed picture of what had happened there, but they knew that some people had not told half of what they knew. So, it was decided that those people would be arrested at later dates.

After finding Brian Rattigan's finger and palm print on the door of Abrakebabra, Gardaí had enough to arrest him and question him about the murder. On 28 August, Detective Sergeant Joe O'Hara and other Gardaí called to Rattigan's home on Cooley Road looking for him. He had been staying at a safe house since the murder, and was not at home when Gardaí searched the house to see if they could find anything to link him to the murder. Gardaí received information that he would be attending Dublin District Court on 4 September 2001. So two officers waited there to arrest him. When Rattigan saw uniformed Garda Paul Lynch and another member, he fled on foot. Sharon Rattigan and Shay O'Byrne were with Rattigan and physically blocked the Gardaí from arresting him. The pair were then arrested and charged with obstruction under Section 19 of the Public Order Act. Later that day Gardaí received information that Brian Rattigan was drinking in a pub on James's Street in Dublin 8. Joe O'Hara arrested Rattigan on suspicion of Declan Gavin's murder, and he was taken to Sundrive Road Garda Station, where he was photographed and fingerprinted.

Detective Sergeants Peter O'Boyle and Joe O'Hara took Rattigan into the interview room. After being cautioned about his rights and speaking privately with his solicitor, the interview commenced. Rattigan told the detectives that he did nothing wrong, and that he used to eat in Abrakebabra but was not there on the night of the murder. He claimed that he was with a married woman at the time, but would not name here because he did not want her husband to find out. He refused to take part in an identity parade. He then quoted the Bob Dylan song 'Hurricane' about the black boxer Ruben Carter, who was wrongly convicted of murder in 1967 in New Jersey. The two hours of interview did not yield much, and Joe O'Hara and Peter O'Boyle took a break. They were replaced by Detective Inspector Dominic Hayes and Detective Garda Marcus De Long from the National Bureau of Criminal Investigation, a specialist unit that investigates serious crime and murders. Rattigan told the two officers that he couldn't remember where he was when the murder happened, and then said that he was with a married woman but would not name her.

He then changed his story and said he was at his brother's 18th birthday party for the whole night and never left it. He swore that he hadn't been near Abrakebabra for months. He was supremely confident throughout the period of questioning, until he was told that Gardaí had recovered his palmprint from the window of the restaurant, and it was in Declan Gavin's blood. The colour drained from Rattigan's face at this point, and he quietly said that if this was the case then 'it's all over'. The interview concluded shortly afterwards. Then Rattigan was visited by Dr James Maloney, in the presence of DS Joe O'Hara. He was asked for his consent to provide a blood sample but he refused. He agreed to be examined by the doctor in private, and Joe O'Hara took this time to speak with Detective Superintendent Denis Donegan, who authorised that a sample be taken from the prisoner under Section 2 (4)(a) of the Criminal Justice (Forensic Act) 1990. Rattigan again refused to comply. He then consulted privately with his solicitor by telephone, and was again asked for a sample, and again he refused.

He was returned to his cell without having given blood, and was given food and tea. He was then visited by an aunt for ten minutes. Around 9.00pm Denis Donegan extended the period of Rattigan's detention, and he was taken back into the interview room. DS Joe O'Hara and DG Eamonn Maloney interviewed him for a period of nearly three hours. During this interview, Rattigan repeatedly said that he 'did not do anything wrong', and was definitely not in Abrakebabra on the night of the murder. He again refused to take part in an ID parade and said that Gardaí had planted his fingerprint. Again, he used the Ruben Carter example. When he was told that there were several witnesses who placed him at the murder scene, he said that when it came to the crunch they 'will never say it'. He smiled at the Gardaí and told them to, 'Prove it, that's your job.' At around midnight Dominic Hayes and Marcus De Long took over. Rattigan again declined to give a blood sample, but he did hand over a strand of hair voluntarily. He said he would wait to see what was in the book of evidence. This interview concluded at around 1.15am, and about an hour later Joe O'Hara and Eamonn Maloney tried again. Rattigan was at his most talkative during this interview. He told the detectives that 'rats' must have given them their information. He told them that he 'guaranteed' that he would not be charged with the murder and said that Gardaí would be going around in bulletproof vests because: 'There will be another one. If I get done tomorrow one of them will get it, that's the way it is.' After being given a cup of tea, he was asked about his opinion of Declan Gavin. He said that his former friend was a 'rat who got caught' and had 'loads of tax and insurance' offences but he didn't do any time. The interview finished with Rattigan saying that if any witness said they saw him at the scene they 'will be naming the wrong person'. The interview was completed around 3.00am, later Rattigan was released on the murder charge, but was charged in relation to an existing bench warrant for his arrest. He was put into custody in the Bridewell Garda Station, and was given bail the following afternoon after a court appearance.

At the same time that Gardaí were searching Brian
Rattigan's family home on Cooley Road, a different search
team called to Mr X's house, just a few minutes away from
Rattigan's. Nobody was present when the Gardaí called, so a
team, led by Peter O'Boyle, forced their way in, but nothing
of evidential value was found. On 7 September, Mr X called
to Sundrive Road Garda Station and told the Garda on front
desk duty that he wished to speak to a member of the Declan
Gavin murder investigation team.

Accompanied by Detective Garda Eamon O'Loughlin,
Joe O'Hara invited Mr X into an interview room. He
explained to him that he was not under arrest and was free
to leave at any time. The two detectives obviously thought
that Mr X was there to talk about the murder a couple of
weeks earlier, but when he sat down, Mr X wanted to know
why Gardaí 'went up to me house and smashed the window
for nothing'. He then said that he had nothing else to say to
them and refused to sign the memorandum of interview.
With that, he sauntered out of the station. The following
afternoon, Joe O'Hara spotted Mr X on the Crumlin Road,
just yards from the Garda station, and arrested him on
suspicion of murder. He was taken to the station and
searched, and was found to have two documents in his
possession. The first was a note from a doctor stating that he
had examined Mr X on 7 September and found no evidence
of external injury to his body. The second document was a
note from a solicitor, signed by Mr X and dated 7 September,
stating that Mr X was innocent of any involvement in
Declan Gavin's death and 'did nothing wrong'. When Mr X
was first interviewed, he remained silent for long periods and
said that he just came to the station to see why Gardaí had
searched his mother's house. During his second interview, he
maintained that he had nothing to do with Declan Gavin's
death and said he was not at Abrakebabra on the night of
the murder, and that whoever told this to Gardaí was lying.

He refused to give a blood sample, but said he would think about taking part in an identification parade. He then said that witnesses would not pick him out 'because I wasn't there the night he was killed'. After being interviewed on the second occasion, Mr X refused to see a doctor to be medically examined, and consulted with his solicitor. His period of detention was extended and he was photographed and fingerprinted. He was interviewed for the third time by Detective Gardaí Eamonn O'Loughlin and Ronan Lafferty. He told the officers that he was with a few mates on the night of the murder but refused to name them. When he was told that people in Abrakebabra had named him as being there, he said they were drunk and mistaken. He confirmed that an ex-girlfriend of Shane Maloney owned a 93 D silver Nissan Micra, but other than that not much progress was made, so the interview concluded around midnight. Mr X then spoke to his sister on the telephone. Before being placed in a cell for the night, he was asked to remove his runners, which is common practice to make sure that prisoners do not attempt suicide. He pleaded with the two detectives that his runners were 'only new' and he would be 'freezing' without them. So Gardaí let him keep them on overnight. The following morning, before being released, Mr X was interviewed one more time. A number of witness statements placing him outside Abrakebabra were read to him, but he said the people 'must have been drunk'. He continued, saying that he did nothing wrong and goaded Gardaí by saying, 'Why don't you just charge me and I'll take my chances in court? Prove it.' At around 10.30am Mr X was released without charge, was rearrested and then charged with an unrelated previous offence. He was taken straight to Dublin District Court, where he was given bail soon after.

On 29 September 2001, Shane Maloney called to Sundrive Road Garda Station with his father and a solicitor. Detective Sergeants Joe O'Hara and Peter O'Boyle invited the three men into the station, and the group went into an interview room. Shane Maloney told the detectives that he had nothing to discuss with them and knew nothing about Declan Gavin's murder. His solicitor then intervened and said his client was not going into an interview involving questions and answers. The interview was then suspended and the three men left the station. While Shane Maloney was walking away from the Garda station, Joe O'Hara arrested him on suspicion of Declan Gavin's murder. During his interview, Maloney repeatedly said that he had nothing to say, or 'I can't remember', to most questions. When witness statements placing him outside Abrakebabra were read to him, he said they 'must be mistaken' and denied having driven a 92 or 93 D registered silver-coloured Nissan Micra. He was shown a picture of the burnt-out getaway car used in the murder, and claimed he did not know whether it was his or not. 'Youse have me car now', he said. During this first interview, he spoke privately with his solicitor on the telephone. During his second round of questions, he became violent and aggressive in front of Detective Garda Barry Butler and Garda Paul Lynch, shouting: 'I told you everything I know. What's your problem? I have nothing to say to you, Lynch.' Paul Lynch knew Maloney well from his years patrolling the Crumlin and Drimnagh area. Maloney then calmed down and refused to answer most questions, and twice said: 'I didn't do anything wrong.' When he was interviewed for the third time, he repeated the mantra 'I have nothing to say.' Just prior to being released, he agreed to provide a blood sample. After being freed, Maloney was immediately rearrested for an unrelated bench warrant. He was taken to Dublin District Court the following day, where he was given bail.

On 3 October 2001, John Roche was arrested at his home at Kilworth Road by Joe O'Hara and taken to Sundrive Road Garda Station. Prior to being interviewed, Roche spoke with his solicitor by telephone, and was visited by his brother Noel, a well-known 23-year-old criminal who was centrally involved in the feud. When he was asked about Joey Rattigan's 18th birthday party, Roche said that he knew 'nothing about any party'. He said he could not remember where he was on 25 August, when the murder took place, and could not remember going to Abrakebabra on that date. When several witness statements were read to him, which pointed to him being at the restaurant, John Roche said they 'must be lying or something'. He said he couldn't remember ever being in Shane Maloney's Micra. He denied ever calling Declan Gavin 'a rat' outside Abrakebabra. During an interview later in the day, Roche told Gardaí that he had memory loss and was innocent of all the allegations being made against him. He said he did not know Shane Maloney and had never even heard of Cooley Road. He also denied knowing Karl Kavanagh or his sister Catherine. He also claimed not to have known Declan Gavin, 'but I think he was stabbed at Abrakebabra, wasn't he?' Gardaí asked him how long he had suffered from memory loss for. Predictably, 'I can't remember', was his reply, and he could not detail any other occasion when he forgot things. Roche was a pro when it came to brushing off Garda questioning. He told officers that he couldn't remember anything at all, but if he did he would be sure to tell his solicitor. He was released without charge that evening.

By the beginning of October, Gardaí had gone through the hundreds of witness statements they had taken and were not satisfied with the cooperation of a number of witnesses, especially some of those present at Abrakebabra. Gardaí believed that at least six eyewitnesses had vital information about the murder after seeing events first-hand, so it was necessary to make arrests. A total of six witnesses were arrested during the Garda investigation. All were detained under Section 30 of the Offences Against the State Act

1998, for offences contrary to Section 9 of the Act: 'Having failed, without reasonable excuse to disclose to Gardaí information in their possession which would have been of material assistance in securing the apprehension, prosecution or conviction of a person for a serious offence (involving loss of human life).' Gardaí knew that some of these witnesses were probably intimidated by members of the Rattigan gang to make sure they stayed quiet, and there was little doubt that they were all afraid, but detectives felt there was no other option.

John Malone had spoken to Brian Rattigan just seconds before the murder, so he was one of the most important potential witnesses. On 10 October 2001, Detective Sergeant Joe O'Hara arrested Malone at Cathal Brugha Barracks. During his five interviews, Malone claimed that he had been recently abducted by two armed men wearing balaclavas while out jogging near his home. He said that he was threatened and knew that the people were involved in Declan Gavin's murder, but he would not name them or even make a complaint about the 'abduction'. Malone confirmed that he knew Shane Maloney, John Roche and Mr X, but swore he didn't see them outside Abrakebabra on the night of the murder. After a visit from his parents, Malone had a change of attitude. He agreed that the Micra was owned by Shane Maloney, and that Mr X was also in the back seat. He then stated that Brian Rattigan was in the front passenger seat and that he wore a balaclava and had a knife, and that he was the man who had stabbed Declan Gavin. However, he refused to sign the memorandum of the interview. Malone told Gardaí that he feared the people who murdered Declan Gavin would come after him, because they knew who he was. He admitted that the supposed abduction never actually happened, and said that he made up the story because: 'I thought you'd let me out if I said I was threatened.' He confirmed that he had not been threatened, but he would not go on the record and name Rattigan as the killer, because he was 'not a rat'. John Malone's parents were present during the interview where he named Brian Rattigan and they agreed to give statements to Gardaí. John Malone's mother confirmed that her son told Gardaí that Brian Rattigan had a knife and had stabbed Declan Gavin. John Malone's father gave a statement recalling his son naming Rattigan as having stabbed Gavin, Shane Maloney as having driven the Nissan Micra and Mr X as being in the back of the car. When this was put to John Malone, he said he would not sign his interview notes. He said that he would not go to court and that if he did, he would say that he lied during his Garda interview and that his parents were also lying about what they had heard him say. He was released without charge.

James Fullam from Crumlin had driven from Finglas with his friends. In his original interview on the morning after the murder, he told Gardaí that he had seen the knife-man get out of the car and run back into it, but he had not actually witnessed the stabbing itself. Detective Sergeant Peter O'Boyle detained Fullam at his home at around 8.00am on 12 October 2001. During his detention, Fullam spoke of witnessing the incident, and said: 'It looked as though Declan Gavin had put his hand up and deflected the knife.' He then described a secondary attack at the door of Abrakebabra, during which Gavin appeared to be having trouble getting through the front door and appeared to have been stabbed again. He said that after the incident he gave John Malone and Andrew Murray a lift home. He said that someone in the car, 'I don't want to say who', said that Brian Rattigan was the man who stabbed Deco Gavin. He said that the day after the stabbing he met with a number of people at Poddle Park in Crumlin, where the incident was discussed. Brian Rattigan's name was mentioned as the knife-man, but Fullam said he wasn't sure who said it.

Detective Sergeant Seán Grennan arrested Justin Beatty

at his home on the morning of 12 October, and he was taken
to Sundrive Road Garda Station. Beatty said that he knew
John Roche and Shane Maloney but hadn't seen them
arguing with Declan Gavin during the initial verbal row
outside Abrakebabra. He conceded that he knew more about
the incident than he had initially told Gardaí but said he was
'not a rat... There's nothing lower than a rat.' He also stated:
'The fella that did this already killed someone. What's to stop
him killing me?' Beatty said that he had since spoken to John
Malone about the incident and the events leading up to it,
and Malone told him who the knife-man was. Beatty didn't
want to tell Gardaí his name but gave his initials – BR. 'You
know who he is. He was arrested for it wasn't he?' Justin
Beatty went on to identify himself from CCTV stills captured
at the scene, and described seeing John Malone speaking to a
passenger in the Nissan Micra. Brian Rattigan then got out of
the car and pulled a balaclava over his face. He was carrying
a knife, Beatty said, while Mr X got out after him. Rattigan
then ran at Gavin, who 'wouldn't run away. He'd never do
that.' He didn't see the actual stabbing but said that Mr X was
standing at the Nissan Micra, 'making sure no one went for
Brian Rattigan'. He named the four occupants of the Micra
as: Shane Maloney, Brian Rattigan, Mr X and John Roche,
and described where each man was sitting. He said this off the
record and wouldn't include it in his statement as he feared
for his life because: 'I seen what they were capable of.'

Andrew Murray, the soldier, was rearrested on 23
October. During his detention at Crumlin Garda Station,
Murray said he was 'not naming names', even though he
knew them, because he was afraid of his life. He confirmed to
Gardaí that he knew Declan Gavin well. He agreed that he
had previously told Gardaí, off the record, that Brian
Rattigan had carried out the stabbing, and that Mr X and
Shane Maloney were also involved. He said he would not go
to court and did not care about his army oath 'to protect the

state and all that'. He claimed that Brian Rattigan did not threaten him, but refused to say if anyone else did.

Gardaí believed that roughly 90 minutes remained unaccounted for before Shane Maloney, Brian Rattigan, John Roche and Mr X drove back to Karl Kavanagh's after the murder. Attempts to question those at the 18th birthday party and subsequent house party did not yield any extra information.

The majority of witnesses were evasive and unco-operative, with some telling blatant lies placing Brian Rattigan at Cooley Road, when he could not possibly have been there. Statements by people in the house and those who later attended the gathering at Karl Kavanagh's house differed spectacularly. A decision was taken that anybody suspected of not telling the full truth should be arrested – so 13 people were detained. Gardaí believed that if they could take individuals into custody for one-on-one interviews that there might be a chance that some of them would crack. This turned out to be exactly the case.

Detective Sergeant Joe O'Hara arrested Karl Kavanagh on 26 September. When he was initially interviewed, he stated that he was at the party in the Rattigans' until about 2.30am on the night of the murder. When he was arrested, he said that he was sure about his timings, because 'my sister told me the following morning it was that time'. He later said that he couldn't tell the truth as 'they'll burn down my house', and refused to elaborate. He said that prior to the murder, he got a taxi to the Kestrel pub in Walkinstown at about 10.30pm, where he met up with Shane Maloney and John Roche. They went to Coco's Nighclub in Tallaght, and at around 2.00am headed to Abrakebabra. The group ran into Deco Gavin outside the chipper, and John Roche and Gavin had a verbal row, with each calling the other a 'rat'. He said that Declan Gavin insisted: 'I'm not a rat. I'm going down for ten years for the stuff that was found.' Karl

Kavanagh said that when Shane Maloney drove back to the Rattigan house, he did not go in but went home to bed. The first he heard about the murder, he claimed, was the following day. He said he had not discussed the murder with anyone and was released without charge. On 1 November, a warrant was obtained at Dublin District Court by Superintendent John Manley of Crumlin Garda Station for the re-arrest of Kavanagh, because Gardaí had received new information about his movements, after interviewing others who were present at the Kavanagh house following the party at the Rattigans'. During his time in custody, he said he would tell the truth after consulting with his solicitor. He said that Brian and Joey Rattigan, Mr X, Greg Bourke, Mark O'Reilly, Shane Maloney and possibly John Roche went to his house after the Rattigan party. He denied that Maloney's car was at his house or that he went out to assist in burning the car. He stuck to his original story about not hearing about the murder until the following day, saying he heard it on the radio. He then changed his mind and said that Greg Bourke and Joey Rattigan were the last to leave his house, at around 7.00am. He said he heard Brian Rattigan, Roche and Mr X talk about Gavin's murder in his house, but said he could not talk to Gardaí about it. He again denied that he had helped to burn Shane Maloney's car. He said the four suspects in the murder all went to his house because he had a 'free gaff'. He said that while in the house they spoke about Declan Gavin being stabbed and said, 'They were the ones who did it.' He said someone told Shane Maloney to 'look after the car'. Karl Kavanagh refused to sign any of the memorandums of interview and was released without charge.

Mark O'Reilly was only 17 at the time of the murder and when he was interviewed on 20 September, he refused to make a statement or say whether he was or was not at the house party in the Rattigans'. He was arrested six days later, and an adult was present at Terenure Garda Station during each interview. He said that he had previously been 'moked' [arrested], with Joey Rattigan and Shane Maloney. He confirmed that he was at Joey's birthday party, but claimed he couldn't remember much. He answered 'don't know' to most questions and said that he smokes 'a reefer or two' of hash a day, and that he couldn't remember most things, although he was going to give up the smoking. After Gardaí had interviewed others present at the party, they knew that O'Reilly wasn't being truthful. Detective Superintendent Denis Donegan obtained a warrant for his re-arrest on 31 October 2001. O'Reilly's mother was present during his interrogation at Crumlin Garda Station. She urged him to tell the truth. He said that he was at the house party in Karl Kavanagh's after the murder, and that they were listening to the radio when, 'Something came on the news about a man stabbed at the shopping centre. Everybody went quiet. There was a bit of panic, and somebody said that we have to get rid of the car.' He volunteered to burn Shane Maloney's car, and drove it the morning after the murder, but would not name his companion. He said he burnt out the Nissan Micra somewhere in Tallaght. He said he bought a bottle of orange, emptied it, and filled it with petrol to burn the car. After the job was completed, he said he and his unnamed friend went back to the Kavanaghs'. The following day, Mark O'Reilly returned voluntarily to Sundrive Road Garda Station with his mother. He said that what he had told Gardaí the previous day was 'all lies. I just wanted to go home.'

Greg Bourke originally told Gardaí that he was at Joey Rattigan's party from 9.30pm until 2.00am, at the latest. He went to his house and fell asleep afterwards and did not wake up until the following morning. Sergeant Colm Fox arrested him on 27 September. Bourke eventually said that he went to the Kavanagh house party at about 1.30am. At around 2.30am Karl Kavanagh and Kenneth Clare went out to Abrakebabra to get food. They came back with Shane

Maloney and John Roche, who told the group that there had been a slagging match with Declan Gavin. Bourke said that the row 'got very personal'. He said that somebody then called to the house and Shane Maloney left. He returned at 5.00am with Brian Rattigan. Bourke said that he left the house at 8.20am and 'went for a walk to clear my head'. On 31 October Detective Superintendent Denis Donegan obtained a warrant for Bourke's re-arrest, and he was detained the following morning. While in custody, he said that while he was at the Rattigans', Shane Maloney, Karl Kavanagh, John Roche and Kenneth Clare went to Abrakebabra. When they got back, he went with them to Karl Kavanagh's house. While there, he learned of the dispute that John Roche and Shane Maloney had with Declan Gavin. He said that Brian Rattigan, Mr X, Shane Maloney and John Roche left Kavanagh's 'from quarter to three on', and when they returned, 'Brian had stabbed Deco.' When the group got back, around two hours later, he did not see any of them bleeding or wearing blood-stained clothes. After hearing on the 7.00am news that Gavin was dead, 'Brian said to Shane to get rid of the car', and 'Mark [O'Reilly] and Karl [Kavanagh] went with him [to do this].' When the three men returned later, Bourke walked home. He told Gardaí that both Brian Rattigan and Shane Maloney had approached him since his first arrest to find out what he had said. John Roche and Mr X 'said nothing except to say to anybody who asks that they were not there [at the party]'.

Catherine Kavanagh was arrested on 28 September, after Gardaí came to the opinion that she had not told them the full truth in her initial statement. While in custody, she said that she had not attended Joey Rattigan's 18th birthday party but had stayed in her own house with Joey's brother and her boyfriend, Ritchie Rattigan. The pair spent the night drinking beer and watching a film. She said that her brother returned home at about 2.00am. She said that when she got up the following morning, Greg Bourke and Joey and Brian Rattigan were there, and she asked them to leave. Later during questioning, she changed her mind and conceded that she got up at 4.40am and saw Brian and Joey Rattigan, Greg Bourke, Mr X, John Roche, Shane Maloney and Mark O'Reilly in the kitchen. She got up again at 7.00am, and the same group were still in the kitchen. She then told Gardaí : 'I heard it on the news about the stabbing at the shopping centre in Crumlin. I knew there was something up, because the lads were quiet. One of them said that Declan Gavin was dead.' In a later interview, she expanded on this and said that Brian Rattigan and John Roche had cheered when the radio broadcast the news Gavin's death. She then heard Brian Rattigan tell Shane Maloney to 'go and get the car burned'. Shane Maloney and Mark O'Reilly then left the house, and she noticed that Maloney's car was gone. Later she heard Brian Rattigan phone Maloney and 'tell him to get a taxi to up the road and not to come back to the house'. Catherine Kavanagh signed the memorandums of the three interviews she gave, and apologised for not initially telling the truth, saying: 'I just didn't want to get involved.' Catherine Kavanagh's revelations were a serious boost for the Gardaí, because they now had someone in the inner sanctum of the Rattigan family effectively telling them that Brian Rattigan had murdered Declan Gavin. Two days after the revelations, Catherine's boyfriend, Ritchie Rattigan, was detained.

Ritchie Rattigan was interviewed on three occasions, and, unusually, signed his interview sheets. He confirmed that the group of men Catherine said were in her house were present and were talking about Declan Gavin. Ritchie said he had been told that his brother Brian, John Roche, Shane Maloney and Mr X had a row with Declan Gavin after an incident earlier in the night. He heard that John Roche and

Shane Maloney had been involved in the original dispute, and that they returned to Abrakebabra with Brian Rattigan and Mr X. When they arrived at the restaurant, he heard 'there was killings. When Brian got out of the car they all scarpered.' After the stabbing, Brian said that the knife was 'well gone'. Ritchie also said that his younger brother told Shane Maloney to get rid of the car and told Mark O'Reilly to go with him. He denied that he had assisted Brian Rattigan in destroying any evidence or changing clothes. Ritchie said that he couldn't remember who actually said that Gavin had been stabbed, and that he 'heard Brian say "the knife is well gone," sort of in the background like', and that Brian was not speaking directly to him. Ritchie Rattigan said he was shocked when he heard that Declan Gavin was dead.

Sharon Rattigan was interviewed by Gardaí and said that she arrived at Cooley Road at around 3.00am with Shay O'Byrne, and that her brother Brian and Mr X were there. She claimed she fell asleep at 3.15am, and said Brian was not there the following day. She didn't see him for three days after this. She said she called to Natasha McEnroe's aunt's house on 25 August, after Brian rang her and asked her to meet him there. She was arrested on 19 October. She denied any knowledge of what happened on the night of the murder. She said that nobody spoke to her about it, and that she first heard about Gavin's death after watching teletext. She maintained that she was not covering for Brian and was released without charge.

Brian Rattigan's partner, Natasha McEnroe, was first interviewed on 2 August, on the basis that she was at Joey Rattigan's 18th birthday party. She said that she met Brian at Cooley Road, and headed off in a taxi at about 3.00am or 3.15am. This was also verified by her aunt, who she lived with. Natasha said she did not see Brian for a few days after the murder, and did not discuss it with him. McEnroe said she hated the ground that Declan Gavin walked on because 'he was only a rat'. In a later statement, she described how Sharon Rattigan arrived at her house on 25 August with a mobile phone number to contact Brian on. She phoned him on the number, but insisted that she didn't ask him where he was or who he was with. When she finally met him, three or four days later, she maintained that she never asked him where he was for the last few days or what he had got up to. Detective Garda Seamus Houlihan arrested Natasha McEnroe at her house on 19 October 2001, and was she taken to Crumlin Garda Station.

While in custody, McEnroe said that Brian Rattigan had never discussed Declan Gavin's murder with her. She said it was not unusual for Brian to go missing for a few days at a time, and that she would often stay in Cooley Road when he was not there. She said that in the days that Brian was lying low she spoke to him on the phone as often as four times each day. She said that Declan Gavin 'was a bleedin' rat', and whoever murdered him, 'should have got a motorbike and done it right. I hated him.' She told Gardaí that a lot of people could have murdered Declan Gavin, because 'everyone hated him'. She was released without charge.

On 2 October 2001, Gardaí Thomas Lynch and William Hernon were on patrol when they noticed a silver coloured Volvo S40 car with the registration plate 97 CW 1280 parked on Beechfield Road in Crumlin. After carrying out a check on the reg, it was found that the plate was false. The two Gardaí searched the vehicle. They found a sawn-off shotgun and four rounds of ammunition under the front passenger seat. The car also contained a taxi roof-sign. Detective Garda Desmond Tracey of the Garda Technical Bureau examined the car and its contents. On examining the newspaper in which the bullets were wrapped, he identified prints on the paper as matching a sample of prints previously taken from Brian Rattigan. It emerged that the car had been taken during the course of a burglary in Naas, Co. Kildare, on 1 February 2001, along with other items of property. The firearm had been taken during a burglary at Castlebellingham, Co. Louth, on 5 October 1999, and the barrel had subsequently been sawn-off to make it easier to transport. The owner of the taxi-roof sign was traced. He said that it was stolen outside his home on 9 April 2001. Residents on Beechfield Road said that they had noticed the car parked in the area on a number of occasions and in a number of different positions in the week or two before Gardaí discovered it. On one occasion, they saw a man get out of the Volvo and go to the boot, before getting into a wine-coloured jeep. However, the description of the man was not very good.

On 14 November 2001, a detective submitted a report about confidential information he had received linking Brian Rattigan, John Roche, Shane Maloney and Mr X to the vehicle. According to the source, it was being used to transport drugs around the country. The informant further stated that since the death of Declan Gavin, the Volvo had been used by Brian Rattigan and his friends to store two firearms, a sawn-off shotgun and a .38 calibre pistol. The guns were being stored in the car, which was being parked around the Walkinstown area at different addresses ready for use if it was needed. Members of the Rattigan gang had received death threats from Declan Gavin's gang since his murder. The threats did not all come from one side though, and Rattigan and his men were quite active themselves. On 15 November, Darren Geoghegan's house on Galtymore Drive in Drimnagh, was fired at in a drive-by shooting. Fortunately, nobody was injured, but the prime suspects in the incident were Brian Rattigan and John Roche. It was the second time in five months that Geoghegan's house was shot at, and it is likely that the gang knew that he had spoken to Gardaí about what happened on the night of the Gavin murder.

Gardaí decided to arrest all the men who had been linked to the Volvo. On 22 November, Gardaí made their move in a major dawn operation involving the simultaneous arrest of the suspects by local Gardaí, backed up by NBCI detectives. John Roche, Brian Rattigan, Shane Maloney and Mr X were detained under Section 30 of the Offences Against the State Act on suspicion of possessing a firearm.

Joe O'Hara arrested Brian Rattigan at his home that morning, and he was taken to Sundrive Road Garda Station. After being processed, Rattigan was brought into an interview room by Detective Inspector Dominic Hayes of the NBCI and Detective Sergeant Sean Grennan. Rattigan was in typically belligerent form, and said he did not know where Beechfield Road was, because he was very bad on locations generally. He was not sure what a Volvo S40 looked like, and he said he thought he got out of prison on 1 February 2001, the day that the Volvo was stolen. He said he couldn't ever remember being in Naas or Castlebellingham, where the car and the firearms had been stolen from. Rattigan was asked which newspapers he liked reading. This question was to link him to the paper that was found with his prints on it and had been used to store the shotgun cartridges. He said he was a daily reader of the *Irish Daily Star*, the *Mirror* and the *Evening Herald*. He said his favourite newspaper on a Sunday was the *News of the World*. During the course of this interview, Rattigan was photographed, fingerprinted and was given a cup of tea, before being examined by a doctor. After this Peter O'Boyle and Joe O'Hara took over the interview. Rattigan told them that he hadn't left Dublin since getting out of prison in February, and that the confidential information that was received, linking him to the stolen Volvo and firearms, was wrong. He said he knew nothing about the shotgun or cartridges. The conversation moved on to Declan Gavin. Rattigan confidently declared, 'I've no worries about Declan Gavin.' After being given a rest and some food and drink, the interview resumed, with Dominic Hayes and Seán Grennan asking the questions. They told Rattigan that his fingerprint had been found on the newspaper in which the cartridges were wrapped. He responded to this by saying, 'You planted my print again like ye did above in Abrakebabra.' It was put to him that it was a bit of a coincidence that his fingerprints appeared on the newspaper, but he said he 'could have been reading that paper'. He couldn't offer any other explanation, but pointed out that Gardaí would have a difficult job linking him to the gun, because his print was 'only on the newspaper, not the gun'. He then laughed and said he'd have to buy himself a pair of gloves. He was dismissive of the worth of the fingerprint revelations, saying: 'I don't give a bollix. You said it the last time. I was in about the Gavin thing, and you said my prints were there as well.' The interview then broke up, and Natasha McEnroe and his sister, Sharon, visited him separately. Later that evening, he was interviewed again, and when he was told that some of his family and friends had been interviewed since his first arrest on 4 September, he replied, 'F***ing rats, all f***ing rats.' The Gardaí asked him how come his prints were found on the window of Abrakebabra after the Gavin murder. He said, 'I don't give a f*** whose blood it was. I wasn't there that night.' At around midnight his period of detention was extended, and Brian Rattigan was allowed to sleep in the cell for the night. He awoke the following morning at 9.00am, and was given some breakfast, before being brought into the interview room again. Joe O'Hara and Peter O'Boyle conducted the interview, and Rattigan spoke about what he called the 'gang warfare' going on in Drimnagh. 'I can't go out, that's why I am in the bunker [keeping a low profile]. I can't even go down to get a Deco kebab or a Deco burger.' He laughed at this sick joke about Declan Gavin, a man who was one of his best friends before the deadly falling out. He was asked what he thought of Gavin and replied: 'F*** him, I hate him. I am not going to admit the murder or having that gun or anything. He had it coming. I did what I had to do. I'll not do time for him, no one will give evidence.' While the memo of that potentially very incriminating statement was read back to him, he told Peter O'Boyle: 'That's f*** all use to you. I am not signing it anyway.' He added, 'If that tape was working I wouldn't say any of that.' The interview was not being recorded on tape – at the time it was not unusal to not record an interview. All interviews are now recorded. This interview ended at 10.48am, and Rattigan was taken back to his cell and given food, before being brought back into the interview room by Dominic Hayes and Sean Grennan. Rattigan said that the 'government is setting me up', and added that nobody aside from the Gardaí was saying that he was the killer at Abrakebabra. The two detectives then showed Rattigan the notes from various people, including his two brothers, which implicated him in events on the night of the murder. 'I didn't stab anybody. I might have been up there but I didn't stab anybody', he said. Anyway, he shrugged, if witnesses did give evidence, 'I'll have to do the time. What can I get, ten years? ten years is nothing. Time would fly.' He then conceded that he went to the house party at the Kavanaghs' on the night of the murder. The interview ended in the afternoon and Rattigan made a phone call and had a visit from one of his aunts. About an hour later he was taken back for further questioning by O'Boyle and O'Hara. He was told that there was a significant amount of witness evidence against him. 'I don't give a f*** what they say in their statements. If it goes to court they will say f*** all', he answered. He was told that Justin Beatty had given a statement saying that he had seen him at Abrakebabra. 'He saw what he saw, that's up to him.' Gardaí asked Rattigan why he didn't he just tell the truth. He replied, 'Why are you asking me? You have the story.' He was asked to repeat the alibi he gave when he was first arrested, but he didn't remember what he said then. 'At this stage I'd like to tell you what happened, but that's not the way I am', he told the two Gardaí. 'You know what you know. If I go signing statements, I'll go down for life.' He then said that he could remember what happened, at the Crumlin Shopping Centre during the murder but he was not going to tell the Gardaí. This interview broke-up shortly before 7.00pm, and after eating a meal, Rattigan was brought back into the interview by the same two detectives. Speaking about the night of the murder, Rattigan said: 'I was pissed; I admit that I had a load of bud. I did about 20 lines [of cocaine]; I got a great buzz out of it. I normally would be f***ed after that and fall asleep.' 'But that night you didn't Brian, did you?' asked O'Hara. 'No, shit happened. I am not naming names. I am not going to go down that road; I can't tell you about the shopping centre. Say if I told you lot, what do you think would happen?' Rattigan asked. At this point Dominic Hayes and Sean Grennan took over the interview, and Rattigan told them that the Gavin gang 'are all a shower of rats'. When it was put to him that the evidence indicated that he murdered Declan Gavin, Rattigan said: 'It's too late to worry about that now. I don't give a bollix about Declan Gavin; I'll go to jail if I have to. Shit happens. It happens to the best of us.' He then looked down at his hands and said: 'When I get out of jail after this, I'm going to cut me hands off. They have me in all this shit.' Rattigan was referring to the fingerprints that he left at both the murder scene and in the stolen Volvo. On 23 November, Brian Rattigan was released without charge. Shane Maloney, John Roche and Mr X were also all released without charge, after making no admissions while in custody.

With Rattigan and his gang spending most of their time trying to evade the law and escape a charge over Declan Gavin's murder, Gavin's associates were planning to avenge his killing. The investigation into Brian Rattigan continued, and a file was prepared for the DPP. Gardaí were confident that they would get a charge, but in the meantime tensions were high, and it was only a matter of time before Deco Gavin would be avenged.

FIVE

A brother for a brother

After Declan Gavin's murder his gang declared war on Brian
Rattigan's mob. It was decided that the only way to seek
revenge would be an eye for an eye. Gavin would have to be
replaced as leader. It was decided that Freddie Thompson
would step forward and take charge. 'Fat' Freddie was born
on 16 December 1980. He lived on Loretto Road in
Maryland, in Dublin's south-inner city, for most of his life.
Thompson had 27 previous criminal convictions for
offences, ranging from road traffic incidents to public order
and assault. Although he was just five foot eight in height,
Thompson was a powerful and violent man who was a good
fighter and often inflicted savage beatings for little or no
reason. He also had ready access to lots of firearms. Despite
the fact that Thompson was a blow-in and didn't come from
Crumlin or Drimnagh, his no-nonsense nature and sheer
aggression in relentlessly targeting Brian Rattigan and his
gang meant that he was the unanimous choice as Gavin's
successor. From an early age, Thompson sold newspapers on
Clanbrassil Street, and was a familiar face to many local
residents. He never had a full time job and lived off the
proceeds of crime, although he did start work as a butcher's
apprentice when he was 16, but this didn't work out. Freddie
first came to the attention of Gardaí when he was just 13
years old. He was involved in petty crime and general anti-
social behaviour, and his brashness and fearlessness led

Gardaí to mark him out as a future big player. Thompson was one of four children. He has two brothers and one sister. His mother, Christine, was a lone parent. His father had left the family home when Freddie was a young lad. He is very close to his mother and siblings. One of his uncles acted as a father figure to him when he was growing up. Even though he was frequently under threat, Freddie liked to spend as much time as he could at his family home surrounded by his brothers and sister. He is involved in a long term relationship with Vicky Dempsey, who is from a well-known Crumlin family, and they have one child. Freddie has an active interest in boxing and martial arts, and trained with a local boxing club in his teens and was very fit. Where some other gang members have endearing qualities, Gardaí, who deal with Thompson on a regular basis, say he is obnoxious when they are interviewing him and is not friendly or in any way a sympathetic character. He has the reputation of being utterly ruthless. When he started to associate with the Crumlin gang led by Declan Gavin, he got sucked in in a big way. He really embraced life as a gangster, and revelled in it. As he grew more notorious, he especially liked to see his name in newspapers. Declan Gavin's murder was a big personal blow to Thompson, because he worshipped Deco and would literally have done anything for him. From the day of the murder, Brian Rattigan was public enemy number one. Freddie and his senior lieutenants were obsessed with getting justice – they would stop at nothing until Rattigan was six feet under.

Rattigan might have been expected to keep his head down after Gavin's murder because he was a marked man, but he did the opposite and went on the offensive. He believed that if he could inflict another murder on a member of the Gavin gang, then it would be weakened forever and he could take over its territory, especially now that the two groups had broken up completely and were not working together. Each group had established themselves as separate entities with separate drugs routes, customers, firearms and strictly separate social scenes. It was almost as if they had never been friends.

On 23 February 2002 at around 2.10am, members of the extended Rattigan family were returning after a night out to Brian's aunt's house. On the way to her house, words were exchanged between Brian and two brothers, Brian and Joey Rattigan got a hold of bricks and other weapons and viciously beat the pair. A man appeared to help the brothers, and he was savagely beaten and later required 80 stitches to a head wound. During the altercation Brian Rattigan produced a black revolver. Searches of the Rattigan home on Cooley Road were carried out under Section 29 of the Offences Against the State Act, and a black revolver with three blank rounds was found. Both Brian and Joey Rattigan were detained. On the night of St Patrick's Day, 2002, Brian Rattigan learned that a number of Freddie Thompson's gang were drinking in Judge Darleys pub in Parkgate Street. He drove past the pub and fired a number of shots at it. He was stopped by Gardaí shortly after the incident, at around 1.00am, but there was no evidence to hold him, so he was told to go home. Following the pub shooting, Rattigan was unaware that Freddie Thompson had held a meeting and decided that tonight was the night that Rattigan would be taken care of. It was just before 4.00am, and Rattigan's house was quiet. Joey Rattigan was lying on the couch in the front room watching television, while Brian Rattigan and Natasha McEnroe lay asleep in a downstairs bedroom. Sharon Rattigan and Shay O'Byrne were sleeping in an upstairs room and Dinah Rattigan was also fast asleep. Joey was about to turn in for the night when he saw a man coming up the driveway wearing a balaclava. He jumped up and ran into the back bedroom, where his brother and Natasha McEnroe slept. As he entered the room, he heard a number of bangs from the direction of the front door. He shook Brian Rattigan but couldn't wake him, although McEnroe quickly woke. Joey shouted: 'Natasha, get up quick. There's fellas outside with Ballys and guns. They're coming in.' Joey was visibly shaken and jumped out a back window into the back garden, where he hid behind a bush. Natasha desperately tried to wake Rattigan from his slumber but he would not move. She ran into the adjoining en-suite bathroom and heard the front door being smashed with three or four bangs. She had the toilet door partly open and saw two men go into the bedroom where her boyfriend lay sleeping. The light was on in the bedroom and bathroom, so McEnroe had a good view. A couple of seconds later, she heard the sound of a gunshot and knew that Brian had been shot. After another couple of seconds, the two shooters ran past her. She shouted, 'You dirty bastard, come back here', at them and ran into the hallway towards the front door as the men were leaving. The two gunmen were wearing dark clothes and balaclavas. As they turned around towards her, one of the men had pulled his mask up revealing half of his face. He stared at her and just laughed. He was quite small in size with a fat head. She later told Gardaí that she didn't know who he was, but if he saw him again she would be able to recognise him. The second gunman was a lot taller and was carrying a shotgun in his right hand. The pair then left the house and sped away in a waiting car.

Natasha ran back into the bedroom and found Brian covered in blood lying on the bed. She quickly rang 999 and asked for an ambulance and the Gardaí.

Sharon Rattigan was woken upstairs by the sound of loud banging and the unmistakable noise of breaking glass. She was afraid to leave her bedroom to investigate what was happening. She heard the gunshot coming from the vicinity of her brother's bedroom downstairs. She then heard Natasha screaming, and after a few minutes she went down, and saw Brian covered in blood. Sharon never saw the gunmen. Shay

O'Byrne was in bed beside Sharon and also woke up when the loud noise started. He was afraid that whoever was downstairs was going to come up. He could hear footsteps on the wooden floor downstairs, and after a loud bang he heard Natasha McEnroe crying out. He then heard a car being driven away. He ran down and saw Brian lying critically injured. Dinah Rattigan also got a rude awakening and heard the words 'they're shooting', coming from a room below. She ran down to confront the gunmen. She was too late, however, and looked out the front-room window to see three men wearing balaclavas running away. Fearing the worst, she ran into the back bedroom and saw Brian. There was a large hole in his back with blood oozing out of the wound. It was obvious that his condition was extremely serious.

At 4.00am the crew of the Sundrive Road patrol car, Gardaí Michael O'Donovan and Michael Reidy, responded to a call reporting a shooting at Cooley Road. They were met at the front driveway by a visibly upset and distressed Joey Rattigan. Garda Reidy went into the house and found Brian Rattigan with blood coming out of an open wound. Garda O'Donovan observed five shotgun cartridges on the ground outside the house, and the scene was sealed off. Shortly afterwards, Jerome Rouiller and Dermot O'Reilly from the Dolphin's Barn fire station arrived at the scene, after receiving notification of the call eight minutes earlier. They observed that the victim had gunshot wounds to his stomach and back. After dressing the wounds, they rushed Rattigan to St James's Hospital. When he arrived at the hospital, Rattigan's injuries were thought to be life threatening, and doctors feared that he would not survive. He had suffered a gunshot wound to the left side of his back, with the bullet exiting through the abdomen. Because the shot was from very close range, it would not have been at all surprising if he died. There was little doubt that his shooting was a bona-fide murder attempt, not just a warning.

Over the next few days, his condition gradually improved, and although it took nearly three months of recuperation, Rattigan would live to see another day. His would-be assassins had failed, and there was little doubt that Rattigan would strike back.

A technical examination of the scene recovered three different types of bullets, indicating that three firearms had been used by the assassination team. There was evidence that at least five shotgun rounds had been fired outside the house and inside the hallway. A .44 calibre round was recovered from the floor. A .32 calibre bullet was taken from the mattress. This was the round that hit him in the back and exited through his stomach. Because Brian Rattigan was asleep when he was shot, he did not know who his attackers were, although he no doubt had a good idea who was responsible. He did not cooperate with the Garda investigation, and inquiries led Gardaí to suspect that Freddie Thompson and Paddy Doyle were the gunmen, and that two other people were involved: one armed with a firearm and the other driving the getaway car.

When Gardaí initially quizzed McEnroe on the afternoon following the shooting, she told them that she did not recognise the gunman. On 8 August, she was again interviewed, and told detectives that she did recognise the man who had shot her boyfriend, but she was afraid of him at that time and was still afraid of him to this day. She said that the man with the fat head was Freddie Thompson from Maryland, and that she didn't shout, 'You dirty bastard, come back here', as she initially indicated, but rather said: 'Come back here you bastard, Frederick Thompson', but Freddie just laughed at her. She said that Thompson was only four feet away from her when she saw him, and she was certain that he was in the house and was carrying a handgun. Freddie Thompson had been detained on suspicion of carrying out the shooting the day before McEnroe's revelation, and was in

Sundrive Road Garda Station when McEnroe was re-interviewed by Gardaí, who were hoping that she would remember something more. Freddie Thompson was well versed in dealing with police interrogations. During seven rounds of interviews with detectives, he replied, 'Nothing to say', to each and every question, and refused to sign the notes of the interview on each occasion as well. He was initially held for 24 hours with his period then extended for a further 24 hours by Chief Superintendent Noel Smith. On the second day of interrogations, Gardaí told Thompson that McEnroe's statements implicated him. He did not flinch. At the eighth and final interview, which like all the previous ones, was recorded on video, Thompson stuck to his script. He knew his time in custody was nearing an end, and was looking forward to going home. When the camera was turned off, Thompson turned around and said to Detective Garda Paul Gilton: 'Natasha McEnroe will never go to court with that statement. This will never go to court.' When asked what he meant, Thompson replied: 'Mark my words, she won't go to court with that.' Thompson was then released without charge, pending a file being sent to the DPP. In correspondence with the DPP's office, Detective Garda Ronan Lafferty said: 'This case rests solely with Brian Rattigan's girlfriend, Natasha McEnroe, who recognised one of the intruders into the house on Cooley Road, Dublin 12, on the 17 March 2002 and [who] shot Brian Rattigan. She knows Frederick Thompson for a number of years, and in her initial statement she described him and admitted she would recognise him again. In a second statement she names the culprit as Frederick Thompson [who she says was] armed with a handgun. She stated that she was too scared to name him in the first statement. I recommend that Frederick Thompson be charged with Aggravated Burglary, Unlawful Possession of a Firearm with Intent to Endanger Life and Attempted Murder.' Gardaí were hopeful that, with Natasha

McEnroe's statement, they would be able to do what had never been achieved, so far – putting Freddie Thompson behind bars. However, Gardaí were disappointed when the DPP came back and directed that no charges should be brought. Freddie Thompson's prediction was right: The case never did get to court.

With Brian Rattigan temporarily out of the way, Freddie Thompson and his gang quickly gained the upper hand in the feud. They took advantage of the fact that their leading rival was severely weakened to exert their supremacy on the streets.

While Freddie was establishing himself as the top dog in drug dealing in Dublin 12, fate intervened and took the life of the man who had inadvertently kicked off the whole gang war. At 10.35pm on 22 May 2002, a lone gunman entered a portacabin outside Kilworth Road in Drimnagh, and fired two shotgun rounds at close range to the chest and leg of 26-year-old Derek Lodge, who was repairing a second-hand TV. He died instantly, after a round pierced his heart. Four years previously, Lodge had set fire to Declan Gavin's motorbike, which led to the gang splitting in two with tragic results. While Declan Gavin had gone on to lead his side of the gang and continue to sell drugs, Lodge had distanced himself from the Rattigan gang, and gradually left the feuding behind. He spent a lot of time in his unofficial workshop, which led to frequent rows with some of his neighbours, because it blocked most of the road.

Lodge had a six-year-old son from a relationship that had ended. Gardaí believe that he wanted a life free from crime so that he could watch his son grow up.

Although he was not involved with Brian Rattigan and the others, he had not completely given up on breaking the law. It is believed that Lodge had become involved in a dispute with a local man, and that Lodge was constantly threatening and harassing the man and his family, and making their life hell. Gardaí believe that a hitman was paid to shoot Lodge as a warning and to make him back off. However, the hitman went too far and shot Lodge dead, instead of just shooting him in the leg, as had been intended. On 25 May 2002, Gardaí received a phone call informing them that 'The man who did the murder in Tallaght on St Stephen's Day got a thousand euro to shoot Derek Lodge.'

The man referred to was Shay Wildes, a notorious hitman from Tallaght. On St Stephen's Day 2001, Wildes, who was born in December 1967, walked up to Joseph Cummins outside the Dragon Inn and shouted, 'Merry Christmas,' before shooting him in the head from close range. Wildes then fired two more shots into Cummins as he lay on the ground, killing the father of five. Wildes later claimed that he carried out the murder as revenge, because Cummins allegedly raped a woman 18 months previously, although there was no evidence to back this up. In September 2003, Wildes received two life sentences after he was found guilty of the murder and possession of the murder weapon, a .22 semi-automatic handgun. Gardaí believe that Wildes operated as a gun for hire, had links to the Continuity IRA and was behind protection rackets in and around Tallaght. In April 2003, Shay Wildes coldly shot dead 32-year-old Declan Griffin in a packed pub in Inchicore. Wildes had been paid by a gang that Griffin owed money to, and lured the victim to the pub, saying that they would offer him protection. Griffin was suspicious and arrived expecting trouble. He was wearing full body armour and had a pistol in his waistband to protect himself. But before he got a chance to take it out, Wildes calmly shot him in the head, through his right ear from close range with a .38 pistol, before strolling out. A jury later found him not guilty of the murder. Witnesses due to give evidence in the case had been intimidated, and Gardaí were also threatened. Although he was later arrested in connection with Derek Lodge's murder, Wildes replied,

'Nothing to say', to every single Garda question. He was released without charge. Nobody was ever charged with Derek Lodge's murder. The investigation remains open.

In the eyes of Fat Freddie's gang, anybody involved or suspected of being involved in Declan Gavin's murder was fair game. On 28 May 2002, a man, who the gang believed had telephoned Rattigan on the night of the Gavin murder informing him that Deco was outside Abrakebabra, was shot. There is no evidence that such a phone call ever took place, but the victim was shot in the chin with a .38 round when he opened his front door at 3.00am. The victim refused to make a statement or cooperate with Gardaí, but members of the Thompson gang were the Gardaí's prime suspects.

Even though Brian Rattigan was still recovering from his injuries and was out of the picture for the moment, the Thompson gang was on high-alert to finish him off, should he be seen anywhere near Crumlin. He was staying in a safe house and keeping a low profile. In July 2002 the opportunity arose to take out Rattigan's beloved younger brother Joey. It wasn't a chance that the Thompson gang were going to pass up.

On 16 July 2002, 18-year-old Joey Rattigan was sitting at home with his girlfriend when he received a call asking him to go down to Dublin 8 for a few pints. He went to the Pimlico Tavern pub, in the heart of Dublin's south-inner city. There Joey met 21-year-old Paul Warren, the man that had made the phone call. Warren was with 26-year-old Ritchie Edwards and 22-year-old Paddy Fogarty. Paul Warren had been Gavin's friend, but Joey Rattigan didn't know the extent of this friendship. He believed that he was perfectly safe having a few pints with the trio, as he looked upon Warren as a mate. Joey was very much mistaken though, and it was this error that would cost him his life. After Declan Gavin's murder and the permanent split of the gang, allegiances were still being formed, and it was hard to know who to trust. In the wake of the Gavin murder, friendships were cheap, and a person who you think is on your side one minute can suddenly turn against you the next. Joey Rattigan thought that Paul Warren was on his brother's side, but in gangland there is no such thing as real friendship, and loyalty is not a commodity that is in rich supply. Unbeknownst to Joey Rattigan, Paul Warren was a turncoat.

Warren, Edwards and Fogarty had been in the pub since 8.00pm. At around midnight Joey Rattigan rang his girlfriend and asked her to come and meet him in the pub. She got a lift in and arrived at about 12.15am, and met her boyfriend and his three drinking companions at the door of the pub. Ritchie Edwards said he would give Rattigan and his girlfriend a lift back to Rattigan's house. When he dropped the couple there, he told them he was going to Islandbridge to leave Paul Warren off at his flat. However, there is no evidence to prove that Paul Warren was dropped off at Islandbridge. A while later Paddy Fogarty rang Joey Rattigan's mobile, and said that he and Ritchie Edwards were on their way back to Drimnagh to collect his girlfriend and drop her home. The pair arrived at Cooley Road, picked up Rattigan and his girlfriend, and dropped her safely home. The three men then drove to Ritchie Edwards' apartment in Inchicore and stayed there for a short time. Gardaí believe that all the complicated lifts was a guise to buy time, and that Paul Warren had arranged for Joey Rattigan to be murdered and was putting a plan in place to have him shot. The exact plan that was put in motion is unclear, but it is known that Rattigan, Fogarty and Edwards left Inchicore shortly before 2.00am, and that at 2.05am Joey Rattigan got out of Ritchie Edwards's van at the bottom of Cooley Road, just metres from his home. As the van pulled away and left, somebody who had clearly been expecting and awaiting Rattigan's arrival came out of the shadows and approached him. A female neighbour later told Gardaí that she heard a loud bang and looked out her window and saw a male lying injured on the footpath. Joey Rattigan had suffered a single gunshot wound to the head from close range. By the time the neighbour got out of bed and peered through her window, both the gunman and Joey Rattigan's lift had gone.

Gardaí received the 999 call informing them about a possible shooting at Cooley Road at 2.18am on 17 July. Gardaí Carolyn Cullen, John Fitzpatrick, Ciaran Nunan and Kelly Dutton arrived at the scene within minutes, with an ambulance from the Dublin Fire Brigade not far behind. It was clear to members of the emergency services that Joey Rattigan was not in a good way. There was a large gunshot wound to the front of his head, and it looked like a pistol was used to inflict the wound. The injured man was rushed to St James's Hospital. Senior Gardaí from the 'G' district, which encompasses Crumlin and Drimnagh, rushed to the scene. It was the opinion of senior officers present that they would soon be launching a murder inquiry. An incident room was immediately established at Sundrive Road Garda Station, under the command of Detective Superintendent Denis Donegan. The investigation was led on a day-to-day basis by Detective Inspector Tom Mulligan, with Detective Sergeant Joe O'Hara running the incident room on a full-time basis. On the morning of 17 July, approximately 30 Gardaí came together for a case conference to review the evidence. Detective Garda Eamonn Maloney was appointed family liaison officer and he dealt with the Rattigan family. Dinah Rattigan was heartbroken that her son was in a critical condition in hospital, as were other members of the immediate family. Sources say that Brian Rattigan was apoplectic with rage that his younger brother was targeted, and immediately ordered his closest associates to find out exactly what happened – so that revenge could be swift and brutal. It soon became clear that Joey Rattigan was being kept alive by a life support machine. He was brain-dead and had little chance of ever recovering. The Rattigan family had a meeting as Gardaí were holding their case conference, and the decided that Joey's machine should be switched off. The extended Rattigan family were at Joey's bedside when he lost consciousness for the final time, and Dr Ryan pronounced him dead. An hour later a relation of Dinah Rattigan identified Joey Rattigan's body to Garda Alan Kerin, who in turn identified the remains to Dr Marie Cassidy at the Dublin City Morgue. A murder investigation was immediately launched, while a grieving and furious Brian Rattigan launched his own witch hunt. What had started out as a feud among close friends had now resulted in two murders, and there would be no going back. It was a case of a brother for a brother, and the feud was now a full-blown war.

Because Joey Rattigan was involved in the drugs gang controlled by his brother, there was little doubt that he was murdered as revenge for Brian Rattigan's role in Declan Gavin's killing. Joey Rattigan was well known to Gardaí, not because he was a serious criminal or found himself getting into trouble every week: he was known because of his infamous brother. Brian Rattigan doted on his younger brother, but this love did not go as far as making sure that Joey kept on the straight and narrow and stayed out of a life of crime, a life that the older Rattigan had made sure was permanent for himself. Although Joey was not a criminal mastermind, he was still well able to move drugs around, sell small quantities of ecstasy and generally take the adulation that comes on the street when your bigger brother is an up-and-coming gangster. Gardaí describe Joey as Brian Rattigan's gofer. A kid who was handy for running errands and passing messages, but not somebody you would trust to help run a major drugs empire. Apart from his arrest for assaulting the two brothers at Basin Street with Brian, Joey Rattigan had never been in serious trouble with the law. He was stopped twice for being drunk and disorderly, but the offences were so minor that he was cautioned by Gardaí rather than taken to court. His most serious offence occurred on 20 August 2001, just five days before Declan Gavin's murder, when he was stopped by Gardaí on the Crumlin Road on suspicion of handling stolen property. The offending item was a bundle of 25 copies of the *Irish Independent*, which had been stolen from a nearby newspaper seller. It hardly qualified as the crime of the century, but nevertheless, he was summoned to appear before Dublin District Court. He was fortunate – the only witness against him failed to show up in court. Whether he had heard about the family's reputation is open to debate, but Joey escaped a conviction. Indeed, when he died, he did not have one single criminal conviction registered against his name. His softness was highlighted when Brian was shot. Instead of getting psyched up and taking on the gunmen who were trying to break down the door while his mother slept upstairs, Joey ran for his life and hid in a bush, while his brother was nearly killed. He then started bawling crying when Gardaí arrived, which is a no-no among criminals who never like to show Gardaí emotion or let the police know that something had got to them. Joey's softness and inexperience in dealing with hardened and experienced murder detectives was obvious when he was arrested in connection with Declan Gavin's murder on 2 October 2001. He had originally lied to the Gardaí. During his time in custody, Joey was interviewed on four different occasions, and naïvely agreed to sign two of the memorandums of interview. It didn't take the younger Rattigan long to break down and admit that he had lied in his original witness statement. He named everyone who was at his 18th birthday party and admitted that he went to Karl Kavanaghs' at 4.30am because he had a 'free house'. He also named everyone at the Kavanaghs'. The group, he told Gardaí, 'were all talking about what happened at Abrakebabra, that Deco Gavin had been stabbed. They all

seemed very happy.' Rattigan said that most of the talking
was being done by his brother and that they heard about the
stabbing on the radio when the 7.00am news came on. He
also described how someone told Shane Maloney to burn his
car, but claimed that he did not know who this was. He said
that Maloney 'had arranged to meet someone else up the
road,' and then went with that unnamed person to burn the
car. Joey also told Gardaí that Brian Rattigan left the family
home to go to the Kavanaghs' at 2.30am, but he did not
arrive until around 4.30am. This was the exact timeframe in
which Gardaí believe that Rattigan went to Abrakebabra,
murdered Gavin, disposed of the evidence and then went
back to Cooley Road. Joey Rattigan was released without
charge, but detectives could not believe how different he was
to his brother. Brian Rattigan would never help the law or
give them any nuggets to investigate. Joey had all but
implicated his brother in the murder and he was naïve at
best. He was certainly innocent, but definitely guilty of an
unforgivable crime in the eyes of serious criminals –
cooperating with Gardaí. The arrest just showed how the
young Joey Rattigan was out of his depth. Joey Rattigan was
singled out not for what he did; he was killed because who he
was. Put simply, he was collateral damage.

A post-mortem examination on Rattigan confirmed that
he died as the result of a single gunshot wound to the head
from a .38 calibre pistol. Gardaí at least knew what sort of
gun they were looking for, and the motive for the murder
quickly became apparent. Although the possibility that
Rattigan was killed because of some mysterious feud that he
alone was involved in was not ruled out, the most likely
cause of his death was the revenge theory. Two hundred and
seventy nine questionnaires were completed by residents and
neighbours of the Rattigans'. A number of witnesses reported
hearing the screech of tyres just seconds after a loud bang,
which led Gardaí to believe that a vehicle had been present

at the murder scene and was probably used when the gunman or gunmen made their getaway. There was little initial progress made in the case. Nobody saw the gunman or was able to identify the vehicle that left the murder scene at high speed. A search team carried out an inch-by-inch search of Cooley Road and Kilworth Road, where the vehicle had been heard leaving the scene, but nothing materialised. After speaking with a confidential informant after completing the first case conference, a detective learnt that Rattigan had been drinking with three men on the night he died. The detective also found out about the lift Rattigan had received just before he was shot dead. The name Paul Warren was not new to detectives from Sundrive Road. Gardaí knew that he had associated with Declan Gavin before he died.

Warren was a minor criminal who came from Francis Street in Dublin 8, and was considered to be a junior member of the mob now controlled by Fat Freddie Thompson. Opinion was divided about whether Warren was capable of coldly walking up to a man and firing a shot into his brain. Some Gardaí believed that he was, while others felt that Warren had merely been a go-between and had given the information about Rattigan's movements to Freddie Thompson or one of his gang. Gardaí felt the possibility of a hitman being paid to carry out the killing could also not be ruled out.

After getting the names of the men that had spent the evening drinking with Rattigan at the Pimlico Tavern, it was decided that Ritchie Edwards, Paddy Fogarty and Paul Warren should all be detained for questioning on 17 July. Edwards was arrested under Section 30 of the Offences Against the State Act on suspicion of being in possession of a firearm with Intent to Endanger Life at the murder scene on Cooley Road. Gardaí interviewed him on eight separate occasions. He answered 'Nothing to say', to each question put to him. Patrick Fogarty was arrested at his flat in Inchicore for the same offence, and during the course of his questioning at Sundrive Road, inconsistencies began to emerge in his story. During his first interview, he told Gardaí about the night spent drinking with Rattigan, and how he and Ritchie Edwards dropped him to Cooley Road in Edwards' van at around 2.00am. He claimed that Ritchie Edwards drove off as soon as Rattigan got out of the van. Detectives knew that this could not have been the case, because a number of residents told Gardaí that they heard a van speeding off after a shot rang out. During his fifth interview, Fogarty agreed that he was in the white van and that they drove off after Rattigan was shot. Later during the same interview, he denied this, and said when Rattigan got out of the van they drove off and heard nothing. In the next interview, he contradicted everything that he had said in the previous five interviews, and said that he was at the scene when Rattigan was shot. He said he 'heard a bang, looked out the window, saw someone running down Cooley Road, saw Joey on the ground, panicked and told Ritchie to drive'. During his next interview, Paddy Fogarty claimed that after leaving Joey off he went to Edwards' apartment, where they turned on the teletext to see if 'anything had happened'. He then claimed that the first he heard of the shooting was the following day, when his girlfriend told him.

Detective Gardaí Eamonn Maloney and Michael Fitzgerald were making serious progress at this stage. Fogarty described how he heard a shot and saw the gunman run down Cooley Road. He then admitted to having a conversation with Paul Warren and to telling him that he was on the way to drop Joey Rattigan home. He also conceded that although Paul Warren was dropped off at Islandbridge earlier on the night of the murder, he had not actually seen him going into his girlfriend's flat. This fact was later confirmed by Paul Warren's girlfriend, who said that she didn't see him on the night of the murder but that

he phoned her at about 3.30am, asking if he could stay the
night. This was a full hour after Joey Rattigan was murdered.
It would have given him time to do the shooting, dispose of
the murder weapon and clothing, and then look for a bed for
the night. Patrick Fogarty eventually told the two detectives
that Paul Warren was the person who he had seen running
away from Joey Rattigan after he had been shot. Fogarty was
then released without charge

After Gardaí had made their breakthrough in securing
Paul Warren's name from Paddy Fogarty, Warren was taken
into custody. He said that he arrived in the Pimlico Tavern
at 8.00pm on 16 July, and joined Richard Edwards, Patrick
Fogarty and a couple of other people. He stated that Joey
Rattigan arrived in the pub at 9.00 or 10.00pm, and claimed
that Patrick Fogarty had a prior arrangement to meet
Rattigan that night. He said that Rattigan's girlfriend arrived
at the pub, after being dropped there by three men, and that
Edwards dropped the couple back to Cooley Road. He then
claimed that he was dropped off at his home at St Theresa's
Gardens, in the south inner city, because he wanted to pick
up some hash he had in his bedroom. This was completely
different to the account given by Fogarty, who said that
Warren was dropped off outside his girlfriend's flat in
Islandbridge. Warren then stated that he later got a
phonecall from Edwards and Fogarty, saying that 'Joey had
rung them looking for some coke and asking them to drop it
to the house.' Again this is contradicted by Rattigan's
girlfriend's statement, in which she said that Paddy Fogarty
rang Rattigan, telling him that he was going to drop her
home. There was not enough evidence to charge Warren at
this stage, and he was released without charge.

On 26 August 2002, Gardaí at Crumlin Garda Station
received a phone call reporting a vehicle that had been
abandoned at Windmill Avenue in Crumlin. Garda
Diarmuid Maguire went to investigate and found that a

Silver Volvo, bearing a false registration plate, 97 D 1251, was locked and secured. When Gardaí searched the Volvo, they recovered a .38 Smith & Wesson handgun from the glove box. A Smith & Wesson .38 is a weapon that used to be issued to all Garda detectives, before the Sig semi-automatic pistol was introduced a number of years ago. It is regarded as a reliable weapon, and one round fired from close quarters would easily kill a person. A forensic examination of the weapon confirmed that it was used in Joey Rattigan's murder, five weeks previously. Every gun leaves a unique characteristic on a bullet it fires. It was also determined that the .38 was also used in the attempted murder of two brothers in the Coombe area on 13 June 2003. Gardaí contacted Interpol with a view to determining where the weapon originated, but the search came up blank. It was likely that the gun, as with most firearms used in gangland operations, was imported into Ireland along with drugs shipments from the Netherlands or Spain. A balaclava was also found in the car, as well as DNA traces of two unknown males. A baseball bat with a bloodstain on it was also recovered, as was a cigarette butt, but detectives were not able to match the DNA to Paul Warren. Further investigations led officers to believe that members of Freddie Thompson's gang regularly used the Volvo. Gardaí do not know if the car was the getaway vehicle used by the person who murdered Joey Rattigan. It seems unlikely, because it is common practice for such cars to be set alight to destroy all forensic evidence. Equally, it is not usual for a weapon that has been used in a gangland murder to be simply left in a car that could – and probably would – be found by police. The fact that there were several DNA matches in the car also puzzled investigators. It is possible that the Volvo was left on Windmill Road for somebody to collect, but a resident reported it to Gardaí, who got to it before any gang member could. Because of the intelligence indicating that members of the Thompson gang used the Volvo, a number of suspects were arrested for questioning. The list reads like a who's who of Crumlin criminals. Gavin Byrne, a 27-year-old senior member of the Thompson gang was detained. He had an address on Windmill Road. He gave Gardaí a sample of his DNA but it came back negative.

Declan Gavin's brother, Aidan, was also arrested. From an early stage Aidan Gavin's name began popping up in the Rattigan murder. Gardaí knew that Aidan Gavin was centrally involved in the feud, and that Paul Warren was a friend of his. They believed that he was instrumental in organising the murder to get revenge for his own brother's killing. He also submitted a DNA analysis, but it came up blank. Freddie Thompson himself, his right-hand man, Paddy Doyle and Darren Geoghegan were also arrested for questioning. All denied involvement in any criminal acts and all readily gave DNA samples, which all came back as not matching the DNA found in the Volvo.

Because DNA found on the murder weapon did not match Paul Warren's, the main suspect in the murder, the Garda case hit a dead end. There is little doubt that Warren either set up Rattigan to be murdered or actually pulled the trigger himself. When first arrested, the story he gave to Gardaí was riddled with inconsistencies. His own friend identified him as the man who shot Rattigan. Nevertheless, without any hard evidence, the DPP decided that there was not enough to secure a charge against him. Gardaí interviewed for this book have a number of theories as to what happened on the night of 16 July 2002. Some say that when Paddy Fogarty and Ritchie Edwards dropped Warren off at Islandbridge, less than two hours before Joey Rattigan was murdered, it was not to go and stay with his girlfriend. It is believed that a member of Freddie Thompson's gang was waiting for him after being phoned by Warren from the Pimlico Tavern and told that Rattigan was there. Warren and the other gang member then drove to Cooley Road, knowing that Rattigan would be dropped off at his house later in the night. When Ritchie Edwards dropped Rattigan on Cooley Road, the gunman stepped out of the shadows, fired a single shot to Rattigan's head and, was driven away from the scene by the senior gang member in a waiting car. Warren either pulled the trigger or drove the getaway car. In the years since the murder, the name Paddy Doyle has frequently been mentioned to Gardaí as the man who murdered Joey, but it is not known for certain.

Other Gardaí believe that a professional hitman was hired at short notice to carry out the assassination, and the 'Merry Christmas Murderer', Shay Wildes, has been nominated as the most likely hired gun. It is possible that Wildes carried out the murder and gave the Smith & Wesson back to members of the Thompson gang, who then wiped it clean of the DNA of any potential suspect and planted in the glove compartment of the Volvo, knowing Gardaí would find it. This makes sense, considering the Volvo and murder weapon were not found until six weeks after the murder, and were discovered in a residential area where an abandoned car would naturally attract a lot of attention. The unusual amount of DNA could have been purposefully left in the car by the Thompson gang who made sure that it did not match them, so the murder weapon or suspected getaway car could never be linked to them. Again this makes sense, when all the criminals arrested willingly gave Gardaí DNA samples, especially when cooperating with Gardaí, in any way, is most unusual for these gangsters.

Freddie mightn't have been the man who was in possession of the gun used to murder Joey Rattigan, but 2002 ended on a sour note for him. In early December, he was disqualified from driving for 20 years at Carlow Circuit Court.

* * *

Brian Rattigan's life was thrown into chaos following his brother's murder. He quickly went off the rails, and began using serious amounts of cocaine, which just added to his paranoia. In the months after Joey's murder, Brian Rattigan got a massive tattoo of Joey's face on his chest, with the words 'Joey', 'brother', and Joey's dates of birth and death in large writing. Despite the fact that he was still in pain after being shot the previous March, and had to wear a colostomy bag because his stomach had been so badly damaged, Rattigan swore revenge and told his gang that he wanted the bodies to pile up. He carried out his own internal investigation into Joey's murder and concluded that Paul Warren was to blame. On 14 August 2002, just a month after his brother's murder, Gardaí from the Bridewell arrived at Cooley Road after receiving a tip that Brian Rattigan was in possession of a large amount of heroin. Detective Inspector John McMahon led the operation, backed up by Detective Sergeant Pat Lordan. Gardaí arrived at the house with a search warrant. When they found the front door slightly open, they burst in. Brian Rattigan obviously wasn't expecting them or had become sloppy with grief, because he was lying in bed asleep with a sock in his hand. The sock was found to contain €27,000 worth of heroin.

It was a hammer blow: because the amount exceeded €10,000, he was facing a mandatory ten-year sentence. It was a schoolboy error on his part, but it was a massive victory for Gardaí, who knew that Rattigan would soon be off the streets for a long stretch. They hoped his absence would bring some respite from the feuding. He was arrested, taken to court and bailed.

Realising that he wouldn't have his freedom for much longer, Rattigan really lost the plot and seemed to have lost the will to live. He was certainly a subdued figure and was a shadow of his confident former self.

On 15 February 2003, at around midday, an unmarked

patrol car from Kilmainham Garda Station driven by Garda Paul Maher, and Garda Patrick Smith, came across a suspicious-looking navy Nissan Sunny in Inchicore. Four men were travelling in the Nissan, and the squad car sounded its siren and signalled for the vehicle to pull over, so that the two Gardaí could perform a routine check on the vehicle to make sure that it wasn't stolen. The Nissan sped off in the direction of the Bluebell Road, and the patrol car radioed for back-up and gave chase. The Nissan drove into a cul-de-sac off the Naas Road. Garda Maher stopped his squad car behind it, as it came to a halt at the end of the road. Without warning, the Nissan reversed at speed and crashed into the Garda car. The impact of the collision was such that substantial damage was caused to the Garda vehicle. Fortunately, the two Gardaí were uninjured. The Nissan then spun around and headed onto La Touche Road at high speed, where it struck the car of an innocent passing motorist. Again the driver was uninjured, although the car was badly damaged.

Detective Gardaí Brian Hearne and Jim Matthews were driving an unmarked car and they rushed to the area to help their colleagues. Brian Rattigan, who was sitting in the back seat, opened up the window and began firing at the detectives with a pump-action shotgun. A total of five rounds were fired, with three of them hitting the car. They could have easily killed the two plainclothes detectives, but luckily all the rounds missed their targets. The unmarked car was rammed three times, as Rattigan and his associates desperately tried to get away. The men abandoned the Nissan at the Bernard Curtis flats complex on the Bluebell Road, adjacent to the Grand Canal, and the four men all fled on foot. Detective Gardaí Hearne and Matthews cornered Brian Rattigan. Rattigan pointed his weapon straight at Matthews and cocked it, ready to fire. The detective ordered Rattigan to drop his firearm, but the deranged criminal continued to point it at the officer. Detective Garda Matthews had no option but to fire a warning shot from his official-issue pistol. The sound of the shot seemed to bring Rattigan back into the real world, because he dropped his gun and was overpowered by the two officers and taken into custody. The fact that Brian Rattigan was prepared to shoot at Gardaí showed just how out of control he had become after Joey's murder. On 18 February, he was charged with the possession of a Mossberg pump action shotgun with intent to endanger life, at Kilmainham District Court, as well as the possession of five shotgun cartridges. Detective Inspector Gabriel O'Gara did not object to bail, but Rattigan did not apply for it and was remanded in custody. Garda intelligence suggests that Rattigan was on his way to carry out an attack on Aidan Gavin when he was arrested. Two of the other three men with Rattigan in the car that night were 18-year-old Wayne Zambra from Maryland, a petty criminal. He was the driver. The other was 19-year-old Wayne McNally from Loreto Road in Dublin 8, who was regarded as a key Rattigan associate and a violent and dangerous young man. McNally later pleaded guilty to allowing himself to be carried in a stolen vehicle and claimed that he did not know that his friend, Rattigan, had a gun. He told Gardaí he only realised that there was a gun when Rattigan fired shots at the Garda car. He was sentenced to four years. There was insufficient evidence to charge Wayne Zambra, which puzzled many criminals because the three men were detained together.

In May 2003, Rattigan was jailed for six years for the heroin that was found in his sock at his home. It meant that he would only serve at least four years. This news brought great relief among Gardaí across South Dublin, but there was disappointment that the mandatory ten year sentencing guideline had been ignored. However, there was a further boost to come. Within two months of Declan Gavin's murder, a complex Garda investigation file, which ran to six

volumes had been sent to the DPP. Following the submission
of follow-up statements from expert witnesses and technical
experts, and after other preliminary-files were received, as
requested by the DPP, directions were finally given to charge
Brian Rattigan with the murder. On 18 September 2003,
Detective Sergeant Joe O'Hara and lead investigator
Detective Inspector Tom Mulligan charged Brian Rattigan.
He was arrested in Mountjoy Prison. He was then
transported to Court 46 at Dublin District Court. The court
heard that he replied, 'No, dirty f***ing rat', when he was
charged. He was remanded in custody back to Mountjoy
Prison.

In February 2004, Rattigan pleaded guilty to the two
charges in relation to the Bluebell incident the previous year.
Rattigan's senior counsel, Brendan Grehan, told Judge
Joseph Matthews at Dublin Circuit Criminal Court that his
client had been the victim of a shooting in March 2002, and
that his brother had also been murdered that same year. He
told Judge Matthews that he could not give him any more
details about the two previous incidents, in case Rattigan was
part of 'a horrible scenario where he is walking around with
a gun because he is expecting to have his head blown off'. He
also said there may be future legal cases against his client.
Grehan said that despite the fact that Brian Rattigan pulled
his gun on Garda Matthews, 'he did not take the ultimate
step of pulling the trigger'. He added that it later emerged
that Rattigan's gun was empty when he cocked it, and the
court should not speculate as to whether or not he would
have fired it, had it been loaded. Brian Rattigan received a
four-and-a-half-year sentence in relation to the incident,
although the DPP later unsuccessfully appealed the leniency.
This was to run consecutively with a six-year term Rattigan
was handed for possession of the €27,000 of heroin the
previous year. This meant that Brian Rattigan would be in
prison for a minimum of seven years, which was a massive

personal blow, as well as a serious body shot to his gang. Although he was off the streets, Rattigan's power was not diminished, and he soon showed that he was able to control his side, even from behind prison bars.

SIX

Rattigan's revenge

With Brian Rattigan locked up and out of the way, the feud quietened down. After the incident involving Rattigan and the Gardaí in Bluebell in February 2003, the rest of the year passed quietly. Freddie Thompson and his gang were now the dominant players in drug dealing from Crumlin to the south-inner city. Rattigan's men seemed happy with this arrangement; they shipped significant amounts of drugs around Drimnagh and made their money without any bloodshed. Although Thompson was enjoying the feeling of dominating the streets of Crumlin and Drimnagh, he couldn't actually enjoy the benefits because he was serving a two year-jail sentence after being found guilty of endangerment and assault, after he drove his car at a Garda in Rathmines in August 2002. He was sent to prison in February 2003. So, with himself and Rattigan off the streets, there was a much-needed lull in hostilities.

The following year, 2004, got off to a bloody start though. It was a sign of things to come – the next two years would be the bloodiest in the history of the feud, with conflict starting again at a pace that was much quicker than before. On 15 January at approximately 1.45am, a number of shots were fired through the window of an apartment in Dublin 8. The apartment was home to a 43-year-old woman and her relation, a 19-year-old girl, who was also Mr X's girlfriend at the time; one of Rattigan's senior henchmen, but nobody was injured. Garda intelligence suggests that Paddy Doyle was responsible for the shooting. Although he was arrested, there was no real evidence against him, so he was never charged and the incident was not solved. On 30 January, the Garda intelligence branch, Crime and Security, received information that there was a threat to the life of Darren Geoghegan. Detective Sergeant John Walsh from Sundrive Road subsequently met with Geoghegan at the station on 3 February. He told Geoghegan the news, before offering him advice on his personal security. Geoghegan laughed when he was told about the threat to his life. He stayed in the station for all of 30 seconds. There was serious bad blood between Brian Rattigan and Darren Geoghegan, and he had been targeted the most out of all the members of Thompson's gang. Gardaí had no doubt that Brian Rattigan's side was behind this latest threat. On 10 February, Crime and Security again got in touch with DS John Walsh and told him of intelligence that Mr X's life was now under threat. John Walsh telephoned Mr X and asked to meet him, but he refused, so Walsh had to give him security advice over the phone.

However, the following day Mr X's mother went to Sundrive Road and she was given more advice concerning the safety of her son. Freddie Thompson's gang were thought to have been behind the threat. On the same day that Crime and Security got in touch about Mr X they also relaid information that Michael Frazer's life was in danger.

Michael Frazer, who was 29 and from Knocknarea Avenue in Drimnagh, had been on the periphery of the Rattigan and Gavin gang when it had just formed. He was no longer associating with either side at this stage, although he had been close to Declan Gavin. The day after Gardaí received the warning from Crime and Security, Frazer called to Sundrive Road station and was given security advice from DI Brian Sutton. He refused to acknowledge the fact that he was involved with any criminal group and expressed surprise that anybody would want to hurt him. However, when he was pressed further he said that if anything were to happen to him, it was because of the Drimnagh feud and his former friendships with people like Brian Rattigan and Freddie Thompson. The intelligence passed on by Crime and Security was spot on. Just four days after he was given security advice, armed and masked men fired three shots outside Frazer's home, and shouted, 'Tell Mickey he's gonna get it.' Gardaí could never fully determine who was responsible, but Shay O'Byrne, Sharon Rattigan's partner, was the prime suspect.

Ever since Joey Rattigan had been murdered, Paul Warren was a marked man and knew that if any of Brian Rattigan's gang saw him alone, he would be vulnerable. However, he had managed to avoid bumping into any of the rival gangsters in the 18 months since he had set up Joey Rattigan to be murdered. On the morning of 25 February 2004, the 24-year-old got up out of bed as normal, having no reason to suspect that this would be the day when fate finally caught up with him. He went to work at Hennessy Glass, on the Lower Kimmage Road, at about 8.20am. He had worked as a glazier for the company for the previous two years. He liked his job and the people he worked with. He went to do a job in the south-inner city at about 1.15pm. He decided to go Gray's pub, on Newmarket Square, for a pint and a game of pool. Warren knew Gray's as the Red Lion, and before that as Bonnie and Clyde's. He grew up not far away in St Teresa's Gardens. He was a regular in the pub, and was well known there. Warren had had an accident a few weeks previously, when a pane of glass had fallen on his head, resulting in stitches. He had an appointment to go to St James's Hospital to get the stitches removed, but he was enjoying the few pints and decided to skip it. His boss had already said it was okay to have the rest of the afternoon off. Warren was also supposed to meet with his probation officer that afternoon, but again decided to give it a miss, even though it meant that he could get in trouble, if the probation officer decided to take things further. He spent the afternoon playing pool with random customers. At about 7.00pm, a friend of his called to Gray's and asked Warren if he would go with him to Crumlin with another mate to try to sort out a dispute that he was having. Warren was always willing to do a pal a turn, so the three men drove to Crumlin, looking for the rival group. There was no sign of the group, so they went back to Gray's to continue drinking. Champions League football was on the telly, and the group were in the mood for a few more games of pool.

Things had been going well for Warren of late. He'd managed to put the events of the last 18 months behind him. He was trying to get on with life as normal. Warren was originally from Fatima Mansions but moved with his parents to St Teresa's Gardens when he was a young lad, along with his four sisters and brother. He had only recently moved in with his girlfriend and they were renting a house together in Clondalkin. He had been in trouble with the police on and off since he was young. He had managed to chalk-up 23 convictions in his 24 years – 20 of those were for road traffic offences, and the other three for the simple possession of drugs. He had never served a lengthy jail sentence, and was regarded as a bit of a messer, and certainly not a serious criminal. He was way out of his depth getting involved in the Joey Rattigan murder. No matter how smoothly things were going at that time, being blamed for setting a man up to be killed was surely never far from his mind.

Gray's pub was not busy and there were only ten people present when the football kicked off. Warren and his two friends drank and played pool, and Warren occasionally spoke to the barman. The barman later recalled that 'he was in good form. There was a good atmosphere, a normal atmosphere.' At about 8.00pm, a man called Jonathan

Mooney came into the pub with his girlfriend at the time. He looked at the other customers and noticed Paul Warren, whom he knew from around the area. Mooney was a criminal who had spent time in jail with Brian Rattigan, and associated with known members of the Rattigan gang. Mooney took his girlfriend's mobile phone and made a call. About ten minutes later, the phone rang. Brian Rattigan was on the other end, even though he was in a jail cell in Mountjoy Prison. Rattigan asked Mooney if Paul Warren was in the pub. When Mooney confirmed he was, Rattigan inquired as to what clothes he was wearing and where he was sitting in the bar. Customers noticed that Jonathan Mooney spent a lot of the night going in and out of the pub talking on the mobile. Paul Warren was playing pool while keeping an eye on the football – oblivious to the fact that the phone call Jonathan Mooney made had sealed his fate. Although Brian Rattigan had had to wait for a year and a half to avenge his brother's death, he was determined that Warren would not walk out of Gray's that night.

* * *

Gary Bryan's girlfriend, Valerie White, was looking forward to a quiet night in, when her boyfriend's mobile phone rang at around 8.15pm. Gary Bryan never said where he was going, but assured her that he wouldn't be long. While White sat watching TV, she was unaware that Brian Rattigan had phoned her boyfriend. A plot was being hatched to murder Paul Warren, who was in Gray's pub, only a short drive from the flat Valerie shared with Bryan on the South Circular Road. Gardaí believe that Bryan went out to meet John Roche, and that the pair were in communication with Brian Rattigan, formulating how they would murder Paul Warren. After about 45 minutes, Bryan came back to the one-bedroom apartment, went to the bedroom and, detectives believe, took a Magnum handgun, which he kept in the house, from the back of the wardrobe. He left again without telling his girlfriend where he was going, and she gave out to him for leaving so soon. It is believed that Bryan and John Roche spent the next hour or so deciding on how the murder would go down, while driving around in John Roche's car deciding on the best route of escape after they had carried out the assassination. After this they went back to Bryan's apartment. They had a pair of balaclavas and each man had a loaded gun. Phone records would later show that several calls were made between Bryan and Brian Rattigan, before the killing took place. Ten minutes before the murder, Gary Bryan rang Jonathan Mooney's girlfriend and asked to speak to him. He double checked to make sure that Paul Warren was still in the pub. He made the call at 10.47pm, it only took 52 seconds for him to get confirmation that the hit was still on. Bryan left his apartment with John Roche and drove the short journey to Gray's in a stolen silver-grey Ford Mondeo. Just before 11.00pm, Bryan and Roche arrived at Newmarket Square, a quiet area with very few houses. It had been agreed that John Roche would do the shooting, but before they went into the pub, Gary Bryan said that he was taking over. John Roche was over 6 ft tall, Bryan at just 5 ft 8" was far smaller. They both put on their balaclavas and gripped their handguns bursting through the front door of Gray's pub. Because Gary Bryan knew that Paul Warren was over by the pool table, he ran straight for him. Warren saw the movement, looked up and knew instantly that he was in serious danger. He ran to the opposite side of the pub, towards the toilets, just as Bryan opened fire with the Magnum for the first time, but the bullet missed its target. While Bryan went to take care of Paul Warren, John Roche covered the entrance to the pub. He shouted at the frightened customers: 'Don't move.' Some of the dozen customers in the bar screamed in terror, and a couple ran towards the ladies' toilets to hide, which was at the opposite side of the bar to the men's. The barman ducked into the cellar behind the bar, so as not to be caught in the crossfire. The execution was over in a matter of seconds. As Paul Warren ran into the men's toilets, Bryan caught up with him. Bryan fired a shot at close range, which struck Warren in the back, just underneath the neck. Even though he had been fatally wounded, Warren kept going. He made his way into a cubicle and tried to push it closed, in the hope that the gunman would panic and leave the pub. Bryan stuck his hand in behind the half-open door and fired a shot into Warren's face, hitting him in the right cheek. Bryan knew instinctively that his mission had been achieved, and he didn't even stop to make sure that Warren was dead. According to witnesses in the pub, when Bryan ran out of the toilet, he said to Roche: 'I got him. Let's get out of here.' Both Jonathan Mooney and his girlfriend were present when the murder took place, but left before the Gardaí arrived. As the two gunmen were making their escape, customers were already starting to recover from the shock of what had happened. Several went into the men's toilet to check on Warren, but the large pool of blood that had flowed under the cubicle door and down towards the main toilet entrance told its own story. Paul Warren was dead.

At around 11.00pm on 25 February 2004, Garda Caroline Mulpeter of Garda Command and Control, based at Harcourt Street, received a 999 call informing her that there had been a shooting at Gray's pub. Gardaí Joseph Duignam and Deirdre McMenamin were dispatched, and arrived at the pub, just one minute later. Dublin Fire Brigade had also been informed of the incident, and firefighters Phil Evans, Terry Dent, Liam Anderson and Ian Duffy arrived at the scene in two ambulances. They tried to administer first aid to Paul Warren, but he was already lying dead in the toilet cubicle. GP Dr Lionel Williams officially pronounced him dead at 11.55pm.

The following afternoon, when Gardaí had finished the

technical examination of the pub, Warren's body was taken from the scene to the Dublin City Morgue in Marino. That evening, Warren's father identified his son's body to Detective Inspector Gabriel O'Gara from Kevin Street Garda Station. DI O'Gara, an experienced murder detective, was the Garda in day-to-day charge of the case. Within minutes of the shooting, a murder inquiry was launched from Kevin Street. Over the next 48 hours, a number of case conferences were held that were attended by local Gardaí and detectives, as well as specialist plain-clothes officers from the National Bureau of Criminal Investigation (NBCI). Because Gardaí from Crumlin and Sundrive Road had been investigating Paul Warren in relation to Joey Rattigan's murder, it soon became apparent that Warren was murdered in revenge for his role – or perceived role – in that killing. Over the next few months, Gardaí from Kevin Street, Sundrive Road and Crumlin would work very closely together: comparing notes, information and anything they learned from talking to touts on the streets. All Gardaí involved in the murder were acutely aware that tensions between the Rattigan and Thompson gangs would be unbelievably high, and that revenge attacks were not just possible, but inevitable.

Warren's funeral was a tense affair. There was a large number of Gardaí, both plainclothes and uniformed, on duty, to ensure that it passed off peacefully. A tradition had developed in Crumlin and Drimnagh that when a person died in a gangland incident, the funerals should be big occasions. They were generally more like show funerals, with massive floral tributes and old style hearses pulled by horses.

Many shops and pubs in the area either closed out of respect to the dead, or were intimidated into closing their doors. Members of the Garda Surveillance Unit routinely photographed mourners at the feud funerals. The pictures gave Gardaí a good understanding of which people were affiliated with which gang. This was invaluable, especially after the first few murders, when individuals could and did change allegiances. In several funerals the priest officiating used the pulpit to plead for an end to violence, and for members of the community to assist the Gardaí in their investigations. On more than one occasion, gang members actually walked out of the church in disgust upon hearing this.

In the weeks after Paul Warren's murder, armed Gardaí patrolled the streets of Crumlin, Drimnagh and the south-inner city, to try to keep a lid on what was a powder keg just ready to explode.

While Gardaí were actively trying to catch Paul Warren's murderer, Gary Bryan was busy covering his tracks. When the murder was completed, Bryan and John Roche went back to Bryan's apartment, where they spoke for a while, before Roche left. Gary Bryan changed his clothes and put them in a bag at the back of the wardrobe. He then stayed up until the early hours taking cocaine with his girlfriend. He eventually told her that he had killed Paul Warren. He woke up the following afternoon, and after carrying out a few errands, he took the bag from the back of the wardrobe and travelled by taxi to his family home at Brookview Crescent in Tallaght. He then spoke to his father, Michael. Bryan then went to the back garden, got some petrol and burned the bag containing the clothes that he wore while carrying out the assassination. There is no evidence to say that Bryan spoke with his father or anyone else about what he did. Another bag lay in the wardrobe containing spent cartridges from the Magnum and one of the balaclavas worn by John Roche during the murder. Bryan realised he would have to get rid of them, so he asked Valerie White if her sister Elaine would take the bag in her house and hold on to it for him. Elaine didn't know what was in the bag, but she agreed. On the evening of 9 March, they drove to Elaine's house in nearby Weaver's Square, and left without the bag. Valerie White was not happy to be getting involved with covering up a murder. She certainly didn't want to get her family dragged into it, but she desperately wanted to help her boyfriend, whom she deeply loved. So she went along with Bryan's pleas to get Elaine to hold on to the bag. As the pair left Weaver's Square to go back home, they failed to notice the two unmarked Garda cars that had been following them for the last few days.

The Garda investigation was progressing well. Senior detectives agreed that the two gunmen had prior intelligence that Paul Warren was drinking in Gray's. All the customers present in the pub at the time of the murder were interviewed, including Jonathan Mooney and his girlfriend. Statements given by some of those drinking, confirmed that the gunmen had prior knowledge about where Warren was in the bar. The barman told detectives: 'When he [gunman] came into the pub, he just looked straight at Paul and ran for him. He seemed to know exactly where he was.'

Officers received their first break just days after the murder, when a confidential informant told them that Gary Bryan was the man who had shot Warren. Gary Bryan was well known to members of the District Detective Unit at Kevin Street, who were aware that he was involved in the drugs gang controlled by Brian Rattigan.

* * *

Gary Bryan was born on 11 December 1975 to Michael Snr and Veronica Bryan. From an early age Bryan was nicknamed 'Tipper'. He was brought up in Tallaght and was from a large family. He got involved with a bad crowd in his early teens and drifted into drugs and criminality. He was a drug addict, using a variety of illegal substances, including cocaine, heroin and codeine. He was trying to kick his drugs habit, and was receiving methadone each day at a drug treatment clinic in Pearse Street.

Bryan had amassed 17 criminal convictions, the first in October 1993, when he was just 17 years old, and the last on 20 May 2003. Most of the convictions were for relatively minor offences, such as driving without a licence, having no insurance, dangerous driving, unauthorised taking of a vehicle and a number of offences for theft. On 16 December 1998, he was sentenced to three years imprisonment for aggravated burglary, and an extra six years for possession of firearms with criminal intent and false imprisonment. The following June, Bryan received another four years for attempted trespass. Bryan never had a steady job and collected social welfare each week. While in prison he met Brian Rattigan and other members of his gang. When he was released, he began to associate with them and gradually got sucked more and more into the murderous feud that had recently developed. Bryan wasn't like a typical member of Brian Rattigan's gang. He didn't have any day-to-day involvement in the shootings and other criminal incidents that frequently happen because of the feud. He tended to keep himself to himself, and only got involved when John Roche or Shay O'Byrne called upon him. He was a drug dealer but worked for himself, and was not supplied by Rattigan. Gardaí always thought that Bryan was more of a hired gun than a central gang member. He was now the main suspect in the Paul Warren murder. The cold precise manner in which that execution had been carried out, made detectives certain that Warren was not the first man that Gary Bryan had murdered.

* * *

After the tip that Gary Bryan was the shooter, detectives immediately placed Bryan's apartment under surveillance. Inquiries and intelligence from Sundrive Road Garda station had determined that he shared the flat with Valerie White, a 29-year-old originally from Crumlin. On the night of 9 March 2004, Gardaí observed Gary Bryan and Valerie White leaving their apartment. Bryan was carrying a white Puma bag. They drove to Valerie's sister Elaine's house, and when they left, detectives observed that the bag, which they had taken into the house, was not with them any more. The pair drove back to their apartment, and a few minutes later Bryan left again. Gardaí later arrested Bryan in Tallaght in relation to a separate offence. Detectives knew that Bryan would not crack under pressure. They wanted to build evidence against him before he was detained and questioned about the Warren murder. With Bryan in a cell in Tallaght, early the following morning, Gardaí obtained a search warrant for his apartment. There they discovered a Taurus .357 Magnum handgun, with six rounds of live ammunition wrapped in a blue and pink plastic bag. They also recovered a black balaclava. Valerie White was present during the search, and at around 4.30pm DI Gabriel O'Gara arrested her on suspicion that she had information in relation to the Paul Warren murder. This was later amended to the unlawful possession of a firearm, and White was detained for 24 hours. She was interviewed a total of 12 times while in custody. She was released without charge the following day, 12 March, after refusing to comment during her round of interviews. Nevertheless, Gardaí had recovered a firearm. They hoped that ballistics tests would confirm that it was the weapon that was used to murder Paul Warren.

On the day that Valerie White was released without charge, her sister Elaine was arrested. Gardaí were aware that Gary Bryan had left a bag at Elaine White's apartment. On 12 March, after securing a search warrant, a team led by Detective Sergeant Adrian Whitelaw searched the premises. The Puma bag was found and it contained four live rounds and 12 spent cartridges from what appeared to be a handgun. A Nokia mobile phone and a Meteor SIM card were also recovered. A mobile phone manual was also found in the bag, as well as a black balaclava.

Witnesses in the pub said that the gunmen had both been wearing balaclavas, and detectives were confident that they had now recovered both of these. Elaine White was detained for possession of information in relation to an unlawful offence and was taken to Kevin Street. She made a statement and told Gardaí that she received the bag from Gary Bryan on 9 March. She was able to describe what was in the bag and told detectives of the dilemma she faced: whether to contact them and tell them about the bag or to just dump it. She didn't want to have any hand, act or part in whatever Gary Bryan had got himself involved in. She was then released without charge.

The investigating detectives were very pleased with the work they had done over the last 24 hours. As well as the Magnum, they now had both balaclavas and the phone they believed was used to plan the murder of Paul Warren. The case was steadily starting to come together, but Gardaí got an unexpected and spectacular boost the following day when Valerie White turned up at Kevin Street and said that she wanted to tell the truth about what happened on the day of the murder.

Valerie White was furious – and felt very guilty – when she found out that her sister had been arrested for agreeing to hold Gary Bryan's bag. After being cautioned about her legal rights, White made a signed statement to Detective Sergeant Adrian Whitelaw and Garda Linda Williams. She gave a graphic, comprehensive and damning account of her boyfriend's role in the slaying, and by the time she had completed her statement, the case against Gary Bryan was effectively sewn-up.

She said that she came voluntarily to Kevin Street Garda Station to 'tell the truth' about the night of the Paul Warren murder because her family were 'getting dragged into it'. White described how she and Gary Bryan had moved into the flat on the South Circular Road in September 2003 and how the first few months went brilliantly. At that time, Gary wasn't associating with members of the Rattigan gang like Mr X and Shay O'Byrne. However, he gradually began to talk to them on the phone and Shay O'Byrne visited the flat in early December 2003. Gary then started to see more of the criminals, and, on the night of his birthday, on 11 December, he came back with €250 worth of cocaine, which Shay O'Byrne had given him as a present. Valerie said that both she and Gary used the drugs and then started to take cocaine more regularly. She described that first night as 'the death of us'. Soon afterwards, Gary brought a gun into the flat and showed it to his girlfriend. He said it wasn't his and that he was just holding it for somebody. Valerie was an honest woman and a law-abiding citizen and was disgusted that her house was being used to store a gun. She told Gary to get it out of her sight and they had frequent arguments about it over the next few weeks, but nevertheless, Gary kept the gun hidden in the wardrobe of their bedroom. Gary then started to get sucked more and more into the Rattigan gang, and Shay O'Bryne and Mr X would regularly ring Valerie's phone looking for Gary. Brian Rattigan would also contact him from his prison cell. Then Bryan started leaving the flat for several hours at a time and wouldn't tell Valerie where he was going or who he was with. In early 2004, things settled down again until the night of the Paul Warren murder. At around 8.00pm that night, Gary got up and left without saying where he was off to. He came back about a half an hour later and went into their bedroom for about ten minutes, before leaving again. When Valerie asked where he was going, he replied simply: 'Out.' Gary Bryan didn't arrive back until about 11.00pm and headed straight into the bedroom without saying hello to Valerie. She knew that something was up and picked up some washing off the radiator and went into the bedroom, but Gary was there with another man. Valerie described him to Gardaí as 'a tall fairly

stocky fella with short brown hair. I know now his name is
John Roche, from Drimnagh, 'cause Gary told me his name
later on that night when he was gone'. Valerie looked on the
bed and was shocked to see two guns. One was the same
weapon that Gary had been holding in the wardrobe, while
the second was smaller and was black in colour. When she
saw the guns, she dropped the clothes and went straight back
into the sitting room. A few minutes later, Gary came in and
spoke on the phone to somebody while pacing between the
bedroom and sitting room. He asked the person for money,
and, when he got off the phone, he arranged for a local drug
dealer to sort him out with some cocaine. John Roche had
left the flat by this stage. Gary and Valerie left the flat and
went to a nearby flats complex to pick up four bags of
cocaine from the dealer. He told them that the Gardaí were
everywhere because Paul Warren had just been shot. Valerie
said that Gary looked at her and that she 'knew by his
manner, the way that he was going on, that he had
something to do with it'. They went back to the flat and
started to take the cocaine, and Valerie asked Gary if he was
involved in the murder. At first he wouldn't answer her and
then asked if she would think any less of him if he was
involved. She told him that she wouldn't, but she had
already vowed to herself that their relationship was over.
Bryan then opened up and went into detail about the murder
he had just committed. Valerie told the two detectives: 'He
started to talk to me then. I asked him what they did. He
told me John Roche stood at the door of the pub. He said
that Roche wanted to do the shooting but he done it
himself. I asked him what gun he used, and Gary told me,
'The Magnum.' I asked him how he knew he was in the pub.
Gary told me that Johnner Mooney had made the call from
the pub to let them know where he was.' Valerie then really
started to quiz Bryan about what had happened, but he
became angry, telling her to shut up. Before they went to bed

for the night, he started to talk a bit more. Valerie said: 'I remember asking Gary did Paul Warren see them coming in. Gary told me that he was standing at the bar, saw them coming in and tried to run. Gary said he fired a shot at him in the pub, but he didn't know if he hit him or not 'cause there was a pillar or something. Then he ran into the toilets, sat down and tried to hold the door closed. Gary said he put his weight on the door to get it open and just put his arm in and shot him. Gary didn't tell me any more than that.' The following day, Gary headed over to his father's house in Tallaght. After that, they didn't leave the house much, but the day before Paul Warren's funeral, Gary went out to get some coke. As he arrived back to the flat, he was approached by three men in a BMW. One of them opened fire with a gun, but Gary escaped and made it back to the safety of the flat. He was white and shaking with the fright and started to wear a bulletproof vest from then on. Bryan knew that there was a contract out on his head, and the couple went to stay in a hotel for a few days because he feared for his life. Valerie then went on to tell Adrian Whitelaw and Linda Williams about going to her sister Elaine's house because Bryan wanted to leave a bag there. She said that he stayed only a short while and then left. After signing her statement, she left the Garda station.

On 14 March the day after Valerie White's explosive statement, Gardaí obtained a search warrant for the Bryan family home at Brookview Crescent. The search took place at first light, just after 7.00am. Officers found the remains of a fire in the back garden. After the search of the Bryan family home was completed, DS Declan Smith arrested Michael Bryan Snr, Gary Bryan's father, under Section 30 of the Offences Against the State Act 1939, for the unlawful possession of information in relation to a criminal offence, the offence being the possession of firearms at Gray's pub on the night of Paul Warren's murder. He was taken to Kevin

Street Garda Station. During his 24 hours in custody, Michael Bryan Snr was interviewed under caution on 12 separate occasions. During one of these interviews, he said that his son called to the family home on 1 March 2004 with a bag, and that he got petrol and burnt the bag in the back garden. Michael Bryan Snr denied having any knowledge of the murder or what was in the bag. He was released without charge. Four days after Michael Bryan Snr was released from Garda custody, Michael Bryan Jnr was arrested for being in possession of information about the firearm used in the murder. While in custody, he said he remembered his half-brother Gary calling to the house, and on the same night seeing glowing embers in the back garden and hearing three or four loud bangs. This confirmed what his father had told Gardaí. Michael Jnr was also released without charge.

After Valerie White made her statement, Gardaí applied for and received records of all phone calls made and received by Jonathan Mooney and his girlfriend on the night of Paul Warren's murder. They showed that he had been in contact with a number of people connected to the murder, namely Gary Bryan, John Roche and Brian Rattigan who had been communicating with the gang via mobile phone from Mountjoy prison. Maloney had been interviewed after the murder as a potential witness, because he was present in the pub when it happened. The Gardaí did not know at that time that without Mooney's help, the murder could not have taken place.

On the morning of 7 April 2004, Sergeant Mark Kelly arrested Jonathan Mooney for being in possession of information relating to the unlawful possession of firearms at Gray's pub on the night of 25 February 2004. He was taken to the investigation headquarters at Kevin Street and was interviewed a total of 13 times while in custody. During this period he made two statements to Gardaí. In his statement, Mooney gave officers a list of the people that were present in

Gray's pub before the murder, including Paul Warren. He then said that he received a phonecall from an associate named Anthony Cannon while in the pub, but that Cannon rang his girlfriend's phone. Cannon asked him questions about Paul Warren being in the pub.

Anthony Cannon was a 21-year-old from Robert Street in Dublin 8, who was climbing the ranks of the Rattigan gang and had a reputation as a hard man. Mooney then said he received several more phonecalls from Brian Rattigan, even though Rattigan was locked up in a prison cell at the time. Rattigan asked him about Paul Warren, and enquired as to where he was sitting in the pub. He told Mooney that if Paul Warren got up and left, he should immediately phone him on his mobile in Mountjoy. Mooney admitted to detectives that he was aware that Paul Warren and Brian Rattigan were enemies. He also knew that there were suspicions that Warren had set up Joey Rattigan's murder. Jonathan Mooney said he knew that giving the information about Warren being in the pub to Brian Rattigan it would cause something bad to happen to him, but he claimed that he thought the worst that would happen to Warren would be 'a few slaps'. Mooney went on to say that a few minutes before Warren was murdered, he received a phonecall from Gary Bryan, who again asked him if Warren was still in the pub and still sitting in the same place. After Bryan and Roche went to the pub and murdered Warren, Mooney again got call from Brian Rattigan, who asked, 'Did Warrener get killed?' Rattigan then told Mooney to make sure that he got rid of the mobile phone, so that it could never be recovered by Gardaí. He did as instructed. his girlfriend's phone was never found. On the day that Mooney was arrested, a detailed search of the landing in Mountjoy, that Rattigan called home was undertaken in an attempt to find the mobile phone he had used to communicate with Mooney and Bryan on the night of the murder. It was never found. It is suspected that Rattigan destroyed it. Gardaí were sure that Rattigan had been in phone contact from his cell, because Mooney had told them so, and when they triangulated the calls that he and Bryan had received, they were found to have originated from a cell tower close to the jail.

The day after Mooney's arrest, DS Adrian Whitelaw detained his girlfriend, for possession of information. She was interviewed 11 times at Kevin Street Garda Station. She made a statement, saying: 'I asked him [Mooney] who rang that night, and he said "Brian Rattigan". He said that Brian Rattigan asked him to point out Paul Warren to the fellas coming into the pub that night and he said "Yeah." I asked him why he said yeah and he said "I don't know." I then asked him what it was over and he said that Paul was supposed to have set up Brian's brother two years ago.'

By admitting to setting up Paul Warren to be killed – whether he knew it was going to happen or not – Jonathan Mooney walked himself into a lengthy prison sentence. Although he was released without charge on 9 April, a file would be prepared and sent to the DPP. Gardaí had no doubt whatsoever, that they would be told to charge him in relation to the phonecall informing Rattigan and his gang that Paul Warren was enjoying a quiet pint and game of pool in Gray's. That is exactly what happened in July 2005. Gardaí initially recommended that Mooney be charged with the murder of Paul Warren, telling the DPP: 'Jonathan Mooney played an integral part in the murder of Paul Warren. He has the *mens rea* (Latin for 'guilty mind', basically meaning the intent). When he was disclosing Paul Warren's whereabouts he knew Mr Warren would be attacked. He also knew the attack was in revenge for Paul Warren's involvement in the murder Joey Rattigan, so he knew the degree of attack would be serious. Brian Rattigan is one of the most vicious criminals in Dublin at the moment, and Jonathan Mooney is aware of this. Any revenge attack orchestrated by him will be serious. It is recommended that Jonathan Mooney be charged with the murder of Paul Warren.'

Although the DPP declined to charge Mooney with the Warren killing, they did charge him with assisting an offender and withholding information. Jonathan Mooney was sentenced to five years in prison, after pleading guilty to assisting an offender. He also pleaded guilty to withholding information in relation to the murder, and was handed another five-year term. The 23-year-old was present in court to hear that his sentences would run concurrently and would be backdated to June 2004. Prosecuting counsel Paul Coffey told the court: 'Mr Brian Rattigan masterminded the shooting from Mountjoy Prison.' Coffey added that Gardaí had established that Mr Rattigan made six calls to Jonathan Mooney between 10.23pm and 11.06pm, with five of the calls occurring before the murder, and one following the execution of Warren. Detective Inspector Gabriel O'Gara told the court that Mooney knew Brian Rattigan, because he spent time with him in jail, and also knew the two men who had carried out the murder. O'Gara said that Mooney claimed that he gave Brian Rattigan information about where Warren was drinking in the pub and the type of clothes he was wearing, because he was 'in fear' of him. The court also heard that Mooney and his mother were threatened with fatal consequences if he said anything untoward about Brian Rattigan. Defence counsel Mary Ellen Ring said that Mooney 'expressed his regret for the shooting of Mr Warren'.

Jonathan Mooney was born on 16 May 1982. He lived with his mother at Thomas Court Bawn in Dublin 8. His father died two years before the murder. He had been involved in a long-term relationship with his girlfriend, but this ended following the murder. He was unemployed and collected unemployment benefit each week. Mooney was regarded as a petty criminal; he had chalked up 24 previous convictions for minor offences, mainly road traffic breaches. He had two convictions for larceny, one for assault and one for breach of the peace. All had been dealt with at the less serious District Court level, and Mooney only served jail sentences of a few months at a time. Unfortunately, he met Brian Rattigan during one of those jail stints. Foolishly, Mooney had kept in touch with Rattigan and other gang members when he was released.

By mid April 2004, Gardaí finally had all the evidence against Gary Bryan collated. The DPP had decided that he should be arrested and charged with the murder. On 21 April, DS Adrian Whitelaw arrested Bryan, under Section 30 of the Offence Against the State Act, for unlawful possession of a firearm at Gray's pub on the night of the murder, over two months previously. He was held for 24 hours, which is the maximum time allowed under law before an extension has to be granted by a chief superintendent. This permission was given by Bill Donoghue from Pearse Street, which meant that Bryan could be held for a further 24 hours. Two days under police interrogation was nothing to a criminal as seasoned as Bryan, however, and in the 13 interviews, he refused to answer a single question. When he was preparing to walk out the door of Kevin Street on 23 April, Bryan may well have allowed himself a smug grin, thinking that he had beat the murder rap. Little did he know that detectives had already been in touch with the DPP and had been given permission to charge him. Bryan was out of Kevin Street for less than 20 seconds when he was rearrested, taken inside and handed a charge sheet, which informed him of the news. Needless to say, he was not happy. Gary Bryan was taken straight to Dublin District Court where he was formally charged with the murder of Paul Warren.

The case against Gary Bryan was very strong. When Detective Garda Tom Carey recovered a bullet covered in

Paul Warren's blood on the floor of the men's toilet of Gray's pub in the hours after the murder, it was obvious that this was a vital piece of evidence. This proved to be exactly the case. When officers recovered the Taurus .357 Magnum handgun, along with six rounds, from Bryan's home on 10 March, it was hoped that the bullet used to murder Warren would match the Magnum. It had already been determined that a Magnum handgun was the murder weapon. When the gun found at Bryan's apartment was test fired, it was found that the bullets used in the murder and the test had the same characteristics, but he could not give a conclusive match. The Puma bag recovered during the search of Elaine White's house on 12 March contained 12 spent cartridge cases. Detective Garda Carey compared them to the cases, which he test fired using the Magnum handgun found at Bryan's apartment, and found that eight of the 12 cartridge cases exactly matched the ones he test fired from the Magnum. Also, five rounds found in the Magnum handgun were Federal .38 specials and were found to be of the same manufacture and head stamp as the four spent cases found in the Puma bag taken from Elaine White's house. There was also fingerprint evidence linking Gary Bryan to the murder. Detective Garda John Grant examined the plastic bag in which the Magnum handgun was found wrapped for fingerprint evidence and found fingerprint impressions on it. Those impressions turned out to match Gary Bryan's fingerprints that he gave Gardaí when he was arrested and taken to Kevin Street. DG Grant also examined the Puma bag and found Bryan's fingerprints on an O_2 booklet and a Meteor SIM pack box. The Nokia phone and SIM card found in the Puma bag would later be confirmed as the number that rang Jonathan Mooney's girlfriend's phone ten minutes before Paul Warren was murdered. There was also a large amount of telephone traffic between his girlfriend's phone, which was used by Jonathan Mooney, and Brian Rattigan and Gary Bryan's phones. Witnesses at the pub said that the two gunmen wore balaclavas, and a balaclava found at Bryan's apartment had his DNA on it. The evidence against Bryan was strong, but the icing on the cake was Valerie White's witness statement implicating him in Paul Warren's murder.

Detectives prepared for the trial in the hope that the outcome would be a murder conviction. However, things took an unexpected turn when the case came to trial in February 2006. The case started promisingly with prosecution counsel Paul Coffey outlining the evidence to the jury about how Gardaí had linked all the pieces together and were in no doubt that Gary Bryan was Paul Warren's murderer. The Central Criminal Court heard how two men wearing balaclavas and carrying guns entered Gray's pub, and that one of them chased Paul Warren into the toilets and fired three bullets into him, with the victim dying less than an hour later. Mr Coffey told the court: 'The prosecution case is that the second gunman who fired all three shots and that the second shot that killed Paul Warren is the accused, Gary Bryan.' However, less than two hours later, the trial was to collapse amid farcical scenes. Valerie White took to the witness stand and said that she would not stand over anything she said in her sworn statement to Gardaí because she was high on cocaine on the night of the murder and could not remember anything. She said that she made her statement and volunteered detailed information to Gardaí because she thought it was what they wanted to hear. Without Valerie White's evidence the case against Bryan was not compelling enough to risk taking before a jury and getting a not guilty verdict. Paul Coffey told the judge that the state had no choice but to enter a *nolle prosequi*, which meant that it would not be proceeding with the prosecution. Mr Justice Paul Carney then excused the jury of six men and six women and there were celebrations from Gary Bryan who was present in court with a large group of friends and relatives.

Gardaí were furious with Valerie White for not standing over her evidence. There were strong suspicions that she had been warned not to give evidence but there was nothing that they could do for the moment. She had signed a deal, whereby she was given immunity from prosecution for cooperating with Gardaí, but had rubbed their noses in it at the eleventh hour. A nolle prosequi meant that the state could prosecute the case at a later date, if they so chose, but without any new evidence, it seemed unlikely that the DPP would risk another public humiliation – not to mention the tens of thousands of euro that had been wasted on the aborted trial.

Gary Bryan looked like a total innocent as he walked out of the court onto Dublin's north quays. With his short hair and conservative glasses, he looked more like a computer technician than a cold-blooded assassin – but Gardaí knew better. Bryan smiled at investigating detectives as he left a free man. He told one detective: 'The song goes, "I fought the law and the law won," but I fought the law and I won.' He didn't know it, but seven months later, he himself would die as a result of the feud, which was now threatening to get totally out of control.

SEVEN

Freddie hits back

Paul Warren's murder was a revenge of sorts for Brian Rattigan, who was intent on wiping out as many of Freddie Thompson's gang as possible. Although Warren wasn't a key member of the Thompson gang, he had been murdered by the rival group, so there was little doubt that another fatality would have to be notched up on the Rattigan side to balance the body count. The wild desperation of the Thompson gang to get even was clear just two days after Paul Warren's murder during an incident at Lansdowne Valley in Drimnagh. A man was set upon by four people with baseball bats and was told, 'You're dead', before being given a good hiding that resulted in serious injuries for which the man needed hospital treatment. While he was being mercilessly beaten, one of the attackers shouted: 'He's not one of them', before the group sheepishly left the scene. Garda inquiries ascertained that the injured party and a friend of his had helped to push start Shay O'Byrne's car earlier that day, and O'Byrne had been seen by a rival gang member. So keen were they to attack Shay O'Byrne that they didn't even bother to make sure they had the right man before they waded in swinging baseball bats. Gardaí never determined who carried out the assault. While Brian Rattigan was serving his sentence in Mountjoy, he wasn't letting time go to waste. On 13 April 2004, Detective Garda Eamonn Maloney was contacted by a man who told him that his brother, who was in Mountjoy, had been threatened in the jail by Rattigan and a number of his friends. The man who approached DG Maloney had been due to give witness evidence in an upcoming case against Eddie Redmond. He had been accused of assault causing harm and false imprisonment. The witnesses claimed that his brother had been told that if he turned up in court, his jailed brother would be murdered in Mountjoy. Gardaí and the prison authorities immediately investigated the claims, but the man in prison was not prepared to make a statement. The case against Eddie Redmond did not proceed because Gardaí could not get any witnesses to go to court, as they were too afraid. The rest of 2004 saw the Rattigan gang on the backfoot, and members kept their heads down because they knew that a revenge attack was inevitable. Gardaí were on high alert, and successfully managed to keep a lid on the tension. In early 2004, Detective Inspector Brian Sutton, who had arrested Declan Gavin for trying to take the 100,000 ecstasy tablets in Ballymount Cross in August 1999, was transferred to Crumlin and was now in day-to-day charge of policing the feud. He replaced Tom Mulligan who had transferred after being promoted. Sutton was an experienced investigator, who made it his business to keep in constant touch with the two gangs and their families to try to convince them to end the feud. Sutton and his boss, Detective Superintendent Denis Donegan, had studied the history of the feud in great detail and believed that proactive policing was the only way to keep the bodies from piling up. The two feuding sides were generally surprisingly receptive to Sutton and a number of young detectives he had brought with him, such as Detective Sergeant John Walsh, Detective Gardaí Barry Butler, David Finnerty and Ronan Lafferty. It was a new departure for the gang to be met by Gardaí who spoke to them on a human level, rather then trying to arrest them every second of the day.

Although Brian Rattigan had been charged with the Declan Gavin murder, things were not going well behind the scenes. The DPP had had possession of the Garda file in relation to the case since February 2002, however, the order to service the book of evidence to Rattigan's legal team had not been complied with by the DPP's office. Superintendent John Manley wrote to the DPP on four occasions, looking for clarification about the book of evidence, without receiving a satisfactory answer about the reason for the delay. Because the state had not given a valid reason for the delay in the service of the book of evidence and full disclosure of all the evidence against him, his legal counsel applied to the courts to have his murder charge struck out, and this order was granted. In such cases the normal process would be to re-enter the charge against the accused, but despite pleas from the Gardaí, the DPP still did not furnish the book of evidence.

Chief Superintendent Joe McGarrity took charge of the Dublin Metropolitan Region South district. He instructed his new Detective Inspector, Brian Sutton, to review all outstanding murders in the Crumlin 'G' district to see if the original investigators had overlooked any lines of inquiry. Brian Sutton undertook this task with gusto with the assistance of his key men, John Walsh, Barry Butler, Dave Finnerty and Ronan Lafferty. The team identified several fresh avenues of investigation and Detective Superintendent Denis Donegan submitted a new file to the DPP that eventually led to Rattigan being re-charged. There was relief all round that the murder charge had been sustained and that Rattigan would eventually be forced to have his day in court. There was no mistake with the book of evidence this time either, and it was served on Rattigan almost immediately. There was now no way that he could worm his way out of this one.

On 26 September 2004, Gardaí became aware that Ritchie Rattigan's life had been threatened. The following day, DI Sutton called to Cooley Road and informed Ritchie and his mother, Dinah, about the information that had been received: that both of them were in danger of being shot by the rival group. He gave them security advice and advised them to review their personal security arrangements. In the course of the discussion, Ritchie Rattigan said that he had received a phone call the previous day stating that there was a contract out on his head. He refused to say who had made the threat but did say that it was to get at Brian in prison. Rattigan also told Sutton that his girlfriend was pregnant, and the two of them would soon be moving to a corporation house in West Dublin. Over the following weeks, Sutton ordered ongoing patrols around the area to make sure that nobody carried the threat out. Gardaí knew that Joey Rattigan's murder had driven Brian as close as he could get to the edge without cracking up. If any more of his family were hurt, he would completely lose his mind, and there was no telling what might happen in those circumstances. In any event, the extra Garda presence made sure that no assassination attempts were carried out on either Ritchie or Dinah Rattigan.

Bringing further Rattigan family members into the dispute was bound to be an incendiary move. The inevitable retaliation came on 7 December at around 4.00am, when two men on a high-powered motorcycle discharged four shots into the front window of Freddie Thompson's mother's house on Loreto Road. Elizabeth Thompson was asleep in bed at the time and was uninjured. A further two shots were shot into a van that had been parked in the driveway of the house. Fat Freddie was still in jail, and was apoplectic with rage when he found out that his innocent mother was being dragged into a feud, which she had never any involvement in. Thompson was released only days after the attack on his mother. Revenge came three days before Christmas, when the front door of Mr X's apartment was kicked in by unknown intruders. Mr X lived at the apartment with his girlfriend. The couple were not home at the time of the break-in. His girlfriend discovered what had happened when she arrived home the following day. She rushed to Sundrive Road Garda Station and reported what had happened to Detective Garda Jonathan Kelly. She was terrified, and Kelly got the impression from her that what had happened was an attempt to exacerbate the feud. Gardaí believe that the break-in was an attempt to kidnap Mr X, but luckily he wasn't home. It was well known that Mr X was a major target. He had already been warned that his life was in danger, and his girlfriend had her house shot up the previous January.

* * *

Things then settled down until March 2005, when the feud escalated in what turned out to be a very busy month. On the first day of the month, Eddie Redmond was outside his house on Cooley Road, when he was approached by a masked man carrying a semi-automatic handgun at around 7.30pm. Redmond saw the gunman in time, and ran through a number of gardens, avoiding three or four shots. He succeeded in hiding in an adjoining garden and the gunman fled, because the sound of shots fired had brought a number of neighbours out of their homes. The gunman escaped in a waiting car. Gardaí are still unsure as to who carried out the attack, although it was clear that a member of the Thompson gang was responsible.

Five days later, 20-year-old Joey O'Brien from Crumlin Park was chased on foot in the Dolphin's Barn flats complex by Freddie Thompson and a number of his associates. O'Brien had loose links to Brian Rattigan. He was regarded as a small-time player, and Thompson and his crew wanted rid of him, but O'Brien managed to escape. He was well able to handle himself both inside and outside prison.

The following day on Kilworth Road, Garda Ciaran Nunan stopped and searched a silver Renault Laguna which was being driven by Eddie Redmond. Redmond had been acting suspiciously and was pulled over. There were two passengers in the car with him – a 29-year-old from Dublin 8 and a 32-year-old from Mulhuddart in Blanchardstown. A search revealed that all three men were wearing navy bullet-proof vests and that they were travelling in a convoy of two cars. The other car was a navy Volkswagen Bora, which was being driven by Mr X's girlfriend. Mr X was the front seat passenger. The two men in the first car were acting as bodyguards for Mr X. The fact that they were going around in convoys and wearing bullet proof vests obviously meant that they knew that something was being planned by the rival group. They were spot on.

At around 12.15am on 9 March 2005, John Roche was walking towards his apartment on Irwin Street in Kilmainham, having returned home in his Fiat Punto after visiting a girl he was seeing. Little did he know that the rival gang had been holed up in an apartment that overlooked Roche's for the last few days, after receiving a tip-off that he was living in Kilmainham. He had moved into the apartment three months previously, and his brother Noel was even staying with him. It was unusual that the pair would risk being seen together. The rival group had spent several days carrying out surveillance of his movements, using an apartment that a close associate of Freddie Thompson coincidently happened to be renting. Because of the ongoing threats to the lives of individual members of the two feuding gangs, it was commonplace that people would regularly move from house to house and never stay in the same place for too long – in case the other side discovered the address. This was especially true of people like the Roche brothers, Freddie Thompson, Darren Geoghegan and Paddy Doyle. They were all young and had no real ties, so they used rented apartments

and houses all across Dublin, in an attempt to keep one step
ahead of the rival gang. Several detectives have said that the
senior members of both gangs would rarely lay their heads on
the same pillow for two consecutive nights – such was their
paranoia that their address would become known. John
Roche knew that he was a marked man because of the Paul
Warren murder, but didn't have a clue that his location had
been compromised. As he walked up to the front door of the
apartment complex, a lone gunman wearing a balaclava
came out of the shadows and fired five shots in quick
succession from a shotgun. Roche was hit three times in the
chest. The fourth bullet entered the window of a nearby flat,
while the fifth round missed the target. The gunman then
jumped into a waiting Saab and sped away in the direction of
Heuston Station. Roche had tried to run when he saw the
gun being pointed at him, and his adrenaline carried him 200
yards before he collapsed on the pavement outside Murray's
bar at Bow Bridge. A number of witnesses later told Gardaí
that 25-year-old Roche cried out: 'Help me, help me', as he
staggered down the road. Other witnesses also told detectives
that they heard what they thought were cheers coming from
an apartment, just seconds after the shots rang out. It is
thought that members of the Thompson gang had witnessed
the murder from the apartment they were scouting from, and
celebrated after the job had been done. Gardaí and an
ambulance arrived at the scene within five minutes, and
Roche was rushed to the nearby St James's Hospital, but he
died from his injuries at around 3.00am. John Roche was well
known to Gardaí. He was born on 27 September 1979, and
spent most of his life living in Drimnagh, although when his
parents sold the house he moved between several different
addresses. Roche first appeared in court in 1996 for stealing
a car. He had several criminal convictions for theft, drink
driving, road traffic offences, possession of an offensive
weapon and threatening behaviour. In June 1998, Roche

walked into a trap set by Gardaí under Operation Cleanstreet, when he sold heroin to an undercover detective at Davitt Road. Operation Cleanstreet was a GNDU anti-drugs initiative aimed at reducing the sale of drugs in some of Dublin's worst trouble spots, including Ballymun, Finglas, Rialto and Inchicore. When Roche was arrested and taken to Dublin District Court, he was not alone. Another 19 drug dealers appeared in court alongside him, all having fallen for the same Garda trap. He was charged with the sale and supply of controlled substances and was later convicted.

* * *

On the night of the murder, Gardaí immediately arrested a female relation of Freddie Thompson, as well as one of her female associates under Section 30 of the Offences Against the State Act on suspicion of withholding information. Detectives believe that it was Thompson's relation and her friend's apartment that was used to carry out surveillance on Roche. Gardaí worked under the assumption that a lookout had seen Roche leave his apartment in the early evening, while the Thompson gang put a plan in place to assassinate Roche when he returned home from his night out. The murder was planned, and the fact that a gunman was hiding in bushes close to where Roche parked his car showed that he might have been under sustained surveillance.

The murder investigation headquarters was at Kilmainham Garda Station and the probe was led by Superintendent Eddie Quirk, with Detective Inspector Gabriel O'Gara in day-to-day charge. He had been in charge of the case that led to Bernard Dempsey being given a life sentence for the murder of former kickboxer Jimmy Curran in the Green Lizard pub in the Liberties, which took place the month after John Roche was shot dead. That case was blighted by murder threats against witnesses and jury-tampering efforts, and O'Gara was widely praised for the way he handled the investigation. O'Gara and his Crumlin equivalent, Brian Sutton, were hardnosed policeman, who closely cooperated with one another in jointly tackling the two feuding gangs that resided across both their districts. Because the feud had spread to his 'A' district, O'Gara familiarised himself with the intricacies of the feud and was well-acquainted with both sides. He was regarded as a top operator and with his right hand man, Detective Sergeant Adrian Whitelaw, and key staff Detective Gardaí, Dessie Brennan, Gavin Ware, Ken Donnelly, Ritchie Kelly, Con Cronin, Bernard Thornton and Willie Brown, was well able to keep up with the likes of the Thompson and Rattigan mobs. They had simply been unlucky that the Warren murder never reached a successful conclusion.

Twelve people were arrested in the course of the investigation into the Roche murder, including former Thompson associate Michael Frazer. Two of those detained were car dealers Sean McMahon from Tallaght and Brian Downes from Greenhills Road in Walkinstown. The pair were best friends and were involved in laundering drugs cash for criminals; 'clocking' cars, which is reducing the number of miles shown on the clock; and 'ringing' cars, which involves changing the number plates and filing down the identification numbers on the chassis. They also imported vehicles from the UK, didn't pay the VRT and sold them on to unsuspecting owners. They were suspected of supplying the Saab that was used as the getaway car in the Roche murder, and which was later found burnt out near the murder scene. Both men would later be murdered in separate gangland incidents.

Gardaí believe that three members of the Thompson gang were involved in planning and carrying out the murder. The suspect for pulling the trigger is a 29-year-old from Dublin 12. This man subsequently fled the country. He has not returned since, and there is a warrant out for his arrest in relation to the Roche murder. Darren Geoghegan is suspected of being the getaway driver, while the third main suspect is Freddie Thompson himself, although he is suspected of planning the murder, not actually carrying it out. Aidan Gavin was also arrested as part of the murder investigation, although he was released without charge, due to a lack of evidence against him.

John Roche's murder resulted in serious political pressure being put on Minister for Justice Michael McDowell. In November 2004, a criminal from Blanchardstown, 23-year-old Paul Cunningham, was gunned down, while his young child and girlfriend slept next to him. Following the savage murder, McDowell told journalists that he didn't believe that gangland crime in the capital was getting out of control. He infamously went on to call the murder: 'The sting of the dying wasp'. This ill-advised statement came back to haunt him and would regularly be used as a stick with which to beat him. For exactly one year after he uttered the statement, 17 people had been murdered in gangland-style killings. Crime went to the top of the political agenda, and after Roche's shooting, Fine Gael's spokesman on Justice, Jim O'Keefe, said: 'This is a worrying recurrence of gangland-style killings in which summary justice is being meted out on our streets.' In response to the political pressure after Roche's killing and other similar slayings, Michael McDowell announced a special Garda operation, codenamed 'Anvil', which was designed to tackle Dublin's rising gun-crime rates. Garda Commissioner Noel Conroy was given 15,000 extra hours of overtime each week, so that his force could 'strike at the heart' of crime gangs, such as the two that were causing death and mayhem in Drimnagh and Crumlin.

McDowell told the Dáil that 'a feature of the gun culture which has emerged is the apparent belief on the part of some criminals that they are not bound by or subject to the laws of the land. Operation Anvil is intended to supplement existing operations so as to ensure that lawlessness does not prevail, that the threat which these criminals pose is met sternly and effectively, and, above all, that human life is respected.' He added that Anvil would be 'focused, sustained, targeted and relentless'. Commissioner Conroy said that the primary focus of Anvil would be 'extensive additional overt patrolling and static checkpoints by uniform mobile and foot patrols, supported by armed plain-clothes patrols'. In addition, 'Intelligence-driven covert operations are also being undertaken, involving Dublin units and national Garda investigative units.' As well as Anvil, Michael McDowell also announced several proposed amendments to the Criminal Justice Act, including minimum sentences for membership of gangs and for modifying shotguns to make them more lethal. Basically, Anvil resulted in Gardaí pounding the pavements and harassing known criminals. Roadblocks were set up outside the homes of gangsters, and they were followed wherever they went. It was a 'get in the face of criminals' operation and would prove to be very successful. The two main areas that Anvil initially targeted were Finglas and Crumlin-Drimnagh. After the Roche murder, the extra Garda patrols were more than welcomed, because the area was incredibly tense in the days and weeks after the slaying. It wasn't just the criminals that were on tenterhooks. Gardaí stopped a BMW car on Sperrin Road in Drimnagh at around 4.40am, four days after the murder. Shane Maloney and three of his friends were in it. In the Gardaí's opinion, the four men were acting extremely nervously, so the Gardaí called for armed back-up. None was available, so the uniformed officers, fearful for their own safety, let the car leave the scene. It subsequently emerged that the BMW had a false number plate. In the early hours of 16 March, Ritchie Rattigan and Karl Kavanagh were arrested in a car, in possession of swords and baseball bats. There had been an incident earlier in the night when one of their friends had allegedly been assaulted by bouncers at a pub in Tallaght, and Gardaí believed that the men were going to seek revenge. They were released without charge, but it just illustrated how tense things were. On 30 March, a shot was fired into the home of a close associate of Freddie Thompson in Dublin 8. On the same night a unit from the Garda Traffic Corps stopped an Opel Vectra on Kildare Street, close to Dáil Éireann. Darren Geoghegan was driving and Freddie Thompson was the front-seat passenger. When they learned who the men were, they were taken to Sundrive Road Garda station for a drugs search. Freddie Thompson had been wearing a wig that made him resemble Noel Gallagher from the band Oasis, and he also wore a bulletproof vest. He appeared to be very nervous and agitated. Geoghegan was wearing a stab-proof vest. Geoghegan was charged with a minor road traffic offence, while Thompson was released. The car had been rented from an agency on the Long Mile Road under a false name. It was seized and taken to the Garda compound in Santry. A few days later, gang member Gavin Bryne unsuccessfully tried to claim it. The following day, a squad car from Tallaght Garda Station stopped a Ford Focus being driven by Aidan Gavin. Freddie Thompson's 35-year-old brother, Ritchie, was a passenger in the front seat. Both were wearing bulletproof vests and both had a set of fresh clothes in the car. The men were arrested, and €5,000 in cash was seized, although they were later released without charge.

On 2 April 2005, three Gardaí stopped Mr X's girlfriend's Volkswagen Bora in Crumlin, which was being driven by Mr X. He was wearing a bulletproof vest and was carrying a concealed Bowie knife. The vehicle was seized and taken to a pound in Parkgate Street. At the same time, Mrs Frazer, the mother of Michael Frazer, who was a former associate of Thompson, went to Sundrive Road Garda Station and alleged that Mr X had threatened her daughter. She said that

Mr X had been driving a Volkswagen, and the incident happened just minutes before Mr X was stopped and searched by Gardaí. While Mrs Frazer was making a complaint in the station, Mr X's girlfriend arrived demanding the return of her car. A row ensued, and Gardaí had to separate both parties. Outside the station, Mr X made threats to Mrs Frazer in the presence of Gardaí.

Detective Superintendent Denis Donegan and Detective Inspector Brian Sutton had adopted a carrot and stick approach in dealing with the feud. On one hand the parents of gang members, local clergy and representatives of both factions regularly met to negotiate peace deals and see if they could find a solution to the feud that was now more entrenched than ever. Donegan and Sutton gave an undertaking that Gardaí would fully support any peace efforts, but warned the criminals that if they were caught engaging in law-breaking they would be prosecuted to the fullest extent of the law. The two senior officers also made it clear that the tit-for-tat killings had to stop. Running parallel with this peace-brokering effort was extensive anti-gang operations by members of Operation Anvil, the Special Detective Unit and local Gardaí, which involved targeted, intelligence led operations, dozens of searches and proactive 'in your face' policing. The officer in charge of the Dublin Metropolitan Region, Assistant Commissioner Al McHugh, personally approved and supported the type of policing being implemented on the streets of Crumlin and Drimnagh. The policy of supporting peace brokering, while having zero tolerance of crime, was thought up by Brian Sutton, who was one of the few trained negotiators in An Garda Síochána. His negotiating skills would be used on several occasions in the feud over the next few years.

On 14 April, 26-year-old drug dealer Terry Dunleavy arrived at the Croke Villas flats complex in Ballybough, at around 10.00pm. He parked his white Volvo and made his way up the stairwell towards his girlfriend's flat. When he got up the first few stairs, a gunman confronted him and fired five shots from a pistol, with a bullet striking him in the chest. Dunleavy desperately tried to escape up the stairwell, but he was pursued and shot again. He fell to the ground as he reached the top. As he lay helpless, the assassin fired three more shots at his head, killing him instantly. The gunman escaped on a motorbike that was driven by an accomplice. When Gardaí searched Dunleavy's car, it was found to contain several blocks of cannabis, worth close to €10,000, and detectives immediately suspected that Dunleavy had been set up by other criminals. The motorbike was discovered in the hours after the murder. It was burnt out at nearby Whitworth Road. The murder investigation was led by detectives from Fitzgibbon Street Garda Station, under the supervision of Detective Inspector Christy Mangan. Mangan had been involved in the arrest of Declan Gavin at Ballymount Cross in August 1999. He was the founding sergeant in charge of the Drugs Unit at Sundrive Road and still had a good knowledge of the feud and the main players. He had since been promoted and transferred to the Dublin Metropolitan North-Central Region.

Terry Dunleavy took pride in the fact that he was regarded as a hard man. He was extremely volatile and inflicted needless violence on hopeless drug addicts if they were late paying him. His fellow criminals regarded him with disdain. He had frequent disputes over drugs and had built up a lot of enemies. Dunleavy sold cannabis and cocaine in and around the north-inner city, but had recently expanded his operation and was now dealing cocaine in several popular nightclubs and bars in the trendy Temple Bar area. He was starting to make a serious amount of money, but was stepping on a lot of toes while he was doing it. A native of Marino, but with an address at Lower Drumcondra Road, Dunleavy had amassed a significant number of criminal convictions for armed robbery and arson, after he burnt down a secondary school. In 2002, Dunleavy went on trial for shooting a man in Fairview Park in 1998, only for the trial to collapse because a newspaper had printed a photograph of him being led back to a prison van in handcuffs after appearing in court. Dunleavy had used firearms on three separate occasions in the weeks before his murder to threaten separate rival drug dealers. He was fond of guns and once threatened a neighbour with a pistol after breaking into his home. It was clear that whoever killed Dunleavy had probably been watching him for some time and was aware that he often went to visit his girlfriend in the evenings. The initial line of inquiry that Gardaí in the investigation took was that Dunleavy had been murdered by a well-known criminal from the north-inner city over a long-running feud between himself and Dunleavy. However, as the investigation progressed, Gardaí ascertained that the getaway bike used in the murder had been owned by Albert Doyle. Doyle, a 21-year-old from Errigal Road in Drimnagh, was Freddie Thompson's first cousin. Doyle was interviewed by Gardaí and said that he had owned the bike up to approximately three weeks prior to the shooting. Detectives then received intelligence that Doyle had handed the bike over to his cousin as part payment for an outstanding debt. This new information led Gardaí to look at Freddie Thompson's gang to see if they might have been responsible. It didn't take much digging before Gardaí discovered that the Thompson gang had indeed been behind Dunleavy's murder. Dunleavy had been supplied with his cannabis by the Thompson gang and owed them €26,000 for a consignment that had been seized just five weeks before his murder. Dunleavy had paid just €14,000 up front for the €40,000 worth of drugs, and had been given the rest on credit. Paddy Doyle went to see Dunleavy on a number of occasions, but he refused to pay up. He made the fatal mistake of slagging off Doyle and Fat

Freddie, and told them that they would not be getting a cent of the cash, and he would shoot them if he saw Doyle near Ballybough again. Paddy Doyle gave Dunleavy one more chance to pay the cash he owed, and when he refused, Doyle told him that there would be serious consequences. Dunleavy's rise up the drug-dealing ladder had obviously affected his brain, because threatening an enforcer from one of the most feared gangs in the country is bound to have a negative effect on your health.

Gardaí have not solved the Dunleavy murder, but Paddy Doyle is certainly high-up on the list of suspects. It is not known who drove the motorbike, and the case remains open. Sources say that Dunleavy was killed to send a message to other criminals being supplied with drugs by the Thompson gang that if you did not pay your bills, you would be shot without mercy. The fact that Dunleavy had been foolish enough to threaten Doyle had sealed his fate. The murder was the first time that the feud had left a person dead who was not directly connected to Crumlin or Drimnagh. It would not be the last time that somebody indirectly involved would be murdered though. The Dunleavy murder illustrates how the Thompson gang had become much bigger and had started to act as a wholesaler to middle-sized dealers across Dublin. With their increased size and influence, they were also becoming increasingly violent and ruthless. John Roche and Terry Dunleavy were murdered within little over a month of each other. The feud had now become so big that its tentacles had spread far and wide. It was becoming harder and harder for Gardaí to determine what was feud related and what was not, especially because there were now so many personalities involved in doing business with both the Rattigan and Thompson gangs.

Although Gardaí didn't find out about the Thompson link to the Dunleavy murder until months after it happened, on the streets of Crumlin and Drimnagh it was well-known, and it only added to the tension and the paranoia of some of the key players.

On 2 May 2005 at around 4.00pm, Eddie Redmond's wife contacted Detective Sergeant John Walsh at Sundrive Road Garda station. She told him she was driving around Crumlin and her car was being followed by a blue Ford Mondeo. She said she was with her husband. She could see three men in the Mondeo, and felt that she and her husband were being targeted. John Walsh and Detective Garda Paul Lynch rushed to the area in an unmarked car and spotted the Mondeo on Herberton Road in Rialto. A 20-year-old from Clanbrassil Street was driving the car. Walsh and Lynch immediately spotted Freddie Thompson in the front seat, even though he was wearing his Noel Gallagher wig and a large pair of sunglasses. As the officers approached the vehicle, Thompson took out the SIM card from his mobile phone and proceeded to swallow it. Paddy Doyle was sitting in the back seat. The passengers and car were searched. A Bord Na Móna firepack, gloves, a balaclava and a leather belt for shotgun ammunition were found in the boot. The trio were arrested and taken to Sundrive Road, but were released without charge. Just half an hour later at 7.15pm, the boyfriend of one of Brian Rattigan's cousins received a severe beating from three men at Grand Canal Lane in Dublin 8. The injured party described one of his assailants as having worn a black curly wig, but he refused to make a statement of complaint, so there was little that Gardaí could do, despite the fact, they believed that Fat Freddie had been responsible.

Freddie Thompson swallowing a mobile phone SIM card before Gardaí approached him might sound like extreme action, but it was not all that uncommon. Members of the feuding gangs change mobile phone numbers every two to three days. They always buy ready-to-go phones, so they do not have to register the number. A criminal buys a SIM card, uses the €10 free call credit that comes with it and then throws it away when the credit runs out. Gardaí refer to these as 'wash-and-go' phones. The feuding criminals know that mobile phone technology is one of the few ways that they can be caught. Gardaí can now triangulate phone signals which means that they are able to tell, almost to the exact point, where a caller was when he used his phone. It is done by analysing the numbers called from individual mobile phone cell sites. It was this technology that helped to convict Joe O'Reilly for the murder of his wife, Rachel. It proved that he was lying when he said he was working at a bus depot in the centre of Dublin. Joe O'Reilly's mobile phone had bounced off a mobile phone mast near his home in Naul, Co. Dublin, where Rachel was murdered in October 2004, so investigators were able to prove that he had lied. These developments hadn't gone unnoticed by criminals, so there were rules that bill-pay mobile phones could never be bought and that phone numbers had to be 'rinsed' every few days, so that Gardaí would never get the numbers. Criminals even went as far as to travel to the UK, buy dozens of ready-to-go SIMs, load them with credit and come back to Dublin with them because they could not be traced by Gardaí.

On 13 June, an article written by this author appeared in the *Evening Herald* newspaper, reporting that the two rival gangs had declared a truce. Senior Gardaí had been liasing with the families – particularly the mothers – of many of those involved in the feud. Local clergymen were also involved. Tentative agreement had been reached the previous month that hostilities should cease, at least temporarily, but Gardaí were not hopeful that the *entente cordiale* would last.

On 15 July, an incident took place, which, although feud related, did not represent a breach of the ceasefire – merely a settling of old scores. Patrick Fogarty was pulled out of his car outside a takeaway at Ravensdale Park in Kimmage, and given a hiding. The 25-year-old had been in the van that had dropped Joey Rattigan off at his house seconds before he was murdered in July 2002. There was widespread suspicion that Fogarty had been involved with Paul Warren in setting Rattigan up to be killed. Warren had been murdered for his perceived role in the slaying, so it was inevitable that Fogarty would be eventually made to pay for the untrue innuendo that he was also involved. The matter was initially reported to Garda James McGeough at Crumlin Garda Station as a random assault. However, on the same night as the assault, Detective Inspector Brian Sutton spoke to Patrick Fogarty's mother who informed him that she believed the incident was connected with the feud. DS John Walsh went to meet with Mrs Fogarty the following day. Mrs Fogarty told him that six or seven youths came upon Fogarty while he was sitting in his car waiting for his girlfriend, who was inside the takeaway getting chips. She said that her son had been economical with the truth, and that it was not a group of youths who attacked him but men in their late teens and early twenties. While Paddy Fogarty was being assaulted, one of the group told him that the beating was for setting Joey Rattigan up and that worse would follow. The group called Fogarty a 'rat' and a 'scumbag'. He received extensive injuries to his face, arms, legs and body, and lost a large amount of blood as a result. However, Fogarty refused to make a statement to Gardaí.

On 22 July at around 10.00pm, five shots were discharged into a house at Grand Canal Bank in Dublin 8, narrowly missing the occupants. At midnight, a person involved on the Rattigan side of the feud, contacted a detective and told him that the occupant of the house, was a relative of Brian Rattigan. The relative was a paraplegic and was confined to a wheelchair. The informant also stated that Eddie Redmond had been contacted that day and warned to keep his head down, because Freddie Thompson had hired two assassins from Limerick to carry out an attack on an unknown member of the Rattigan mob. The informant went on to say that when Rattigan heard that the home of his disabled brother had been shot up, he had put out a €30,000 contract for anyone to carry out a revenge attack on Freddie Thompson, Aidan Gavin or any of their close associates. The truce had lasted just under two months, but it seems that Freddie Thompson's gang was just taking advantage of the lull to plan to wipe out members of Rattigan's gang. Rattigan, being very devoted to his family, was always likely to go ballistic if any of his relations were singled out, especially a paraplegic brother. Around the same time, Garda Crime and Security issued a circular advising that intelligence had been received from prison that Brian Rattigan had told a gang member to plan to wait until at least five members of the Thompson gang were present in the one location before attacking them with grenades, wiping them all out at the same time. This tactic of mass murder had previously been used by the mafia, and the fact that he even contemplated this revealed a lot. The gloves were now off and the revenge attacks were bound to be vicious.

They were not long in coming either. Just five days after Rattigan's relation's house had been shot at, Aidan Gavin was shot in an incident at his house at Foxdene Avenue in Clondalkin. Shortly after midnight, Gavin answered a knock at his front door and was faced with a masked man brandishing a revolver. The first shot missed the target and the second whizzed past Gavin's cheek and grazed the bridge of his nose. Gavin slammed the door and ran out the back of the house into the back garden and jumped over a wall and escaped. His wife and two children were in the house at the time. This was a bona fide murder attempt, and it was a miracle that Gavin survived at all. The gunman escaped in a waiting car, and there was no forensic evidence left at the scene. It is not known who carried out the gun attack.

Aidan Gavin was born in December 1971, and spent most

of his life living on Mourne Road in Drimnagh. He was involved in the feud from day one, and moved large volumes of drugs around the city. He had nine criminal convictions for possession of drugs with intent for sale and supply, simple possession of drugs, burglary, robbery and a conviction for assaulting a Garda. When Declan Gavin was murdered, Aidan took it personally and began to lose the run of himself. He developed a bad drug addiction and got more and more drawn into the world of organised crime, a world that had claimed the life of his brother.

On August 8 2005 at around 5.50pm, Kevin Redmond, a brother of Eddie, was fixing a car outside a house on Knocknarea Road in Drimnagh, along with a man he had recently sold the vehicle to. The pair were hard at work when a motorbike pulled up with two men on it. The passenger on the bike pulled out a revolver and fired a number of rounds at the two men, hitting them both but not causing serious injury. The two men were totally innocent, and Gardaí believe that they were shot in a case of mistaken identity, because Kevin Redmond closely resembled his brother Eddie. Gardaí believe that the attack was in revenge for the attempted murder of Aidan Gavin the previous month.

The day after the shooting, Gardaí recovered the .375 Magnum revolver that was used in the shooting of the innocent men. It was hidden in the garden of a house in Dublin 8. Gardaí seized the weapon and placed the garden under surveillance. A number of hours later, a 28-year-old man from the north-inner city arrived and attempted to recover the gun. He was a close friend and known associate of Paddy Doyle, but he refused to say anything and was later released without charge. Following this shooting, members of the Rattigan gang took photos of the bloodstained footpath where the two men were shot. They then sent the photos via picture message to a mobile phone that Brian Rattigan secretly had in Portlaoise Prison. Rattigan had been transferred to the high-security jail because he was becoming too powerful in Mountjoy. A text accompanying the photos asked him what should be done about his friends and lieutenants being shot at. A couple of weeks after the shootings, there was a random search of cells in Portlaoise and the mobile phone and picture messages were discovered. Gardaí were called in to investigate, and they got a reminder – if they needed any – that it was still the jailed crime lord who was calling the shots in the feud.

A week after the two men were shot by mistake, 24-year-old Daniel Doyle from Clonmacnoise Road in Crumlin, was drinking in Sundrive Park, which is also known as Eamonn Ceannt Park, when he was approached by three men, one of whom was carrying a sawn-off shotgun. One of the trio opened fire from close range with a .22 rifle, hitting Doyle in the thigh and back. He survived, but was left paralysed for life as a result of the incident and will have to live permanently in a care home. When he recovered enough to be interviewed, he gave a statement to Gardaí identifying Paul Hurley, a 17-year-old from Clonmacnoise Road, as one of the three men. Doyle told Gardaí that he had been shot at the behest of the Rattigan gang, after he was blamed for being the man who shot the two innocent men the previous week. Doyle told detectives – off the record – that he was shot because he had recently stopped sourcing his drugs from a close associate of the Rattigan gang and changed to Graham Whelan.

Whelan was with Declan Gavin in the Holiday Inn during the Garda operation in March 2000. He was serving a six-year sentence in Mountjoy, but he was running a drugs operation from his prison cell. Phone records obtained by Gardaí linked Graham Whelan's prison mobile to having contacted a number of well-known feud members, so detectives had little doubt that Whelan was a serious player. Whelan was far from a young man being influenced by more serious criminals – as he had argued in court after the Holiday Inn seizure.

Paul Hurley was subsequently charged with the shooting. On the first day of the trial at Dublin Circuit Criminal Court, the prosecution senior counsel told the jury that Doyle recognised Hurley as the gunman, but he was refusing to give evidence. Detective Sergeant Gerry Quinn took the stand and read out the statement that Doyle had given to Gardaí fingering Hurley as the gunman. He told officers that he recognised one of the men as Hurley but, 'I thought nothing of it because I recognised one of them. As they came towards me, I saw a flash and heard a bang and I started to run. Then the next thing I knew, I was on the ground.' Doyle said that Hurley was not carrying the rifle, but was standing on the left of the group and wore a baseball cap. He said that he brought his hand up to block his face from further shots. 'I heard one of them say, "You got him in the head," so I went along with that. I played dead.' In his statement, Doyle added that he heard one of the group suggest that they take his mobile phone. 'They says, "Hurley, get his phone," and he said "No, I'm not touching him." ' Somebody then turned Doyle over and began searching him. He still had his hand over his face when he was turned, and opened his eyes and saw Paul Hurley. When the group left Doyle, seemingly dead, he dragged himself to the front gate of the park and a passer-by called the Gardaí.

As Detective Sergeant Gerry Quinn read out his statement, Doyle shouted that the Garda was telling lies. When he was questioned by Judge Paul Carney, he refused to answer him and said that if he did, he would be killed. Judge Carney said that the only reason Doyle wasn't spending a night in the cells was because he was in a wheelchair. Judge Carney said that the law gave him no alternative but to acquit Paul Hurley of attempting to murder Daniel Doyle or cause him serious harm. Hurley walked free from court. Gardaí say there is no doubt that Daniel Doyle was intimidated and frightened into not following through on his statement.

Three days after Daniel Doyle was shot, Gardaí searched a house in Portarlington, Co. Laois, after a tip-off, and found a note identifying members of the Rattigan gang and some of their loved ones who could be targeted. A number of individuals were identified in the note, including Mr X. The note listed: *Mr X. Navy Blue Bora which his 'girl' drives. Shay one arm Valley apartments.* This was a reference to Shay O'Byrne, one of Brian Rattigan's lieutenants. The note went on: *Rattigan's sister silver Golf easy got.* This was a reference to Sharon Rattigan, O'Byrne's partner. ****** easy got.* This is thought to refer to Brian Rattigan's disabled relative. He was obviously considered to be fair game because his home was shot up the previous month. It is possible that he was shot after he was included in the seized list; detectives didn't know how old it was or if it had been acted on yet. Another name to appear on the list was *B Rattigan's girl silver Bora easy got.* This was obviously Rattigan's partner, Natasha McEnroe.

* * *

On the same day as the note was recovered, Joey O'Brien went to Sundrive Road Garda Station at around 11.00pm, and said that two cars pulled up alongside him on nearby Keeper Road. He recognised the occupants of the cars as Aidan Gavin, Darren Geoghegan, Freddie Thompson and Thompson's cousin Eoin O'Connor. Also present, O'Brien claimed, were brothers David and Liam Byrne from Raleigh Square in Crumlin. When O'Brien saw some of the men get out of the cars, he ran away and hid in the front gardens of houses that backed onto Sundrive Road Garda Station. He told Gardaí that while he was hiding in a bush, he looked out and saw Freddie Thompson standing nearby, carrying a handgun. Thompson and some of the others searched for O'Brien, but couldn't find him and drove off. When he was satisfied that the coast was clear, O'Brien headed to the Garda station to report the incident. It was the second time in five months that O'Brien had managed to get away from Thompson and his cronies.

On 19 August, the day after Freddie Thompson had allegedly come looking for Joey O'Brien, he was again keeping busy. Freddie's partner, Vicky Dempsey, had been friendly with a man from Crumlin, while Thompson had been serving a jail sentence in 2003 and 2004. When he got out of prison in late 2004, Thompson stabbed the man in the back with a knife, leaving the injured man needing 27 stitches. He did not report the incident to Gardaí because he believed that he and Fat Freddie had sorted out their differences. However, at around 1.00am on 19 August, while he was in the Texaco garage on the Crumlin Road, the man saw a silver BMW car pass by him. Freddie Thompson was sitting in the front passenger seat. The BMW suddenly did a handbrake turn and sped after him. The man managed to jump into a car being driven by a friend and made it home safely. He spotted the BMW driving past his house on several occasions immediately after he escaped. While he was in his house, he received a call on his mobile from Freddie Thompson. He asked Thompson what he had done wrong, and was told that he was going to have his throat slit. The following week, the man was attacked by Freddie Thompson who had a baseball bat. He had done nothing wrong, but Thompson obviously still held a grudge over the man's friendship with Vicky Dempsey.

EIGHT

Thirty-six hours of mayhem

By late 2005, the Thompson gang was making so much money from drug dealing that they literally did not know what to do with it. Gardaí estimate that the gang was making in excess of €250,000 some weeks, although that would be when a major shipment arrived. Other weeks the gang might have been low on supply, and would only be taking home €20,000 or €30,000, while they awaited the arrival of another shipment. Also, if Gardaí intercepted drugs that were destined for the Thompson mob, it would have a major effect on their profit – because the supplier would have to be paid anyway. When there were lots of drugs on the market, the price would drop and profit would be down. If Freddie's gang had most of the product that was on sale in Dublin, they could pretty much charge what they liked and would make serious money. So some weeks were better than others. Being strictly a 'cash only' business, drug dealing can pose major problems in what to do with the profits. A senior gang member cannot go around buying top of the range cars and luxury apartments with used notes, because the authorities would soon cop on and seize them if they cannot be legitimately explained. Any large criminal organisation has people who launder the money for them. These senior figures use a network of dodgy solicitors and accountants to rinse the dirty money and legitimise it, so that when it comes back into the hands of the gang, it is clean and untraceable. Even in a bad week there would be lots of cash that needed to be

looked after. According to Gardaí, it was 27-year-old Darren
Geoghegan's responsibility to take care of the Thompson
gang's loot.

Geoghegan, from Galtymore Drive in Drimnagh, had
grown up with Brian Rattigan and Declan Gavin, but had
been closer to Declan Gavin. So, after Gavin's murder he
pledged his allegiance to Freddie Thompson. He had
developed into one of the most senior, trusted and, arguably,
most important members of the gang. Geoghegan was highly
intelligent and had a good head for figures. Indeed, if his life
had been different, Gardaí say he could easily have worked
for one of the country's top accountancy firms, such was his
grasp of complicated numbers. Sources describe Darren
Geoghegan as purely a businessman who was not involved in
the day-to-day business of running the drugs gang. He would
have been far more comfortable with a pen than a gun.
Although he had been arrested as part of the John Roche
murder investigation, Geoghegan was not suspected of
actually pulling the trigger.

Being the money man for a major drugs gang is one of the
most sought after criminal jobs because it means that you are
indispensable. It is the money man who knows how much
each dealer makes per week and where the cash has been
sent to be cleaned and made legitimate. He has the direct
line to the crooked accountants and the unscrupulous
solicitors; he controls the properties and investments that
have been bought with the clean money. He basically knows
where all the metaphorical bodies are buried – leaving the
dangerous matter of disposing of the real bodies to other
minions. He enjoys the rewards of the trade, without
handling the drugs and without any of the risks that more
'hands-on' gangsters take.

Gardaí only have a basic idea about how Darren
Geoghegan laundered his group's money. This information
has been gleaned from intelligence, and because the CAB

never looked into his activities, we do not know many details of the complicated web used by Geoghegan to cover his tracks. It is suspected that Darren Geoghegan established a property company under the name of a person with no criminal record, and used the clean company to purchase dozens of apartments and several large commercial premises around Dublin for the gang. The properties would be rented out, and the income would be used to buy more drugs from Spain and the Netherlands. Then the profits would be used to expand the gang's property portfolio. Some sources have estimated that he had bought scores of apartments with the drugs money in places as far away as Bulgaria, Latvia and other Eastern European countries, where the authorities do not ask too many questions when foreign business transactions are being conducted. A solicitor, who is based in Walkinstown, and a number of accountants in Dublin are currently being investigated by CAB on suspicion of facilitating property deals for several criminal gangs in Dublin. Gardaí are confident that when the probe is finished, they will be able to link these individuals, especially the solicitor, to Darren Geoghegan and will have a clear picture of exactly how much money he laundered and what he used the money to buy.

Gardaí also believe that Geoghegan had a business relationship with Walkinstown based car dealer Brian Downes, a small-time criminal with major gangland connections. They believe he gave Downes large sums of money to launder through his dodgy second-hand car firm. Downes was in business with several other criminal car dealers. He hatched a money laundering scam for drug gangs, whereby a wide range of high-powered cars were imported into the country but were presented to Revenue officials as lower-specification cars with fake paperwork vouching for the vehicle, so Downes would get away with paying lower rates of Vehicle Registration Tax and VAT. The scam was a lucrative one, and profits of up to €25,000 could be made on each car. Downes was also suspected of providing the Thompson gang with cars that were used as getaway vehicles in several murders, and cars in which to transport drugs. He was shot dead at his dealership in Walkinstown in October 2007, along with his innocent associate Eddie Ward. Like Darren Geoghegan, Downes had been arrested for questioning about the murder of John Roche, on suspicion of giving the Thompson mob the Saab that the killers had escaped in.

Having access to all that cash meant that the Rattigan mob regarded Geoghegan as a key player, and as a result he was one of their top murder targets. Geoghegan had been targeted on several previous occasions. A drive-by shooting on his family home on Galtymore Drive, back in June 2001, was one of the first feud-related incidents documented by Gardaí. The Geoghegan family home was shot up again in November of the same year. Darren Geoghegan rarely returned there after that because he wanted to send out the message that he no longer lived there, so his family would not be targeted.

People who knew Darren Geoghegan point out that he was no thug or lowlife. They say that he was quick to step in and break up fights. And that he looked out for his friends and neighbours, and was incredibly loyal. If he saw people taking drugs in the local park, he would make sure that young kids were moved along to ensure their safety. He was big into swimming and going to the gym, he was naturally well toned and never used steroids or hard drugs. The closest he ever got to drug use was smoking the odd joint. While there was no doubt that there was some good in Geoghegan, he also had a darker side and began to get involved in criminality. It is difficult to pinpoint the exact time when this happened, but when he was 20 he grew tired of his job as a painter and decorator. So he quit and went on the dole. It was probably then that he started to get involved in crime with his other mates, and the gang, then united, started dealing drugs and grew to be a large organisation quite quickly. In early 2001, when he was 21, Geoghegan moved out of the family home. Soon after that, the feud kicked off in a big way, and because of the threat from the other side, Geoghegan moved around a lot and did not call any one place home. He stayed away from Drimnagh and Crumlin as much as possible, and mainly stayed in rented houses and apartments around South Dublin.

Geoghegan had managed to stay under the Gardaí's radar and had only amassed a handful of criminal convictions for road traffic offences. He was suspended from driving for 18 months in September 2001 for dangerous driving, which was the most serious sentence he had received.

Gavin Byrne was Geoghegan's assistant when it came to looking after the drug money. Originally from Windmill Road in Crumlin, Gavin Byrne moved to Clonsilla to try and ensure his safety. Byrne had also grown up with Brian Rattigan and Declan Gavin, but he was not as intelligent as Geoghegan and was never treated with the same level of respect by his own gang. Gavin Byrne had made it to his 30th birthday, which is very unusual for somebody so involved in gangland crime. He was always one step ahead of the law, and didn't have any criminal convictions. He had been in court three times to contest parking fines, and had always left the courthouse vindicated, with the charges being struck out. The fact that he hadn't been caught didn't mean he wasn't involved in serious crime though, and Byrne was a regular target of Gardaí from Crumlin and Sundrive Road. He had been arrested as part of the Joey Rattigan murder investigation in late 2002, when he was linked to a car in which the revolver that had been used to shoot Rattigan was found. He submitted his DNA to Gardaí, obviously knowing that he had never been near the abandoned silver Volvo.

That arrest was part of a Garda exercise to 'round up the usual suspects' because most of his mates, Darren Geoghegan, Paddy Doyle, Freddie Thompson and Aidan Gavin had been arrested, to see if their DNA could be linked to the car, but in the end it was a fruitless exercise for the Gardaí.

Gavin Byrne was never in the frame for the Rattigan murder, but he was able to use violence when the occasion called for it. On 13 June 2002, he was arrested along with Aidan Gavin, after the front door of a house at Park Terrace in Dublin 8, was kicked in, and five shots from a .38 Smith and Wesson were discharged randomly. There were five people in the house at the time. Freddie Thompson's cousin, David Byrne, was the intended target. There was not enough evidence to charge either man, but it would later be determined that the .38 used in that attack was the same gun used to murder Joey Rattigan. So although there is no suggestion that Byrne was involved deep down and dirty in Joey Rattigan's murder, he was certainly no innocent.

Geoghegan and Byrne were very close and were rarely seen without each other. Because of their tightness and the fact that they had access to vast amounts of money, serious tensions began to develop within the gang in early 2005. It is believed that some of the other gang members felt that the pair had become too big. They voiced the opinion that they didn't trust them with the cash, and felt that they were squirreling away money for themselves. There is no evidence at all to suggest that either Geoghegan or Byrne were creaming money off their own side, but gangland is dominated by paranoia, and the unfounded and unproven suspicions of one man can often turn into accepted fact.

On 21 October 2005, both Byrne and Geoghegan were arrested during a joint Garda and Customs operation at Rosslare Harbour in Wexford. The pair had just got off a car ferry and the black Volkswagen Golf belonging to Byrne was stopped and searched. A high-powered Beretta pellet gun and ammunition was found in the boot of the car. Byrne took full responsibility for it and said he had recently bought it in Spain and had it for his own protection. The pellet gun was seized. The incident illustrated that Gavin Byrne probably knew that his life was in danger and he was taking steps to protect himself. It was probable that the two friends were aware that they were under suspicion within their own gang. Geoghegan routinely wore a bulletproof vest when driving around the city, and when he was stopped by Gardaí, they discovered that he was wearing protective clothing. Even though both men probably feared the rumblings of discontent from within their own ranks, it is probably safe to say that the last thing they expected was Freddie Thompson sanctioning their murders.

On Sunday 13 November, Darren Geoghegan and Gavin Byrne drove to the Carrickwood estate in Firhouse, near Tallaght in South Dublin, at around 9.30pm. The men were in a silver Lexus, which had been imported from Northern Ireland. Gardaí believe that they had been told to meet a senior member of the gang to take part in some sort of job on an unknown target on the opposite side of the feud. This is the assumption because the two men were only wearing tracksuits and runners and had no socks on. There were two sets of clothing in a plastic bag in the boot of the Lexus. (Changes of clothes are often brought by criminals when they are carrying out shootings. They usually strip off the first set after carrying out the shooting and burn them, often along with the getaway car.) The fact that both men were wearing bulletproof vests also indicated that they had taken precautions to ensure that they would return safely from whatever job they were going to carry out. Less than two minutes after the Lexus parked in the quiet housing estate, a silver BMW 5 Series, which had been stolen in Northern Ireland the previous week, pulled up alongside the car. Geoghegan and Byrne saw somebody they knew emerge from the BMW. Byrne clicked open the central locking, and the man got into the back seat of the Lexus, leaving the two men in front of him in very vulnerable positions. The fact that the man was allowed to get into the backseat without Geoghegan and Byrne being suspicious, leads to the conclusion that the person was well-known to them and absolutely trusted. Neither Byrne nor Geoghegan were armed, which suggests that they were not expecting a confrontation. The man was in the car only a matter of seconds before he pulled out a Sig Sauer pistol and opened fire. Darren Geoghegan was shot twice in the back of the head. Before he had time to react, Byrne also had two bullets fired into the back of his head. Both men died instantly. They would not have been alive long enough to know what was happening. The gunman got out of the Lexus and walked to the waiting BMW, which sped off towards Clondalkin. The gunman was dropped off and made his escape in another vehicle, while the driver went to Glenvara Park in Templeogue, where he set the vehicle alight causing it to explode, thereby eliminating the possibility of any forensic clues being left behind. The scene of the burning of the getaway car was literally a minute away from Carrickwood. The driver then ran through a field and jumped over a railing onto the main Ballycullen Road, where he was picked up and left the area in a Volkswagen Golf that had been stolen in Bray.

When the fire brigade managed to quell the flames of the BMW getaway car, Gardaí recovered two Sig 9mm pistols in the shell of the burnt-out vehicle. They had been melted by the flames, meaning that there was very little forensic evidence left to be examined. All in all, it was a difficult case for Gardaí to investigate. If a rival gang carries out a murder, it is usually opportunistic in nature or involves planning by several people, which means that information often makes its way into the hands of investigators. This was different. Gardaí initially suspected that Brian Rattigan's gang was behind the double murder, and that Geoghegan and Byrne might have arranged for a meeting with their rivals to discuss a ceasefire and were then ambushed. When this line of investigation hit a brick wall, it soon became clear that it was an internal gang row that led to the deaths.

Gardaí are convinced that Darren Geoghegan's best friend, Paddy Doyle, murdered Geoghegan and Byrne. The theory behind the crime is that the men were executed over an internal dispute about money, and that Freddie Thompson sanctioned the killings. If this is the case, then it is inconceivable that they were murdered before the rest of the gang got to find out where their money was invested. The last thing that Freddie Thompson would have allowed to happen was the loss of two of his top lieutenants without any financial gain to show for it. Detectives believe that before their deaths, Geoghegan and Byrne must have shared information about the gang's cash.

The double murder investigation was run out of Tallaght Garda Station and was led by Superintendent Declan Coburn with Denis Donegan, as the Detective Superintendent in joint charge. The day-to-day running of the probe was the responsibility of Detective Inspector Seamus Kane and Detective Sergeant Tom Doyle in Rathfarnham. There was a realisation among senior Gardaí that there was little prospect of the two killings ever being solved, unless one of the Thompson gang took the unlikely route of turning informer and entering the Witness Protection Programme. There was only one arrest in the investigation – a 28-year-old from Stepaside was detained on suspicion of having information about the getaway car – but this ultimately came to nothing. In the aftermath of the double murder, rumours began to circulate that Geoghegan and Byrne were shot dead by the IRA. There was absolutely no basis for this; whatsoever. The story probably spread because the getaway car had been stolen in Co. Antrim, although the fact was that the man who had organised the theft was from Bray, Co. Wicklow, and was a well-known criminal with no political allegiances.

There was predictable political outrage over the fact that two men could be so coldly executed in a middle-class estate. This was the first time that the feud, which had been going on for five years, had really burst into the public consciousness. Most of the general public would not have been aware of the existence of the two gangs, and certainly not the main players. These two murders changed that, and the likes of Freddie Thompson would soon become household names. Justice Minister Michael McDowell was quick to come out and express his anger, saying there was little doubt that the killings were linked to the Crumlin-Drimnagh war. He attributed the deaths to 'two groups in particular who are engaged in a battle to control cocaine and other drug supplies in Dublin and are willing to use any method whatsoever to bring about superiority over the other,' before adding, 'They are people who are completely amoral. This was a very careful, cold and ruthless trap set for two people in a rival gang. All I can say is the Gardai are putting every resource possible into cracking the gangs behind this feud and preventing them from doing any more damage. They deal in death. Their coinage is death. They don't care if they kill people through dealing hard drugs or soft drugs because it all means large sums of money. They use death to enforce debt collection operations and they use death in order to knock out rivals in this lethal business. Nobody should be under any illusions that drugs lead directly to this.'

McDowell tried to reassure people by saying that the two sides were under heavy surveillance and that Operation Anvil was working. McDowell ordered a squad of 50 Gardaí to patrol the streets and keep key gang figures under constant surveillance. This new Organised Crime Unit was under the control of the National Bureau of Criminal Investigation (NBCI), spearheaded by Detective Superintendent Dominic Hayes.

The opposition used the double slaying to score political points, but Labour's Joe Costello made a valid point when he questioned why the conviction rates for gangland murders were so low. Geoghegan and Byrne were the 17th and 18th gangland murder victims in 2005 alone, yet nobody had been convicted of a single murder. Costello said: 'We need a fundamental review of the Gardai's approach to dealing with the gangs and with gun murders. The conviction rate for those involved in such killings in so low gang leaders know they can order murders with virtual impunity.'

Gangland funerals are always nervous and potentially incendiary events, but Gardaí had special fears about the removal and burials of Geoghegan and Byrne. Because they had been murdered by their own side, tensions within the Thompson organisation would obviously be sky high. These tensions could lead to unpredictable events, and there was nothing to say that the Rattigan gang wouldn't try to take advantage of the split in the rival gang by trying to take out a couple more of Thompson's men.

Three hundred mourners filled St Agnes's Church in Crumlin, as Fr Alan Mowles celebrated Gavin Byrne's funeral. The priest told the congregation: 'If any good is to come of this, it is that the violence should stop. There needs to be an end to this senseless killing. It is not an individual we condemn. We condemn the whole drug culture. It is sad that Crumlin is tarnished by the deaths of so many young people. The community has celebrated youth in so many ways. It is sad that we have to say goodbye.' Byrne's partner and their three children, as well as his parents, were visibly upset when his favourite song, Michael Jackson's 'You Are Not Alone', was played.

None of Byrne's criminal pals went to the funeral to say

their final farewells. Gardaí were not taking any chances though, and plainclothes officers were present in and around the church, while members of the National Surveillance Unit discreetly photographed everybody who went in to the church. The funeral passed off peacefully.

The theme of an end to violence was also strong at Darren Geoghegan's funeral mass at Our Lady of Good Counsel church in Drimnagh. Father Martin Cosgrave appealed to those who had influence to end the killing and suffering. 'Otherwise, we will have more young deaths, more children orphaned, more families decimated. It does not bear thinking about. Darren's family have asked me to associate them with this appeal.' Fr Cosgrave said it was very difficult for any mother or father to see their child die in the circumstances in which Darren Geoghegan had passed. 'No mother wants to see her child kill or be killed. Padraig Pearse, the poet, when speaking of mothers, put it very well when he said: "We suffer in their coming and their going." ' The priest remembered how Geoghegan had been baptised, received his First Communion and Confirmation in the same church. 'No doubt but that these days were filled with hope for Darren that his life would be long and fulfilled. It hasn't worked out as hoped', he added sadly. Darren Geoghegan's friends are adamant that Paddy Doyle was not behind his murder. They say that if Doyle got into the back of the car and shot Geoghegan and Byrne, then his DNA would have been left in the car, but there was none. Gardaí, though, point out that if Doyle was meant to meet the two men to go out on a job, then he would probably have worn gloves. They argue that if anybody approached the car wearing gloves, then Geoghegan would have smelled a rat and realised that something was up. The way the two men were murdered left little doubt that they trusted the gunman; they willingly let him into the back seat, while they were vulnerable in the front. Doyle and Darren Geoghegan were best friends and spent a lot of time together. Friends of both men cannot believe that Doyle would have turned on a man who was almost like a brother. They even say that Paddy Doyle was not even in the country when the two murders were carried out. They say he only arrived back in the country the following day when he learned of the deaths. Gardaí say there is no evidence that Doyle was in the UK when the murders were carried out. An article appeared in a Sunday newspaper in 2008 claiming that Geoghegan and Byrne were preparing to carry out a murder when they were killed. The same article claimed that the two men had both had body waxes, so they wouldn't leave any hair fibres after carrying out the murder they were allegedly planning. The Geoghegan family issued a statement in response to the claims made in the article. It said: 'Three years after this tragedy these false claims are being made about our son and brother. This has caused terrible suffering for our family.' The statement also denied claims that Darren Geoghegan had grown up with Paddy Doyle. 'Darren was never a childhood friend of Patrick Doyle's. Since Patrick's murder our two families are helping each other through our bereavement.'

Numerous detectives interviewed as part of the research for this book say they have no doubt whatsoever that Patrick Doyle was the murderer. The question is if he was not responsible, then who did kill Darren Geoghegan and Gavin Byrne? Friends and associates of both men have put forward other theories on the crime. They say that Darren Geoghegan was questioned over the John Roche murder in Kilmainham in March 2005. Perhaps it was Noel Roche who carried out the shooting as revenge, thinking that Geoghegan had been responsible for his brother's death. This theory doesn't really stack up though, because there is no way that Geoghegan and Byrne would have allowed Noel Roche or any of the Rattigan gang to get into a car with them, and especially not in the back seat. Others have suggested that maybe Darren Geoghegan wasn't even supposed to be in the car with Gavin Byrne that night. Geoghegan was popular within his own gang and was trusted, whereas Gavin Byrne would have been less established.

Another theory has developed over the years, and it is one that some Gardaí give credence to. This theory is that there was a Bray, Co. Wicklow, connection to the double murder. A leading criminal from Bray organised the getaway car that was used after the killings. So what's to say that he didn't organise the hitman as well? In early 2009, information was received, following several feud-related incidents, that a man in his early thirties from Bray might have been responsible for several feud-related shootings. It was suggested that he might have been used by the Thompson gang as far back as the Geoghegan and Byrne murders, although there is nothing to physically link him to the crime scene. Again, you would have to wonder why the two men would have allowed a stranger into the back of their car, unless a second person was with him, perhaps a senior gang member who would obviously have been trusted. People who knew Byrne and Geoghegan maintain that they were not aware that their lives were in danger, and were not showing any signs that there was internal strife in the gang. If the pair knew they were in danger, friends argue, then they would have left the country and headed to England or Spain until the heat died down.

Friends of Gavin Byrne and Darren Geoghegan are very unhappy with the Garda investigation into the double murder. They are frustrated that a reconstruction of the murder was due to be carried out and featured on RTÉ's *Crimeline*, but never happened. It is fair to say that the double murder investigation never really got off the ground, but statistically it is very seldom that gangland murders are solved, unless there is a confession or a gang member breaks ranks, and that is rare. It is possible that in the near future a fresh investigation will be launched into the double murder, possibly by the Garda 'Cold Case' unit, to see if any new evidence comes to light.

On the evening of 15 November 2005, two days after Darren Geoghegan and Gavin Byrne had been shot dead, Noel Roche was preparing for a night out. Roche and his cohorts in the Brian Rattigan gang had spent the previous 48 hours trying to work out what the hell had happened at the housing estate in Firhouse. Two key members of Freddie Thompson's gang lay in a morgue, but Rattigan had absolutely nothing to do with it. It was a mystery, and the only thing that 27-year-old could think was that there was some serious civil war going on within Thompson's mob that would drive them to such lengths to start killing their own. There was no point in looking a gift horse in the mouth, and Roche was probably more than happy that Thompson's gang's number had been reduced by two, and felt sure that the internal strife was not over. He would happily sit back and let Thompson's crew murder each other, but if he got half the chance, he would take them out himself.

Noel Roche had convictions for assault, the illegal possession of a firearm and road traffic offences, and had been disqualified from driving for four years on 6 December 2001. His brother John had been dead for less than eight months. He had not avenged his killing and that was probably one of his priorities. Although he was distraught when his brother was murdered, Roche realised that they were involved in a war and there were bound to be casualties, so he channelled his grief into getting even. It had been a good few days. Roche was in good spirits and was looking forward to his night out; he was going to see Phil Collins in concert at the Point Depot. Although the soulful Collins might seem like a strange choice of musician for a Dublin gangster to be a fan of, detectives spotted over a dozen serious and well-known criminals from across the city going to see Collins perform that night.

According to Gardaí, for some reason there are two songs that really resonate with criminals in Dublin. These songs are a staple of every wedding, twenty-first birthday and wake attended by well-known and petty criminals. The first is 'Eye of the Tiger' by Survivor, which was the theme tune for the *Rocky* films. A high percentage of gangland criminals are serious boxing fans and would always attend championship boxing matches at the Point. Freddie Thompson is a massive boxing fan and regularly travelled as far as Las Vegas to take in the fights of Ricky Hatton and Joe Calzaghe. When Bernard Dunne fights at the Point, or the O_2 arena, as it is now known, there are upwards of 15 armed and undercover Gardaí mingling among the crowd. Literally every criminal across Dublin attends these high-adrenaline events, and this obviously could result in bloodshed if the wrong people ran into each other. When 'Eye of the Tiger' is played at Bernard Dunne fights, the crowd explodes with delight. The tune is a testosterone-fuelled number and brings out the best – or the worst – in macho men who remember watching Rocky and Apollo Creed square off against each other in the film when they were kids. Whatever the reason for its popularity, 'Eye of the Tiger' is a gangster's favourite. It can only be matched in popularity by one song – Phil Collins' 'In the Air Tonight'. 'In the Air Tonight' is a powerful song that tells the story of the singer witnessing an unspecified act, which leads to a death. Collins wrote the song while he was going through a divorce, and several urban myths have developed. Again, it is hard to tell why the song resonates with criminals, but there is an undercurrent of anger throughout, and when there is an explosion of drums going into the final verse, it never fails to bring the criminals to their feet to sing along. Maybe it is the fact that the singer has the power of life over death in the song, which criminals can relate to, or more likely, they just like the beat of the drums. It could also be because Phil Collins starred in the film *Buster*, about the Great Train

Robbery. He played a petty criminal from the East End. It is hard to imagine that Irish gangland criminals would not only listen to his music, but actually go to his concerts.

Noel Roche had arranged to go to the concert with his girlfriend and aunt and uncle. Eddie Rice drove Roche to the gig. Rice was 32 and hailed from Kilworth Road in Drimnagh. Rice was not a central member of the gang, but was a trusted lieutenant who was seen as very loyal to Rattigan, and especially to Noel Roche. He had a handful of convictions for relatively minor offences. His most serious brush with the law had come in October 1994, when he was arrested and later jailed for two years after admitting to pointing a rifle at and threatening two Gardaí who were pursuing him.

Part of Eddie Rice's job was to run errands for Noel Roche, and, to generally make sure that he had everything he needed. While Roche enjoyed watching Phil Collins, Rice would have stood guard, making sure that everything was okay and that his boss had everything that he wanted. Roche was a lazy individual who was happy to have somebody running around and doing menial jobs for him and acting as his chauffeur. If you are making the money that Roche was each week, it is probably easy to let others do the mundane tasks that most people have to do for themselves. At around 9.30pm, Roche and his girlfriend went out to the lobby bar for a drink. While he was there, either he or Eddie Rice saw somebody of whom they were suspicious. It is not known whether that person was a rival gang member or an associate of the Thompson gang, but Roche was concerned enough to leave the concert early for his own safety. He sent his girlfriend to tell his aunt and uncle that he had to head off. He dispatched Eddie Rice to the car park to get the car and pull up out the front, so he could safely leave the area. There is no evidence that Roche feared his life was in danger, but perhaps he was just being cautious and didn't want to put himself in a position where he could be confronted by one of Fat Freddie's men while he was so far from home. A man was waiting outside the Point in his car to collect his parents and noticed a Fiat Punto in front of his car. The man in the front seat was fairly large. There was another person wearing a hoodie and smoking a cigarette going back and forth from the pavement to the Punto. Suddenly a Ford Mondeo pulled up and a man jumped into the vehicle and it took off at high speed in the direction of Clontarf. The man who jumped into the car was described as been about 5ft 9" with black hair and in his thirties. He was on his mobile phone when he got into the car. The Fiat Punto that had been parked in front of the man's car did a u-turn and took off after the Mondeo. He didn't realise it at the time but he had seen Noel Roche leaving the Point, and whoever was in the Punto was probably the person that had seen him at the concert and was now following him.

Roche and Rice were unaware that they had been seen early in the night and were probably under surveillance while they were at the concert. Gardaí do not know who was in the Fiat Punto outside, but it is known that the person made a phone call to Paddy Doyle. He came out of his hiding place after the double murder two days before, and psyched himself up, ready to inflict yet another casualty on the Rattigan gang. He summoned his driver, 21-year-old Craig White from O'Devaney Gardens in Dublin 7. White was a driver for the Thompson gang and was quite low in the gang's hierarchy, but he was eager to learn the tricks of the criminal trade and was happy to do anything to please the gang leaders. He was driving a beige Peugeot 307 that had been stolen from outside a house in Blessington, Co. Wicklow, five weeks previously.

Eddie Rice drove Roche and his girlfriend back across North Dublin to her apartment near Coolock. After dropping her off, Roche told Rice to make his way down the Clontarf Road towards town, and they would head into

Temple Bar for a few pints. They were not being followed and were happy that they had left the Phil Collins concert without attracting any attention from the rival gang.

At around 10.25pm, a Peugeot 307 began to rev up behind Rice's Mondeo, attempting to ram it off the road. It was not their lucky night. After getting the call and picking Paddy Doyle up, Craig White spent half an hour or so driving around to see if he could spot the Mondeo. The Thompson gang knew that Noel Roche had an offside apartment in Coolock, and headed in that direction to see if he had gone back to stay there. It was just sheer luck that they managed to spot Noel Roche on the Clontarf Road. Even though it was late and there were not that many cars on the road, trying to pick out one car in a massive area of North Dublin was akin to finding a needle in a haystack, but Doyle and White were lucky. The Clontarf Road is one of the busiest arteries that lead into Dublin city centre, with thousands of cars using it each morning. It is unclear if Roche knew that Paddy Doyle was in the front of the Peugeot with a gun, but he would have known that he was in serious danger, because he was not armed and was in an old car, and Eddie Rice wasn't turning out to be much of a getaway driver.

Rice desperately tried to get his battered Mondeo away from Doyle and White, but he was no match as a driver compared to White, who would not give up and refused to be shaken off. As Roche and Rice were approaching The Yacht pub, White managed to swerve across their path, so that Paddy Doyle and Noel Roche were side by side in the middle of the road.

Doyle whipped out a 9mm Glock and fired four shots in quick succession. His aim was accurate, and Roche was hit three times in the head, dying instantly. Eddie Rice slammed on the brake as soon as the shooting started. He wasn't hit. He looked to his left and saw that his friend was dead and covered in blood. Although Rice was naturally shocked and covered in Noel Roche's blood, he fled his car. He began knocking on doors, trying to wake householders. Several people answered their doors in their nightclothes, only to quickly shut them when they saw a man covered in blood screaming frantically at them. Rice managed to make it into a back garden and escaped.

After the shooting, White drove the Peugeot to Furry Park in Killester, which was less than a mile away. This was a similar tactic to that used in the double murder carried out two days previously. Burning the car close to the scene of the crime is seen as a must, because the last thing that gang members want to happen is that they speed away from the murder and are passed by Gardaí on their way to investigate. It is too dangerous and leads to the possibility of being stopped, which would definitely result in the person being convicted, because they wouldn't have the chance to burn out the getaway car, dispose of their clothes or get rid of the murder weapon. Destroying the car and the all-important DNA evidence immediately and within the vicinity of the crime is therefore vital to ensuring that there is nothing to link you to the incident.

However, White made a ridiculous error: in his panic to escape, he actually forgot to torch the car. This was despite the fact that he had brought a can of petrol for that very purpose. This would later come back to haunt him. White and Doyle ran down Furry Park Road and got into another waiting car, which was driven by an unknown third accomplice. They were seen by a resident running away, but were gone by the time Gardaí arrived.

At around 10.30pm, Gardaí received a call to say that shots had been fired. Several local residents had heard a number of loud bangs and had assumed that fireworks were being let off. Clontarf is a quiet, affluent area, and the last thing people expected was a gangland slaying to be taking place on their doorstep.

Gardaí rushed to the scene and saw the green Ford Mondeo abandoned in the middle of the road. The driver's door of the vehicle was wide open, the lights were on and the key was in the ignition, but the engine was not running. There was no sign of the driver. Garda Colm Mac Donnacha looked through the driver's window and saw a male slumped backwards on the front passenger seat. It was Noel Roche, covered in blood. It was obvious that he had been shot several times in the head, and his body was lifeless. Garda McDonagh noticed four bullet holes in the passenger window. He moved around to the passenger side and spotted four nine-millimetre bullet casings lying on the ground. Gardaí immediately put out a message across the city for all units to be on the lookout for a man who was on the loose and was potentially injured and armed and dangerous. Armed detectives and members of the Emergency Response Unit (ERU) flooded into Clontarf and began a sweep of the housing estates in and around the murder scene, searching for the car's driver. Garda dogs, specially trained to sniff out even the smallest drop of blood, and their handlers combed through gardens. Gardaí knew that the driver was injured because they had seen a trail of blood, but they did not know the extent of the mystery man's wounds.

Some officers carried bulletproof shields in case the man was armed and attempted to fire at them if he was confused and thought that they were the hitman coming after him. A check on the owner of the Ford Mondeo told detectives that the driver was probably Edward Rice, who was born in August 1973 and had a criminal record. Gardaí in Clontarf would not have known Roche or the players in the Crumlin-Drimnagh feud, but as the car was associated and linked to Rice, Crumlin Gardaí were summoned. They soon indentified the deceased man in the Mondeo as Noel Roche. They were also able to tell investigators at Clontarf that Eddie worked as a driver and general messenger for

Noel Roche, so at least Gardaí knew who they were looking for.

The ERU immediately flooded the streets of Dublin, and every Garda was on red alert to look out for Rice, because it was feared that because he was a potential witness, he might be the rival gang's next target. It seemed like he had vanished into thin air. Gardaí didn't know whether he had been kidnapped by the shooters or had been fatally wounded and was lying dead in a hedge somewhere. The Garda helicopter spent the night searching for Rice from the air but without success.

A woman from Furry Park Road went to the front of her house at around 10.30pm and heard a car speeding past her. It pulled up across the road from her, and two men who looked to be in their early twenties jumped out and ran away. She took the car registration details and immediately phoned the Gardaí.

When Gardaí arrived at the scene, they were amazed to find that the getaway car was still intact. A forensic examination of the vehicle recovered a brown paper bag in the rear driver's side of the car, which contained a balaclava, a Glock 9mm pistol, a tea towel and gloves. A container of petrol was also found in the footwell of the abandoned car. A further search of the area along Furry Park Road unearthed two gloves, which were believed to be discarded by the people that had murdered Roche. Fibres from the Peugeot were later found to match fibres on the discarded gloves, while the four bullet casings found on the road beside the Mondeo were shown to have been fired from the Glock that was found in the Peugeot. It was a veritable treasure trove of forensic evidence and a Garda detective's dream scenario. The contrast to the scarcity of evidence left in Firhouse, two days previously couldn't have been stronger.

Superintendent Nicky Connelly from Raheny Garda Station and Detective Superintendent Mick Byrne from

Santry Garda Station led the investigation into the Roche murder. Detective Inspector Angela Willis also played a key role in the probe. Connelly and Byrne and their team would not have been familiar with the Crumlin-Drimnagh feud, but soon brought themselves up to speed with the help of Detective Sergeant John Walsh and one or two other detectives from Crumlin.

Although there were no actual eyewitnesses to the murder, a tour bus full of Americans did pass by the scene just seconds after the incident, and a tourist filmed the immediate aftermath of the murder on a camcorder. The footage was handed over to Gardaí. It showed the stolen Peugeot doing a u-turn after the shooting took place and speeding off in the direction of Clontarf, breaking a red light.

The forensic evidence found in the Peugeot was crucial. Gardaí later applied for warrants to search the homes of Craig White and his girlfriend, on suspicion of the unlawful possession of a firearm. While he was in custody, White refused to cooperate or say anything. Gardaí had information that Paddy Doyle was the gunman and offered to place White in the Witness Protection Programme, if he cooperated. He didn't take them up on the offer. Gardaí took White's fingerprints and DNA while he was detained, and were confident that they could match it against the items that were found in the stolen Peugeot and that charges would then follow.

Noel Roche's murder meant that his mother, Caroline, and father, Noel Snr, had lost two of their sons in just eight months. Noel and John Roche knew that their central involvement in the feud could result in them both being killed at some point, but they could hardly have imagined that they would both be murdered in the space of just a few months. Caroline Roche is a decent woman who was central to the earlier efforts to broker a truce in the feud with Pauline Gavin, Declan's mother. She knew that her sons were no angels and she also knew the intricacies of the feud. When she arrived at the scene of Noel's murder and saw him lying dead in the car, she immediately told Gardaí that Paddy Doyle was responsible.

With three murders in less than three days, in two middle-class areas, it was obvious that there would be severe political fallout and serious pressure on the Gardaí to make progress in the two cases. Michael McDowell's claims after the double murder, two days before, that the key members were under surveillance were shown to have been a bit wide of the mark. There was little doubt that there would be reprisals from the Rattigan side. Noel Roche's murder was the eighth feud killing, and it was a matter of when, not if, the ninth victim would die. In the 48 hours after Noel Roche's murder, Gardaí carried out two dozen searches on properties around Crumlin and Drimnagh, but gathered nothing of note. It was mainly a political exercise to show that they were doing all they could to prevent bloodshed. CAB was also called in to uncover where the two gangs kept their drugs cash, in a bid to hit the two outfits where it really hurts – their pockets.

A day and a half after witnessing Noel Roche's murder, Eddie Rice walked into Raheny Garda Station with his solicitor. He was arrested and questioned for almost 11 hours, but refused to cooperate or offer any information that would help Gardaí in tracking down his boss's killer. He said that he didn't see who was responsible for the murder and that when he heard shots being fired, he just jumped out of his car and ran for his life. Rice was also offered a place on the Witness Protection Programme but politely declined. He did not want to spend the rest of his life with a new identity, hiding out in some far corner of the world. Rice was released without charge. His silence and loyalty seemed to earn him the respect of the Rattigan gang.

After being fingered for carrying out the three murders in

A young-looking Brian Rattigan with his partner Natasha McEnroe. Rattigan is currently serving a life sentence in Portlaoise Prison.

Eddie Redmond who is a key member of the Rattigan gang.

Shay O'Byrne, Sharon Rattigan's long-term partner. He was shot dead outside their home in Tallaght in March 2009.

Rattigan's 'enforcer', Anthony Cannon, was shot dead in Ballyfermot in July 2009.

Hitman for hire Gary Bryan is suspected of carrying out at least two murders. He was shot dead in September 2006.

Eddie Rice was the driver of the car that was ambushed prior to Noel Roche's murder in November 2005.

Shane Maloney, a key Rattigan ally, is serving a ten-year jail sentence for possessing €1.2m worth of heroin.

Wayne McNally, one of Brian Rattigan's most senior gang members.

Ritchie Rattigan, Brian's older brother.

Brothers John and Noel Roche were leading members of the Rattigan gang. The pair were murdered within eight months of each other in 2005.

Wayne Zambra was shot dead on Cameron Street in 2006.

Pictures of Rattigan from his high-security prison cell, with only his beloved pet budgie, Shrek, for company.

Abrakebabra at the Crumlin Shopping Centre, the scene of Declan Gavin's murder in August 2001.
© Collins

Declan Gavin, the original leader of the gang, was murdered by his arch enemy, Brian Rattigan. This marked the beginning of the deadly feud.

'Fat' Freddie Thompson took over from Declan Gavin as the gang's boss in August 2001.
© picture Gary Ashe/Irish Daily Star

A happy-looking 'Fat' Freddie Thompson on a night out with a lady friend.

A leading member of the Thompson gang, Aidan Gavin, brother of Declan Gavin.

Paddy Doyle, the 'enforcer' for the Thompson gang, was shot dead in Spain in February 2008.

'Fat' Freddie's brother, Ritchie Thompson.

Darren Geoghegan, the Thompson gang's money man, was shot dead in Firhouse in November 2005.

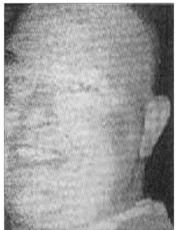

Gavin Byrne was shot dead with Darren Geoghegan in November 2005.

Liam Brannigan, an associate of Freddie Thompson.

Trevor Brunton, a 'minder' for the Rattigan gang, was jailed after he was caught with a loaded gun at a busy Dublin nightclub.

Eoin O'Connor, 'Fat' Freddie's cousin, was left with permanent scarring after he was stabbed by Anthony Cannon at a music festival.

Philip Griffiths was one of the gang members caught in the Holiday Inn raid in 2000.

David Byrne, a cousin and close associate of Freddie Thompson.

Craig White was the first person to be found guilty of a feud murder when he was convicted of shooting dead Noel Roche, in November 2005. He was sentenced to life imprisonment. © Collins

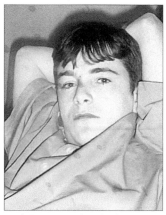

Albert Doyle agreed to give evidence against the Thompson gang after he was shot, only to change his mind.

Paul Warren was shot dead in Gray's Pub, Dublin 8, in February 2004.

Gray's of Newmarket Square in Dublin 8, the scene of Paul Warren's murder in February 2004. The pub has since ceased trading.

A young and happy Eddie McCabe. McCabe was an innocent victim of the gangland feud. He had his eye gouged out in a savage and brutal assault that resulted in his death.

Ian Kenny was murdered after he fell out with one of the new generation of feuding criminals who is nicknamed 'Mad Dog'.

Christopher 'Git' McDonagh was shot dead outside his home in Ronanstown in September 2008 after being labelled a 'rat'.

Terry Dunleavy owed money to the Thompson gang. He was shot dead in a flats complex in Dublin's north-inner city in April 2005.

Detective Superintendent Denis Donegan (now retired) from Crumlin Garda Station was in charge of many of the feud murder investigations. © Collins

Superintendent Brian Sutton, one of the most senior Gardaí involved in investigating the feud. © Mark Condren/*Sunday Tribune*

Detective Superintendent Gabriel O'Gara. Many of the feud murders happened in his Kevin Street 'A' District. © *Evening Herald*

Inspector John Walsh
who has a knowledge of
the feud that is second to
none.
© Mark Condren/*Sunday Tribune*

Detective Garda Ritchie Kelly, Detective Garda Ken Donnelly and Detective
Sergeant Adrian Whitelaw, from Kevin Street Garda Station.
© Mark Condren/*Sunday Tribune*

Brian Rattigan winks defiantly at the camera as he is led from court in December 2009, after he was handed a life sentence for the murder of Declan Gavin. © Collins

less than 36 hours, Paddy Doyle knew he was the most wanted criminal in Ireland, both by the Gardaí, and worse still, the Rattigan crew. Roche and Rattigan had been very friendly all their lives. Brian Rattigan went absolutely beserk when Roche was murdered. A bounty of €60,000 was placed on Doyle's head. For the next few weeks, Doyle travelled around the city and out of the country with his head down and in heavy disguise – often going to such extreme lengths as to dress as a woman. He seldom stayed at the same address for more than two consecutive nights. About a week after the Clontarf Road murder, Doyle went into Crumlin Garda Station and had a meeting with a senior detective. He said that he knew he was in the feud up to his neck and wanted a way out. The detective told him to admit to carrying out a crime, and he would see what could be arranged with the DPP's office. Doyle just looked at him and laughed, and said he would pass and take his chances. He did offer an insight into the way he was thinking, when he said that he thought that Freddie Thompson was a Garda informant and that he did not trust him. He always suspected the worst of people and trusted nobody but himself. When the gangs got so big and began to make so much money, the friendships were replaced by business partnerships. Friendships seemed to be fickle and money was the motivator. That Doyle would have been able to get into the back of a car with two men he considered to be friends and blow both their brains out showed this clearly. Paddy Doyle despised the Gardaí, so the fact that he was even talking to them showed just how desperate he had become. Several senior detectives said they had more time for Doyle than any other gang member, and said he had a way about him that wasn't typical of most of the feuding criminals. He was more genuine, more polite and unlike many involved in the feud. He dressed well, looked well, looked after his two kids, and for want of a better phrase, had a way about him, some might go as far as to say he had a little bit of class. However, the fact remains that he was good at what he did and was a very violent man who would shoot dead anyone who got in his way, without a moment's thought and without a shred of guilt. Several Gardaí said they were always struck by Doyle's vacant stare; he looked you in the eye, but his gaze penetrated you like you weren't even in the room.

They described him as a natural born killer, far more than Gary Bryan ever was. They thought that Bryan was a total junkie who murdered for money, but it was always business with Doyle. Doyle had all the cash he needed, and although he took the occasional line of cocaine and was a steroid abuser, he never went near heroin and was quite health conscious. He was handsome, worked out religiously, ate well and was a keen and talented boxer. When Doyle said that he wanted to get out of the crime game, the senior officer in Crumlin believed him. The detective had heard this story dozens of time before, but knew that Doyle was genuine. Unfortunately, when you get into crime as deep as Doyle did, it is very difficult to get out. He was making tens of thousands of euro some weeks – he had more cash than he knew what to do with. It was believed that he had killed three men and would have to take responsibility for his actions.

A month after Noel Roche died, Paddy Doyle had enough of the pressure at home in Ireland and decided that he would have to leave the country permanently. He boarded a flight bound for Birmingham and then intended to head for Spain. When he passed through security at Dublin Airport, he probably knew in his heart of hearts that because of the massive price on his head, he would not be returning home any time soon.

NINE

Old habits die hard

Wayne Zambra had spent the night having a few pints in his local pub, Morrissey's, on Cameron Street. It was about 1.00am on 19 August 2006, and he had parked his 04 D Honda HRV estate car just across the road from the busy boozer. He opened the door and got into the driver's seat, while one of his good friends, David Little, hopped into the front passenger seat. Zambra didn't have much time to react, but would have heard the screech of tyres, as a silver Nissan Almera pulled up alongside his Honda, and a series of shots were fired. In less than 20 seconds, the 22-year-old was dead, his head slumped over the steering wheel. He had been hit a total of four times in the head and chest. David Little was struck in the leg. He was an innocent victim of the murderous feud. Though shot in the leg, Little managed to open his door and run down the street where he dialled 999. Within minutes the area was flooded with Gardaí and medical personnel. Despite frantic efforts of an ambulance crew from nearby St James's Hospital, there was nothing that could be done for Zambra. After bravely summoning help, Little collapsed. He was rushed to St James's in a serious condition, but would later make a full recovery. The car that was used by the murder team was found abandoned and burnt out nearby not long after the shooting, but its occupants had long since vanished into the night. It was clear that Wayne Zambra had been under surveillance in the pub and that his murder was calculated and well planned.

The murder investigation was launched at Kevin Street and the lead Garda, Detective Inspector Gabriel O'Gara, already had his hands full. He was in the middle of another murder investigation after a pensioner, Vincent Plunkett, had been knifed to death at his flat in Robinson's Court, not far from where Zambra was killed, a few days before. Indeed five people had been murdered in the country in the space of just one week, and Kevin Street Garda Station was undoubtedly one of the busiest.

Wayne Zambra was well-known as one of Brian Rattigan's men. He lived on Lourdes Road in Maryland, right in the middle of Kevin Street's district. He was a familiar face to Gardaí on the beat. He was known to be involved in the distribution of drugs around the south-inner city on behalf of his jailed boss. Zambra and Rattigan would not have known each other growing up, but started to become friendly after Joey Rattigan's murder, when Wayne McNally had introduced them. Zambra was driving the car in February 2003 when Brian Rattigan lost the plot and started shooting at Gardaí in Bluebell. When Zambra was questioned by Gardaí about the incident, he claimed that he did not even know that Rattigan had a firearm on him. However, he kept on driving the car away from the pursuing Gardaí and made no effort to stop. He was of sound enough mind to flee from the area and was not initially arrested. When he was detained, he did not say anything to implicate Rattigan more than he already was. Because of this, he probably earned his stripes and went up in Rattigan's estimation, thus earning him an element of trust. This trust meant that he was permitted to handle large amounts of imported cocaine and heroin for Rattigan when he was sent down over the Bluebell shooting.

Zambra was not a hardened criminal though, and Gardaí described him as slightly naïve and foolish and in way over his head in his involvement with the Rattigan gang. Zambra was a serious heroin addict, who let his need for drugs impair his judgement, so he was happy to be working for Rattigan because it meant he had regular cash in his pocket and also had access to drugs to feed his addiction. Although Zambra was a well-known face to Gardaí, like many criminals he had managed to avoid notching up too many convictions. His most serious conviction occurred after an incident on 16 May 2003, when he was arrested by Gardaí after being involved in a serious assault outside a pub on Wolfe Tone Quay. Zambra repeatedly stabbed a man, causing serious wounds to his chest, right shoulder and upper arm. He was rushed to hospital in a serious condition but subsequently recovered from his injuries. Zambra viciously assaulted his victim in a row over a woman. He was immediately detained by Gardaí. The assault was so serious that he was remanded in custody. When he appeared in court in February 2004, he pleaded guilty and was handed a 30-month sentence. The court heard that Zambra went 'berserk' during the incident. Because he had already been in prison for nine months, the judge suspended the remainder of his sentence and released Zambra on condition that he keep the peace for 18 months. His solicitors argued that Zambra was a drug addict who was receiving treatment in prison. He was released on condition that he live with his parents and sign on at Kevin's Street Garda Station three times per week. Aside from that run-in with the law, Zambra had minor convictions for criminal damage, unauthorised taking of a vehicle and obstructing a Garda, but he never served jail time for those offences. He had also been arrested for being drunk and disorderly and for being a passenger in a stolen car, but was never charged with either offence.

* * *

Wayne Zambra's murder had been the first since Noel Roche was gunned down on the Clontarf Road, the previous November, at the end of the two days of unprecedented bloodshed. A combination of good work by Gardaí involved in mediation between the two gangs and the fact that one of the main players, Paddy Doyle, was now out of the country meant that the feud had largely subsided. There had not been many serious feud incidents in the previous nine months. Two weeks after Roche's murder, Gardaí received information that Shay O'Byrne was planning a revenge hit and was intending to use a silver Volkswagen Passat as the getaway vehicle. The car was recovered at Lansdowne Valley in Drimnagh, and 14 shotgun cartridges were found in the boot. O'Byrne wasn't arrested, and things quietened down after that until the Zambra assassination.

Gardaí initially suspected that Freddie Thompson's gang had shot Zambra dead, and that theory made perfect sense. He was a low-to-middle-ranking member of the Rattigan gang and was moving a fair amount of drugs around the Dublin 8 area, which is lucrative turf. Taking him out would be fairly easy because he lived with his parents in Maryland and was pretty much a sitting duck. However, Gardaí explored every possible avenue, and came up against dead ends in trying to tie Freddie's crew to the murder. In the weeks after the murder, it became obvious that Zambra was probably murdered by his own gang after an internal row. Before he was shot dead, rumours began to circulate that Zambra had been dipping into drugs that he was meant to be dealing, and that profits were down as a result. If he was using Rattigan's drugs, then he was leaving himself wide open to suffering severe consequences. Although Rattigan and the other members trusted him to a degree, this trust was limited, and once he started getting in the way of making money, there was only one way Zambra was going to end up – dead.

In confusing times Gardaí usually go to their trusted informants who give them the off-the-record low down on what actually happened but there was one problem – Wayne Zambra was their main informant. Several sources interviewed, as part of the research for this book, have said that Zambra was providing information about rivals, and also members of his own gang, to several Garda detectives. These detectives provided him with a degree of shelter. In return the Gardaí got valuable information about the activities of senior drug dealers who would then be targeted. If members of Brian Rattigan's gang even suspected that Zambra was a rat it would be an automatic bullet for him – perhaps they had found out. Maybe Brian Rattigan and Wayne McNally began to wonder why they had both been charged over the Bluebell shooting incident, but Zambra had got off scot-free. Perhaps he had given a statement implicating them under the agreement that he would get a free pass. Nothing could be ruled out by detectives. Thirty-two people were arrested as part of this investigation – Wayne McNally was the most high-profile – but nobody was pointing the finger in the direction of the Thompson gang.

Detectives began to draw up a list of possible suspects outside of Freddie's crew, but none of the names that were mentioned made any sense. They looked back at the feud murders from the previous four years and the manner of the murder – the fact that the killing was so precise and took place in a busy area with potential witnesses, led one Garda to mention off-hand that it reminded him of the work of Gary Bryan.

* * *

Gary Bryan, to the best of everyone's knowledge, was still behind bars, after being sentenced to a three-year jail term in April 2004 for the possession of €10,000 worth of heroin. To satisfy themselves Gardaí checked with the prison authorities, who informed them that he had actual been released on 20 July, just one month earlier. The final year of his sentence had been suspended, so Bryan was set free. It was a significant moment. Gardaí knew that Bryan was a professional killer and had been hired by the Rattigan gang to take out Paul Warren at Gray's pub in February 2004. What was to say that they hadn't hired him again to take care of some internal housekeeping?

Bryan was comfortable in jail and used his frequent sentences to wean himself off heroin. In the course of his adult life he served 17 separate jail sentences. These sentences included seven months for four counts of car theft, ten months for drunk driving, three years for the possession of a firearm, three years for criminal damage, four years for aggravated burglary and three years for false imprisonment. When he walked out of Mountjoy Prison, he was 29 years old and determined to lead a straight life. Although Valerie White had told Gardaí that she was finished with him after the Paul Warren murder, the couple had never really broke up and were as devoted to each other as ever. She visited him twice each week in Mountjoy, and was waiting for him outside the prison gates when he was released. Then they went straight back to their new flat on the Lower Kimmage Road. For all of Bryan's undoubted faults, she had decided to stand by her man, and their new flat was meant to signal a new beginning – away from crime, drugs and all the other negative temptations in his life. The new start lasted just a couple of days. Bryan struggled to adjust to life as a free man and started abusing heroin again. He also met up with his old associate Shay O'Byrne, and made it clear that he was available for work, should he be needed. With a heroin problem that was costing him a couple of hundred euro a day, he certainly needed the cash. So, he started selling drugs again, but this time he was being supplied by the Rattigan gang. He started to make a lot of cash and would regularly have thousands of euro in his possession. He started to go on week-long drugs benders. It was in the early days of September that Gary Bryan was first nominated as a suspect in Wayne Zambra's murder. Detectives were in the process of trying to build up a case against him. They knew that they faced a difficult task, because there was no actual physical evidence to link him to the murder. Nevertheless, once officers had started to put his name to confidential informants, the word that came back was that Bryan was being fingered as the triggerman in the murder on the street as well.

This encouraged Gardaí and they thought that although Valerie White had let them down at the eleventh hour before, when she withdrew her statement, if her boyfriend was back to his old tricks and she knew about it, she might be willing to give him up again. Preliminary investigations had determined that Bryan had left his flat the night before the Zambra murder. He said he would be back in an hour, but had not returned for four days. This led them to believe that he had kept his head down in a safe house after carrying out the murder. However, before they could try to get a statement from White or get enough evidence to question Bryan, fate intervened and ensured that the Zambra murder will almost certainly be classed as 'unsolved' forever.

On 26 September 2006, just after 5.00pm, Bryan and Valerie White left their flat and drove towards Crumlin with the intention of calling in to see Valerie's mother, Margaret. They had spent the early afternoon shopping in town and planned to relax for the evening after visiting Margaret White. On the way to Crumlin, they took a detour to the McDonald's drive-thru on the Long Mile Road. Bryan was driving a Blue Nissan Micra, registration 94 D 5139. At 5.45pm he parked outside the ABC newsagents on Bunting Road in Crumlin to pick up a packet of cigarettes. A few minutes later, he got back into the car with Valerie and drove 500 yards to Margaret White's home on Bunting Road on the Crumlin/Walkinstown border. He parked the Micra directly outside the house, with the front of the car facing towards Crumlin village.

The pair went into the White family home. They spent about ten minutes chatting to Margaret and to Valerie's sister, Linda White, along with her two young sons. At 6.00pm, Bryan went outside to fit two new car seat covers on his Micra. Valerie followed him out and spoke to him while he worked on the car. Five or ten minutes later, Bryan looked up and saw a metallic-blue Volkswagen Golf driving slowly past the house. He recognised the driver and said: 'There's a fella that's going to make a phone call. I have to get out of here.' Valerie asked him who he was talking about. He said Graham Whelan was the man driving the car, and that he wasn't safe and needed to leave.

Graham Whelan had been released from Wheatfield Prison on 19 June 2006, after serving nearly all of a six-year stretch. He was sentenced for possession and intent to supply. Back in March 2000, he was caught in the Holiday Inn with Declan Gavin and Philip Griffiths with a drugs haul worth a €1.7m. Although Whelan had served a hefty sentence and Declan Gavin had got off, Whelan did not join the Brian Rattigan side in the dispute. He remained loyal to Fat Freddie Thompson and spent a lot of time with him.

Gary Bryan saw Whelan drive off in the direction of Crumlin village. Valerie told him not to be so paranoid, and went into the house to make him a cup of coffee, and said they would head off after that. Gary took the coffee and continued to work on the car. He was lying on the front passenger seat with the door open, while Valerie was inside the house with her mother and sister. At around 6.35pm, a man armed with a handgun walked up to Bryan and shot him three times in the back, while Bryan was attempting to get out of the Micra. Bryan ran across Bunting Road towards Bunting Park, pursued by his assassin. As he slumped and fell to the footpath, the man leaned over him and fired three more shots to his head from close range, instantly killing him.

Valerie White and her family heard the commotion from inside the house. Valerie ran across the road and saw the gunman. She noticed that he was around 5ft 8", was quite stocky and wore a camouflage jacket with the hood up. She remembered that he also wore a pair of camouflage trousers. He had black hair with a long fringe, although it was possible that he was wearing a wig. He wore large brown sunglasses, in an effort to disguise himself, and his hands were covered by a pair of black gloves. Valerie noticed that the man had a tanned face and a square jaw. He held the gun in his right hand, and it was described as being black in colour with a square shaped barrel. Valerie White shouted at the gunman, and he jumped into the front passenger side of a silver Subaru Impreza, which sped off down Bunting Road and turned right onto Balfe Road. Valerie instantly knew that Gary was dead, and she threw herself on his body and started screaming and hugging his lifeless corpse. She would later have to be forcibly removed from him, because her arms were so tightly wrapped around the dead man.

At 6.41pm, Garda Alan Greally was on duty at Command and Control at Harcourt Square when he answered a 999 call. The caller would not identify himself, but said that opposite Bunting Park in Crumlin, 'There have been shots fired at a house here.' The mystery caller then added that there was 'a male lying on the side of the road'. At 6.43pm, Linda White also dialled 999 and stated that a man had been shot on Bunting Road. Garda Greally immediately circulated the information over the Command and Control radio system to all the mobile patrols in the Dublin area.

Gardaí Tony Kennedy and Sue Kinsella were on patrol in the Crumlin area when they received the radio message. The two officers arrived at Bunting Road at 6.45pm. Garda Kennedy observed a male lying on the grass verge opposite Bunting Park. He was lying face up and appeared to be dead, and there was a lot of blood. Another four Gardaí arrived at the scene within the next two minutes. It was quickly ascertained that the man had no pulse and was dead. Bunting Road was closed to traffic, and the scene was quickly preserved, while Garda Kinsella determined that the dead man was Gary Bryan, from Brookview Crescent in Tallaght. Shortly after the arrival of the Gardaí, Fire Station Officer James Dowling, along with his colleagues, reached the scene at Bunting Road. They parked the fire engine alongside Gary Bryan and used a defibrillator to check for signs of life. It was clear that the dead man was beyond help and it was obvious to all at the scene that he had been shot several times in the body and head. An ambulance arrived a couple of minutes after the fire brigade, and James Dowling requested that they call a doctor to come and pronounce Gary Bryan dead. At 8.00pm, Dr James Moloney officially pronounced Bryan dead at the scene. Later that night, Garda Lorcan McCarthy accompanied his remains to the City Morgue in Marino.

Gary Bryan's parents were immediately informed about his murder. On the morning of 28 September, they identified the remains of their son to Sergeant Karen Barker from Crumlin Garda Station. That afternoon, the post mortem examination on Bryan's remains took place, conducted by Deputy State Pathologist Dr Michael Curtin. Detective Gardaí Tom Carey and Shane Curran from the Ballistics Section, Detective Garda Pat Flynn from the Photography Section and Detective Garda Eamon Hennelly of the Fingerprints Section of the Garda Technical Bureau were also present during the post mortem. Dr Curtis concluded that Gary Bryan had died as a result of multiple gunshot wounds to the head, neck, trunk and left lower limb. These gunshots had caused injuries to Bryan's brain, right lung, heart, aorta and liver. There were a total of 12 gunshot wounds to Gary Bryan's body, six separate entrance and exit wounds. He had been hit in the scalp, the back of the head and had two wounds in the neck, behind his left ear. He had two gunshot wounds in his back, two to his chest, one to the upper left thigh, one to the anterior of the left thigh and one below the chin. Dr Curtin determined that Gary Bryan had no diseases, and toxicology tests carried out on his blood and urine found no traces of alcohol, but a cocktail of drugs was found. Among the substances in Gary Bryan's body were morphine, codeine, methadone, diazepam and benzoylecgonine, which is a metabolite of cocaine. It was clear from the toxicology report that Bryan had not managed to get himself off drugs – he was obviously abusing them in a big way.

In the immediate aftermath of Gary Bryan's death, a murder inquiry was launched from Crumlin Garda Station. Detective Superintendent Denis Donegan and Superintendent Bart Faulkner headed the investigation, with Detective Inspector Brian Sutton in day-to-day charge. Around 50 Gardaí from the local district and national units were involved in trying to catch Bryan's killer. Because Gary Bryan was the main suspect in Wayne Zambra's murder (the previous month), there was absolutely no doubt in Gardaí's mind that Gary Bryan was murdered as an act of revenge. Because it was suspected that Bryan had killed Paul Warren and Zambra, it was always likely that there would be a price on his head. So, nobody was particularly surprised when he was shot dead. Detectives immediately suspected that the Thompson gang had been responsible. The investigation team's initial findings led them in that very direction.

The first and most urgent Garda action was to interview everybody who had been in the area at the time of the murder and may have witnessed anything that could help Gardaí to find Bryan's killers.

A number of witnesses observed the events before, during and after the murder. The most disturbing account came from a couple who saw the murder take place. They were stopped at the junction of Balfe Road and Bunting Road. The couple saw a man working on his car at the footpath on Bunting

Road, and then saw another man approach him. The pair
then became involved in a 'tussle'. A shot was fired and the
man working on his car ran across the road and was pursued
by the man carrying a gun. They heard a number of loud
bangs and Gary Bryan fell to the ground. Both the witnesses
saw the gunman then shoot Bryan twice in the head from
close range. The gunman then jumped into a silver Subaru,
which then drove off down Balfe Road. It was followed by a
01D silver Fiat Punto. The couple were stuck in traffic behind
the Punto. There were two men inside the vehicle. They
pulled their hoods and hats off and started to cheer,
celebrating the fact that Bryan had just been murdered. The
cars then turned left onto the Long Mile Road.

Valerie White and her mother and sister all witnessed
events in the lead up to and aftermath of the murder. Gardaí
obviously felt that what they saw could eventually prove to
be crucial in solving the case. Margaret White told detectives
that she was sitting in her living room and looked out the
window and saw Bryan working on his car. A man wearing a
camouflage jacket, with the hood up to cover his head, then
appeared and 'lunges' at Bryan. Gary Bryan then ran towards
Bunting Park, and Margaret heard a number of loud bangs
seconds later. She then grabbed her two grandchildren to
make sure they were safe and remained in her house.

Linda White was also in the living room, and when she
heard gunshots, she rushed out of the house to bring her
young son back in to make sure he was not caught up in the
mayhem. She then heard four or five gunshots, but could not
see what was going on because Gary Bryan's car was blocking
her vision. She then saw a stocky man in an army camouflage
jacket running away from the scene.

Valerie White told Gardaí what had happened before the
shooting and what Bryan had said about seeing Graham
Whelan.

After interviewing all the witnesses, Gardaí had determined that two cars were used to carry out the murder and execute a safe getaway: a Suburu Impreza and a Fiat Punto. At around 7.00pm on the evening of the murder, Sergeant Aidan Minnock and Gardaí Jason Miley and Declan Leader came across a silver Subaru Impreza, registration 00 D 7814 on fire outside a house at Camac Park in Bluebell. The car was being hosed down by members of the Dublin Fire Brigade.

A check on the registration number established that it was fitted with false registration plates which actually belonged to a Ford Ka. The Suburu was stolen during a burglary on a house in Bray, Co. Wicklow, five days before the murder. A technical examination of the car and false registration plates did not recover anything of evidential value, but it was clearly the car that the Gardaí had been searching for.

On 3 October, Detective Garda David Finnerty located the Punto at Rossmore Lawns in Templogue, Dublin 6W. It was registered to the girlfriend of a member of the Freddie Thompson gang, Liam Brannigan. Brannigan was 24 and from Bride Street in Dublin 8. The car underwent technical examination and fingerprints were lifted from the glass on the back passenger door. Gardaí already knew that the car belonged to Liam Brannigan's then girlfriend, so they compared the prints to a set previously taken from Liam Brannigan. It turned out that the prints taken from the Fiat Punto matched Liam Brannigan's right middle finger. A number of newspapers and other items were recovered from the boot of the Punto, which were sent away for forensic examination.

Forensic evidence is one of the best ways Gardaí have of solving cases, especially murder cases. Detective Garda Shane Curran from the Garda Technical Bureau, located a total of seven 9mm discharged cartridge cases and three 9mm cartridge bullets from where Bryan was murdered at Bunting

Road. A further cartridge case and three discharged bullets were recovered from the grass verge where Bryan had fallen when he died. It was determined that the cartridges were fired from a Luger 9mm pistol. A technical examination of the empty cartridges and the bullets concluded that they had probably all originated from the same weapon and that Gardaí were most likely looking at the scenario that one gun was used to murder Bryan, and that one gunman was probably responsible for his death. Despite dozens of searches being carried out, the murder weapon was never recovered.

After carrying out over 230 lines of inquiry, arresting 10 people and taking 200 witness statements, the Gardai's theory on the murder was that Graham Whelan was driving on Bunting Road and happened upon Gary Bryan working on his car outside a house. Gardaí believe that Whelan made a phone call to one of his associates and told him that he had just seen Bryan. Detectives believe that a 23-year-old from Drimnagh and a 19-year-old from Tallaght were then dispatched to carry out the murder. The 23-year-old pulled the trigger and jumped into the waiting Suburu, which then fled the scene.

Gardaí had come to this theory from mobile phone records and CCTV footage. In the immediate aftermath of the murder, officers had spent a lot of time attempting to trace the movements of the Subaru getaway car. It drove from Bunting Road onto Balfe Road and then turned left onto Walkinstown Road, right into Walkinstown Drive and then on into Walkinstown Green. The driver of the Subaru then dropped the gunman off at a cut through the Long Mile Road, and the gunman escaped on foot up the Long Mile Road. The driver of the Subaru abandoned the car at Kilnamanagh Court at around 6.45pm, and left on foot. A short distance away, the driver was confronted by a local man who asked him what he was up to. He ran back to the Subaru and drove onto the Long Mile Road, turned right onto

Walkinstown Avenue and onto Camac Park, where he burnt the car out. The driver of the Suburu was captured on CCTV footage. The images of the driver were grainy, but Gardaí believe that the driver was a 19-year-old from Tallaght who had links to the Thompson gang. Ironically, he was well known to Gary Bryan. On 3 October 2006, Gardaí featured Gary Bryan's murder on RTÉ's *Crimecall* programme in the hope that members of the general public would provide them with information that might lead to a breakthrough. The programme led to a number of promising leads. The 19-year-old was known as a hothead, who had previous convictions for violence against Gardaí and had once rammed a patrol car off the road. He was detained on 1 November 2006, and again refused to cooperate with Gardaí. He also refused to take part in an identity parade, so Gardaí had no choice but to let him go.

On the same day that the 19-year-old was detained, Gardaí also swooped on Liam Brannigan and his girlfriend. Detective Sergeant Barry Butler arrested the 22-year-old woman from Dublin 8, under Section 30 of the Offences Against the State Act. She was questioned at Crumlin Garda Station and made no reply to the majority of questions put to her. She did say that she was with friends from 5.30pm on the day that Gary Bryan was murdered, and went to a party in Drimnagh with them. The woman was arrested because she was the registered owner of the 01 D Fiat Punto that was seen by six witnesses at the murder scene leaving in convoy with the Suburu. The woman acknowledged that she owned the Punto, but said she hadn't used it since June or July 2006. She was six months pregnant when she stopped driving the car. The car had been stopped by Gardaí on 8 February 2006. A man, who was involved in the Thompson gang, was driving. When he was stopped at Robert Street, he named Liam Brannigan's girlfriend as its owner. Liam Brannigan was stopped at Francis Street, on 27 May 2006, driving the Punto, and he told Gardaí that his girlfriend was the owner. Despite the fact that Gardaí had found the car abandoned in Templeogue after Gary Bryan's murder, it was never reported lost or stolen by the woman. She was released without charge.

Liam Brannigan was arrested at Crumlin Road and taken to Sundrive Road Garda Station. His house, at Bride Street in Dublin 8, was also searched, after Denis Donegan issued a warrant. During 10 interview sessions, Brannigan refused to answer a single question or sign notes of interview or engage with Gardaí at all. He was detained because witnesses had seen his girlfriend's car leaving the murder scene. The vehicle was insured with Quinn Direct, and the policy recorded its owner as being Liam Brannigan. The car had been recovered by Gardaí but had not been reported lost or stolen which was very unusual. Brannigan's fingerprint had been found on glass on the back passenger door side, which proved that he had used the car previously. He has also been stopped by Gardaí while driving the Punto on six separate occasions. Brannigan was released without charge.

Gardaí had issued an arrest warrant for the 23-year-old suspect gunman, but had not been able to track him down. Investigations had linked him to the Suburu. Four days before Gary Bryan's murder, a man was shot in the head and shoulder during a drive-by attack on a house at Windmill Hill in Rathcoole, Co. Dublin. A BMW that was used as the getaway car was found burnt out in a remote field, not far from the shooting, soon after the attack took place. Because of the remoteness of the field, the culprits would have needed other transport to leave the area. Gardaí from Clondalkin called to petrol stations in the area, to see if anybody had noticed the BMW or if anything suspicious had occurred around the time of the shooting. They called to the Esso station on the Naas Road in Rathcoole, and were told that somebody had purchased a can of petrol on the evening of the 22 September, just hours before the shooting. They viewed copies of Esso's CCTV footage, and it became apparent that the petrol was bought by the occupant of a silver Suburu Impreza car with the same registration that would be used in Gary Bryan's murder four days later. Photographic stills were produced from the CCTV footage. Gardaí Kelly Dutton and Pat Fagan later identified the man buying the petrol as a 23-year-old from Drimnagh. This 23-year-old, who Gardaí believe actually carried out Gary Bryan's murder, and the 19-year-old suspected of driving the Suburu away from the murder scene, were stopped together in Waterford a week before the murder. The Garda who stopped the two gave a statement saying that the 23-year-old had a tanned complexion, like he had been away on holidays. This tallied with Valerie White's description that the man who shot her boyfriend was tanned. On 21 January 2007, the 23-year-old was arrested in Co. Wicklow, after a high speed chase in which Gardaí pursued him for over 20 miles (32 kilometres). He was a passenger in the car, which was being driven by the 19-year-old believed to be the getaway driver in the Bryan murder. He was taken to Crumlin Garda Station and was interviewed on seven occasions, but exercised his right to silence and said nothing. He was shown CCTV footage of him driving the Suburu into the Esso station in Rathcoole and buying a can of petrol, but didn't show any reaction. It was the same story when he was told that that this Suburu had been used in Gary Bryan's murder. The man initially agreed to take part in a formal identification parade but changed his mind. When he participated in an informal ID parade, a witness was unable to pick-him out. He was subsequently released without charge.

On 7 February 2007, Gardaí finally had enough evidence to arrest Graham Whelan. Detective Garda Eamonn Maloney detained him that evening. He was arrested under Section 30 of the Offences Against the State Act, for Possession of a Firearm with Intent to Endanger Life at

Bunting Road on the day of Gary Bryan's murder. He was taken to Sundrive Road Garda Station. He refused to provide a sample of blood or DNA, so a doctor was called, and took two buccal swabs from the prisoner. After having his photo and fingerprints taken, Whelan was allowed to sleep for the night. He was interviewed the following morning. He was interviewed a total of seven times throughout the day. The Graham Whelan who 'spoke' to Gardaí was very different to the Whelan that was portrayed in court when he was jailed in 2001 for his involvement in the Holiday Inn seizure. He might have been described as a naïve youngster then, but in February 2007, Whelan was a pro when it came to answering police questions. He didn't. Throughout the course of the day he did not even answer one question from detectives. Any criminal who deals with Gardaí knows that the cardinal rule is to shut your mouth and say nothing. The reasoning is that if you do not give Gardaí the rope, then they will not be able to hang you with your own words. The people who are usually charged with murders on which the evidence is patchy are invariably the ones who engage with Gardaí. An effective way of making sure that you never see the inside of a courtroom is just to remain silent, as is your constitutional entitlement. Graham Whelan knew that Gardaí did not have a smoking gun against him, and that the evidence they did have was circumstantial. Gardaí used all the tricks in the book to try to get him to open up. They asked him about his friendship with Freddie Thompson. Whelan remained silent. They asked him about his girlfriend and whether or not she was aware of his involvement with the murder. Whelan remained silent. He was asked if he had an alibi for the day of the murder. Again, Whelan remained silent. Evidence of his mobile phone use in and around the murder scene was put to him. Again, he said nothing. Gardaí had no choice but to release Graham Whelan and send a file to the DPP, in the hope that they would come back with a direction to charge him.

When detectives analysed the calls made by Whelan's mobile phone on the day of the murder, they discovered that Whelan had been in touch with a man called Stephen Carlisle on 14 separate occasions prior to Bryan being shot dead. The Garda theory of the murder was that Graham Whelan saw Gary Bryan on Bunting Road, and made a phone call to Stephen Carlile, who then phoned the 23 and 19-year-olds, who actually carried out the murder. Carlile was 22 at the time of the murder and was originally from Ballyfermot but was living in an apartment in Áras Na Cluaine in Clondalkin. Freddie Thompson had an apartment in the same block as Carlile, and he often spent time there with his girlfriend, Vicky Dempsey. Stephen Carlile was a petty junkie who had become caught up in the Thompson gang to earn money to feed his serious cocaine addiction. He owed tens of thousands of euro to the gang for drugs. He was used as a mule by the senior members, who knew that Carlile could not afford to repay his debts. In the weeks after the Bryan slaying, he started to appear on the investigating team's radar. He was not known to Gardaí and had just three previous convictions for minor road traffic offences. However, on 24 October, Gardaí, acting on a tip-off, raided Carlile's Clondalkin apartment and discovered over €11m worth of heroin. At the time it was the biggest heroin seizure in the history of the state, and the drugs belonged to a number of serious criminals throughout the city, including Freddie Thompson, Graham Whelan and a Ballyfermot gang led by Karl Breen. It was probably no coincidence that Thompson was in such close proximity to the massive haul of drugs and could keep his eye on them, without ever having to touch them. The haul again showed how criminal gangs throughout Dublin cooperated with each other in importing massive drugs hauls, which were then split up and distributed in each gang's separate and defined territories. Carlile was caught red-handed with the drugs and later pleaded guilty to possession for sale or supply of over €10.6 million worth of heroin, €839,000 of cannabis, and to unlawful possession of a machine pistol, 1,609 rounds of ammunition, four magazine pistols and two silencers. Carlile told Gardaí that he was paid €400 a week to mind the drugs and firearms. The €1,100 a month rented apartment was described in court as 'effectively a drug warehouse in which heroin was prepared for sale'. Carlile was only a minor cog in the Thompson gang, but he knew the score and refused to cooperate with the investigation into the drugs, because he feared that he or his family would be murdered if he named names. Carlile was remanded in custody after the drugs haul and was later sentenced to 12 years in jail.

The week after the seizure of the drugs found in Stephen Carlile's apartment, Gardaí received a massive and unexpected boost after Freddie Thompson was arrested in Rotterdam. He was nabbed in close proximity to seven kilos of cocaine and six machine pistols at an apartment he had rented. The seizure was the result of a phone tap laid by Dutch police and not Garda intelligence after the Clondalkin seizure. It came about through cooperation between the GNDU and their Dutch counterparts that had been going on for over a year. Thompson was arrested on 27 October, although when police swooped, he was in the lobby of the apartment complex in a middle-class part of the city. To cast further doubts on the strength of the case, the drugs and guns were found in a garden adjoining the apartment, but police were confident that fingerprints and DNA would link them to the gang boss. Thompson was in the Netherlands with a 23-year-old female friend from Ireland and an Irish couple – a 51-year-old man and a 41-year-old woman with an address in Hull. The three people were also detained, but were later released without charge. However,

Fat Freddie was remanded in custody by a magistrate while police investigated him. Under Dutch law, suspects can be sent to jail while the authorities try to build a case against them. The remand period can only be for a maximum of three months, however, before the evidence has to be presented to the magistrate who then decides whether there is sufficient evidence to warrant a prosecution. At the time the three people were released without charge, a spokeswoman for the Rotterdam Public Prosecutions Office said: 'They are not allowed to leave the country; they are still suspects in the case and they have to make themselves available for questioning during the investigation. The man we are holding, Freddie T, is the main suspect in the case. He will be brought to court again within 14 days. We will seek to have his period of detention extended. It is going to take some considerable time to complete the investigation and we want him kept in jail.'

A spokesman for the Rotterdam Police confirmed that the Irish authorities had not been in contact with them about extraditing Thompson, and added: 'This is a Dutch case. There was information from Ireland concerning these people's activities and that they were suspected of having large amounts of drugs and weapons, but there was no Irish involvement beyond that. None of the Irish people arrested were armed. They were taken completely by surprise and they had no time to make a run for it. It was a smoothly run operation; there were plenty of officers waiting for them.'

The Dutch arrest was a massive blow to Fat Freddie. He had, seemingly, been caught with a large haul of drugs and was looking at a prison sentence of at least ten years, maybe even life, depending on the quality of intelligence and evidence garnered by the Dutch. It is believed that he was in Rotterdam arranging shipments of drugs to be imported back to Dublin to sell on the streets. It had long been suspected that the Thompson gang moved several million euro worth of drugs through Rotterdam Port each year. The arrest was proof positive, if it was needed. However, not for the first time, Thompson struck it lucky and managed to beat the rap. In the first week of February 2007, the magistrate struck out all the charges. The Dutch police moved too quickly and arrested Freddie while he was in the apartment complex, even though he had not actually touched the drugs or guns. Had they waited and kept him under surveillance, they might have caught him red-handed, but Thompson was too cute. There was also no DNA or fingerprint match, so there was plenty of room for him to wriggle out of any charges. It was a serious error by the Dutch police, and one that the Gardaí would come to regret. Freddie could scarcely believe his luck, and to rub salt into the wounds, Dutch law dictates that if a person is remanded in custody while their case is being investigated they are entitled to a payment of €50 per day when they are released. Thompson was in jail for nearly three months and received the princely sum of over €4,000. He booked himself a business class ticket back to Dublin. He arrived in the airport hopelessly drunk, after treating himself to champagne during the flight. Gardaí from the National Immigration Bureau literally could not believe their eyes when the drunken Freddie fell through customs taunting them. The Dutch police toyed with appealing the decision of the judge, but it came to nothing. They had no choice but to move on – as did Freddie.

On 26 February 2007, Detective Sergeant Barry Butler arrested Freddie's neighbour Stephen Carlile. He was brought from Cloverhill remand prison, and was taken to Sundrive Road Garda Station for questioning about Gary Bryan's murder. He told Gardaí that he had nothing to do with Bryan being shot. He said he owned the phone that had been in regular contact with Graham Whelan. However, he knew better than to name Whelan, and denied that he had ever heard the name or even met the drug dealer. He couldn't explain why he had spoken to a complete stranger on 14 different occasions in only a few hours, but Gardaí had little option but to send him back to jail after he had been interviewed for more than six hours.

David Byrne was also arrested as part of the murder investigation. The 24-year-old from Raleigh Square in Crumlin was Thompson's cousin. He was also a key member of the gang and was one of Graham Whelan's best friends. He was arrested on 14 May 2007, because Whelan's phone records showed that a phone registered to his mother was in frequent contact with Whelan on the day of the murder. Gardaí believed that Byrne had been using his mother's phone. While he was in custody, Byrne refused to answer a single question and would not account for his movements or acknowledge his friendship with Whelan. When Graham Whelan was first arrested in relation to the murder on 7 February 2007, he was held for nearly two days. On 8 February, David Byrne called into Crumlin Garda Station, where Whelan was in custody. Byrne handed newspapers and other items to Sergeant Andrew Duncan for Whelan. Sergeant Duncan examined the newspapers carefully and found a message on one of them which said: 'Loose lips sink ships.' Gardaí believe that Byrne was telling his mate not to cooperate with Gardaí, but there was little in the way of proof, so he was released without charge.

Gardaí also arrested Freddie Thompson in connection with the murder, but he was not taken in until 10 September 2007. When he was questioned, the offence he was held for was not the Gary Bryan murder.

Gardaí got their chance to arrest him after an incident at about 9.00pm, when they received a call saying that a man from Clogher Road in Crumlin received minor gunshot wounds to the chest, after he was hit with rounds fired from a sawn-off shotgun. The incident was to do with Vicky Dempsey's previous friendship with the man Thompson stabbed in 2004; Thompson was still jealous and out for revenge. The shots had been fired from a passing car. Thompson was arrested, not far from the scene at Kildare Road, and was held on suspicion of having information about the shooting. While he was in custody, Gardaí took advantage and quizzed him about Bryan's murder. They had little doubt that while Thompson may not have been directly involved, he knew what was going on as the leader of the gang. That coupled with the fact that an *Irish Independent* newspaper taken from the boot of the Fiat Punto that left the scene of the murder was found to have his fingerprint on it. Even putting questions to Thompson was a waste of time. He was released without charge. He was not charged with either the shooting on Kildare Road or any aspect of the Bryan investigation.

With little prospect of building a case against the actual gunman and the getaway driver for Bryan's murder, detectives pinned their hopes on getting a conviction against Graham Whelan. They were confident that they had built up a decent case against him, and outlined their case in correspondence to the DPP's office. At around 4.45pm on the day of the murder at Old Country Road Dublin 12, Garda Ciaran Nunan and DS John Walsh were on a routine patrol and stopped a 04 D blue Volkswagen Golf. The car was stopped because the driver was speaking on his mobile phone while driving. The driver turned out to be Graham Whelan. Gardaí believe that this sighting was significant because it placed Whelan in the Crumlin area two hours before the murder. Old Country Road is only half a mile from where Gary Bryan was shot dead. Gardaí argued that Valerie White's statement that Gary Bryan had seen Graham Whelan driving by Margaret White's house 20 minutes before his murder was also significant. On 28 September 2006, Graham Whelan was arrested at Liffey Street for the purpose of a search under the Misuse of Drugs Act 1977

–1984. He was taken to Store Street Garda Station for the search. He was released without charge, after it was found that he was not carrying anything illegal. However, Gardaí seized Whelan's Nokia 1600 'ready-to-go' mobile phone. They analysesed it in order to determine what calls Whelan both made and received on the day of Gary Bryan's murder, and to ascertain where those calls had been made from. From 2.32pm to 4.57pm, Whelan's calls were processed through five different phone masts in the Crumlin village area. From 4.57pm to 5.55pm, his calls went through masts situated in Dublin 8, away from Crumlin and the murder scene. From 5.58pm to 6.46pm, his calls were processed through phone masts in the immediate vicinity of the murder scene at Bunting Road. The four masts were located at the Ashleaf Shopping centre, Star Bingo on Kildare Road, Spar in Walkinstown and Crumlin Taxi in Crumlin village. From 6.47pm to 7.25pm, Whelan's calls went through masts at the Long Mile Road, Red Cow Hotel, Firhouse and Rathfarnham Golf Club. Gardaí argued with the DPP that this phone site analysis proved that Graham Whelan was in the vicinity of the murder scene both before, during and after Gary Bryan's murder. When he was arrested for questioning about the murder, he refused to account for his movements around Bunting Road.

On 9 February 2006, Graham Whelan was again arrested and he declined to take part in a formal identification parade. Gardaí wanted a witness who had seen Whelan driving on Bunting Road before the murder, to see if they could pick him out of a line up. The witness had never seen Graham Whelan before the day of the murder and did not know anything about him. At around 1.00pm that afternoon, Sergeant Peter McBrien accompanied the witness to the radio workshop office at Crumlin Garda Station from which they had an unobstructed view of the station yard. Eight volunteers plus Graham Whelan had been lined up to take part in the informal parade. Four of the volunteers walked out in single file, and the witness said that the man they saw on the day of the murder was not any of them. When the fifth man, Graham Whelan, walked into the yard, the witness stated: 'That's him, that's the man.' Sergeant McBrien asked if the witness was certain. The witness answered: 'Yes.'

Gardaí wrote to the DPP's office requesting that Graham Whelan be charged with Gary Bryan's murder. They wrote, 'Graham Whelan is a ruthless criminal. Mr Whelan is heavily involved in the Freddie Thompson/Paddy Doyle gang. He has amassed a total of fifteen previous convictions at 24 years of age. It is suspected that Mr Whelan organised the brutal murder of Gary Bryan along with several other suspects. Due to the nature of the evidence, I would recommend that Graham Whelan be charged with the Murder of Gary Bryan at Bunting Road, Dublin 12, on 26/09/06, contrary to common law.'

Gardaí were confident that they had enough evidence to at least put to a jury for consideration against Whelan. Phone evidence and an eye witness had put him at the scene of the murder minutes before it happened, and although there was no suggestion that he had actually pulled the trigger, detectives felt that the murder would not have happened had Graham Whelan not driven past Gary Bryan when he did. However, it was not to be. After several months the DPP came back and said there was not enough evidence to charge him. It was a blow to Gardaí who had worked tirelessly to try to get justice for Bryan. The case still remains open, but in the absence of new information, it seems unlikely that anybody will have to answer for Gary Bryan's murder.

Gary 'Tipper' Bryan was a tragic figure who was controlled by his drug addiction. Just before he was freed from Mountjoy, after serving his drugs sentence, he had applied for a passport. Detective Garda Terry McHugh, who was the liaison officer attached to the prison, signed the application for him. Bryan told him that he wanted to leave Ireland permanently with Valerie White because he feared for his life. He was only out of jail for a little over three weeks when it is believed that he murdered Wayne Zambra. For all his good intentions, Gary Bryan was a cold-hearted gun for hire who thought nothing of looking a man square in the eye and blowing his brains out. When he was using drugs, Bryan was a changed man. While he was soft-spoken, gentle and never violent when he was sober, he became a different person when he was injecting heroin. Although he did not look like a gangster, he certainly behaved like one, and once the 29-year-old had murdered Paul Warren and Wayne Zambra, it was clear that it was a matter of when, rather than if, Bryan himself would fall victim to a gangland assassination.

Bryan was the ultimate loose cannon, and sources say that he would have shot literally anybody for as little as €2,000. Because he was so addicted to drugs, Bryan had no loyalty and was happy to freelance for anyone who would pay him. That unpredictability and ability to turn on anyone at the drop of a hat is what made him so dangerous. Detectives have described Gary Bryan, as a 'ruthless killing machine' who would murder anybody who got in his way, without conscience or a moment's thought. It is likely that both sides of the feud breathed a sigh of relief when he died. Valerie knew that Bryan was far from an angel. He stopped telling her what he was involved in when he was released from prison, so she never knew for certain whether he had murdered Wayne Zambra. He understood why she felt she had to make a statement to Gardaí about the Warren murder, and he never gave her a hard time over it. Friends of White say she blames herself for Gary's death. She feels that if she had gone ahead and given evidence in court, then he would be alive today, albeit in jail. They were together for six years; Gary was behind bars for 27 months of their relationship.

The couple planned to move away to England and start a new life together. It was not to be. Gary Bryan was murdered before the plans came to fruition. Gary Bryan's new passport arrived in the post two weeks after his murder. He never got to use it.

TEN

Making new friends

Prison authorities took the decision to house Brian Rattigan at the highest security jail in the state – Portlaoise. This decision was made because of his notoriety and the fact that people were being murdered as part of a feud he was directing from behind bars.

Portlaoise Prison was once used to house IRA prisoners, with army snipers on the roof to make sure that nobody attempted to escape. It is still home to convicted members of the Real and Continuity IRA, but today it is not renegade republicans that the Irish Prison Service has to be concerned about. It is the coterie of the country's most serious criminals who are on the notorious E1 landing. E1 reads like a who's who of the criminal underworld. Its 34 residents are the most dangerous and feared criminals in the country. Its most infamous inhabitant is probably John Gilligan, the Don of drug dealing before his empire came crumbling down after Veronica Guerin's murder. Because Brian Rattigan had started out working for 'Factory' John, the pair had a good relationship. Rattigan would have regarded Gilligan as yesterday's man, because he was in prison for so long and was well out of the loop when it came to importing drugs. Gilligan's partner in crime, Brian Meehan, was also an inmate on E1. He had driven the motorbike that was used to transport the hitman to murder the Sunday Independent journalist, and was given a life sentence for his role. Sources say that 44-year-old Meehan and Brian Rattigan do not get on well. There is tension between them, and as a result, both men keep their distance from each other. Harry Melia was another inmate who Brian Rattigan would have heard stories about when he was growing up. Melia was one of 'The General', Martin Cahill's, top henchman and is notoriously violent. He once cut the tips of Seamus 'Shavo' Hogan's ears off to make him resemble a rat, because there were suspicions that Hogan was an informer. Melia has since been released and his drugs conviction quashed by the Court of Criminal Appeal.

Karl Breen was another major criminal housed at Portlaoise. Breen, the so-called 'Champagne Killer', was the boss of a Clondalkin based drugs gang. He was convicted of the manslaughter of one of his best friends, Martin McLaughlin, on New Year's Day 2006, at Jurys Inn in Croke Park. Breen was given a nine-year term. He had spent the night drinking with McLaughlin and others. During a drunken brawl, Breen stabbed his friend McLaughlin three times in the chest. A witness in the case, had to leave Ireland after being warned he would be murdered if he testified against 29-year-old Breen in court. His home was shot at twice, so he moved to Spain following the threats from Breen's associates. Breen has nearly 100 previous convictions and is loosely aligned with Freddie Thompson gang. Gardaí believe that the €11m worth of heroin seized in the apartment in Clondalkin in October 2006, was partly funded by Breen and Thompson. Drug dealers are nothing if not pragmatic though, and despite Breen's business deals with his arch enemy, Rattigan and Breen were on good terms and there did not seem to be much animosity between them. At the end of the day, they were both businessmen who were in serving lengthy stretches, so there was no point in creating more headaches and making things worse by fighting.

One of the biggest modern day gangsters on E1 was 48-year-old Limerick gangland boss Christy Keane. Keane is head of the Keane-Collapy crime syndicate who are at war with the rival McCarthy-Dundon group in Limerick. He was the undisputed head of organised crime in the city until he was arrested in August 2001. Keane was caught walking across waste ground with €240,000 worth of cannabis in a coal bag on his back. The following year he was jailed for ten years and sent to Portlaoise, where he continued to run his drugs gang and oversee murders from behind bars. His own brother, Kieran, was murdered as part of the Limerick feud in 2003. In many ways he was similar to Rattigan, who had also lost a brother because of gangland feuding, and the pair identified with each other.

Christy Keane's son Liam was also a major player in organised crime. The 25-year-old came to national prominence in October 2003, when he made a two finger salute to a press photographer after his murder trial collapsed. The trial collapsed when all the witnesses developed 'collective amnesia', having obviously been threatened and intimidated. Keane was charged with the murder of 19-year-old Eric Leamy in 2001. Because of the reluctance of witnesses to speak in open court, Keane literally got away with murder, and was then free to run his father's drug business. Christy Keane and Brian Rattigan were very friendly in Portlaoise. They decided that their two gangs should cooperate in any way that they could. This involved splitting the money to buy drugs shipments, and even supplying the other side with gunmen, should a sensitive murder need to be carried out. Christy put his son Liam in touch with the Rattigan gang. Rattigan designated Anthony Cannon as his point man in dealing with the Limerick mob, and ordered him to cooperate in any way possible. Cannon was fast becoming one of Rattigan's most trusted lieutenants and was acting as the gang's chief enforcer – keeping dealers in line and making sure they paid on time. Keane and Rattigan enjoyed daily chats in each other's cells, and despite the age gap, the pair developed a strong bond and friendship. Liam Keane and Anthony Cannon wasted no time in putting their two gangs to work together. After Keane's life was threatened in late 2006, he moved to Crumlin, where he was put up at a variety of safe houses controlled by the Rattigan gang. Because Anthony Cannon was one of the gang's most feared enforcers, he spent almost every hour of the day with Keane, watching his back and generally dreaming up schemes to break the law and make money. The two men were both hotheads and were a bad influence on each other. On 21 April 2007, Natasha McEnroe, Brian Rattigan's girlfriend, was on a night out at the Village Inn pub in Crumlin village, with about half a dozen of her girlfriends. Keane and Cannon and a couple of other heavies were drinking with the women. McEnroe, Keane and Cannon were outside smoking, when two men in their early twenties pulled up in a car across the road and started to wolf whistle at Brian Rattigan's girlfriend. McEnroe wasn't really bothered, but Keane and Cannon lost the plot, and the Limerick criminal pulled out a Glock 9mm pistol and ran over to the parked car. Cannon started banging on the window and told the two occupants that they were dead men. Natasha McEnroe, who didn't know that Keane had a gun, ran over and told the pair to stop and go back into the pub. The men in the car apologised profusely and sped off, not realising that Keane and Cannon would have had no problem shooting them. Several bystanders witnessed the incident and Gardaí were called. Cannon and Keane drove to a house nearby and changed clothes, got rid of the firearm and went back to the pub. When Gardaí arrived, they arrested the pair for questioning, but the two men in the car were too afraid to make a formal complaint, so there were no charges over the incident. Nevertheless, it showed just how close the Rattigan and Keane gangs had become. There were rumours that McEnroe and Keane had become a little too close, and graffiti appeared on walls around Crumlin claiming that the pair were sleeping together. There was no truth in this however, and it was a crude ploy by the Thompson gang to infuriate Brian Rattigan, so he would end his relationship with the Keanes. However, he did not believe it, so there was no problem.

When Gardaí learnt the extent of the two gangs' business partnership, they became very worried. They were not the only ones. Freddie Thompson didn't want to take on Limerick criminals while he was outnumbered, so he organised his own tie-in with the McCarthy-Dundon faction in early 2006. Freddie travelled to Limerick and met up with senior members of the gang. It was agreed that 21-year-old 'Fat' Frankie Ryan and 39-year-old 'Fat' John McCarthy, who is the reputed head of the McCarthy family, would be the contact men for 'Fat' Freddie Thompson in Limerick. Freddie and the Limerick mob were only beginning to trust each other when his main contact man, Fat Frankie, was killed. He was sitting in his car in Delmege Park in Moyross, when Gary Campion walked up and calmly shot him twice in the head. Campion was later found guilty and sentenced to life for the murder. It is believed that another contact man was assigned to Freddie after Ryan's murder.

* * *

The Rattigan family is not a large one, but Dinah Rattigan, Brian's mother, is very close to her brothers and sisters and there is a tremendous loyalty between them. The vast, vast majority of the extended Rattigan family are hard working, and have nothing at all to do with crime. To them Brian Rattigan's behaviour is a major embarrassment to the family name. However, one cousin shares Rattigan's interest in crime. Timothy Rattigan was behind one of the most shocking and despicable murders of recent times. Coincidently, he is also an inmate of Portlaoise, but is not regarded as any sort of gangland player, but rather as a fool.

On 3 April 2004, Joan Casey, a 65-year-old grandmother, was asleep in her home on Avonbeg Terrace in Tallaght, when two men armed with a shotgun burst in through her front door at around 6.00am. The intruders made their way upstairs to the landing and tried, unsuccessfully, to break into the old woman's bedroom. Timothy Rattigan pulled out the shotgun and fired two shots through the bedroom door. One shot hit the wall opposite the door and the other struck Mrs Casey in the chest. She later died from her injuries.

Witnesses said that after hearing two loud bangs, they saw two men at Mrs Casey's front gate calmly walk away. One was brandishing a shotgun. The shotgun was later found disassembled in three pieces in a blue bag in bushes close to Rattigan's sister's flat. The bag also contained both live and spent cartridges and a firing pistol. Garda forensic experts were able to match a fingerprint on the gun to 26-year-old Timmy Rattigan. He was convicted of the murder and given a mandatory life sentence. Joan Casey had not been the intended target. It is believed that Rattigan set out to shoot her son Gerard. Gerard Casey often stayed at his mother's house. He was married to one of Rattigan's sisters, and the couple had four children together. Rattigan had been drinking on the night of the murder at a pub in Tallaght with his co-accused, Conor Grogan. They had made their way back to Rattigan's sister's house. It is believed that Rattigan then hatched the plan to shoot Gerard Casey, because there was bad blood between them. Rattigan, from St Dominic's Terrace in Tallaght, had two previous convictions for trespassing and a road traffic offence. When he was found guilty, one of his associates was heard to remark to the Casey family, 'At least we have somebody to visit tomorrow; we won't be visiting a headstone.' Joan Casey's daughter described her as 'the best mum in the whole world'. In another blood shedding incident, Timmy Rattigan's father, Timmy Snr, was shot in the head outside a bookmaker's shop on Thomas Street in the summer of 1997. The 39-year-old had been associating with members of the INLA. No one was ever charged with the murder. Despite being related and both being murderers, Brian Rattigan is said to have little time for his cousin, and does not associate with him in Portlaoise.

Brian Rattigan has quite a chequered disciplinary history in prison and is consistently in trouble. He invariably shows attitude to prison guards, and has been disciplined internally three times for threatening staff. He has one infraction for fighting, just days after he arrived at the jail, and has also been written up for damaging his cell. Sources say that Rattigan rarely gets involved in the frequent internal squabbles between prisoners and prefers to keep his head down than play politics. He does not receive many visitors. Natasha McEnroe regularly goes to see him and has remained loyal to him during his long stint in prison, when many would have been tempted to end the relationship. The years spent in prison have only made Brian's love for his murdered brother grow stronger. Each year on the anniversary of Joey's murder and birthday, Rattigan takes a memorial ad in the *Evening Herald*, along with his mother and other family members. On 24 August 2009, the day that Joey Rattigan would have turned 26, Brian's ad read:

BROTHER
I picture you in Heaven,
With my good friends who have passed on,
But it's still hard to accept,
That you are really gone.
You were just a kid Joey,
And kids aren't supposed to die,
And I can't ever forgive that,
No matter how I try.
It hurts to imagine,
You'd be twenty-six this year,

But there's nowhere to send birthday cards,
And there won't be birthday cheer.
I've plenty of time to think that,
As that is all I do,
I think of ways to let them know,
I'll never forget what happened you.

Happy twenty-sixth birthday baby brother, the heart that truly
loves never forgets, love you always and forever your brother
Brian and Natasha xxxxxx

On the seventh anniversary of Joey Rattigan's murder the
Evening Herald message read:

BROTHER
Did the angels sing amazing grace,
The day you saw the Lord God's face,
Did you know you were not alone,
The day the Lord called you home,
For I was there I watched you go,
And the pain I felt no one will ever know,
I thought of you for the past seven years,
And inside I've cried bitter tears,
I sit today and think of you,
But baby brother that's nothing new,
Because I think of you each day and night,
And how it wasn't even your fight,
Though I made you a promise and what I will do,
I will live each day in memory of you,
I will find a way to make sense of your loss,
It doesn't matter what that may cost,
Because my heart is full of sorrow,
That for you there's no tomorrow.

The heart that truly loves never forgets, your loving brother
Brian and Natasha XXXXX.

The tender poems that were dictated from Rattigan's prison cell are at odds with his hardman reputation, but show that he had a talent. A talent that could have been used to help him lead an honest life – had he not chosen to go down the alternative road that leads to death and destruction.

In September 2006, Gardaí received intelligence that Rattigan had a mobile phone in his cell in Portlaoise. Detectives from Crumlin Garda Station accompanied prison officers as they carried out an inch by inch search of his cosy living space. Sure enough, it wasn't long before they found the phone hidden in his mattress. Rattigan used to put the Nokia mobile up his anus, when his cell was regularly searched, but this time he was taken by surprise, because there was no warning about this targeted search and no other prisoners were bothered. Investigators couldn't believe their eyes when they studied the footage on the phone. Nobody who had dealt with Rattigan had ever taken him for much of an animal lover but there were several videos of him kissing and hugging his green pet budgie. The gang boss can clearly be heard talking to the bird, who he named Shrek. Shrek was one of two budgies kept by prisoners on the E1 landing and Rattigan communicates with his feathered friend through whistling. There are even photos of Shrek inside Rattigan's mouth in a scene like Ozzie Osbourne's famous bat-eating antics. Rattigan didn't bite Shrek's head off though, but seemed to have a genuine affection for the bird. There were also photos and videos showing pornographic material and several pictures of his erect penis. Natasha McEnroe also featured prominently on the phone with three or four photos of her, above which he had typed 'wifey' or 'I love Natasha.' Spending large amounts of time in a cell alone can do strange things to people, and Rattigan seems to be no different. There were videos of him dancing frantically by himself to rave music, as if he was off his head on ecstasy. A fellow prisoner also used Rattigan's phone to film an impromptu jailhouse party, in which Harry Melia is seen smoking and drinking amid cheers and laughing. Rattigan is a big user of steroids in prison, and works out in the jail's gym each day. He has developed a muscular physique. He is obviously proud of it, because upwards of a dozen photos that were found on his phone are of his own naked body, with the tattoo of Joey Rattigan clearly visible. In one photo above the tattoo of Joey, Rattigan wrote the word 'brother'.

Rattigan is not very clever when it comes to hiding his mobile phones from the authorities. He has been caught and officially reprimanded on six separate occasions in prison for having a mobile phone in his possession. In theory, a prisoner caught with an illicit mobile can have an extra five years added to their sentence if they are convicted in court, but Rattigan obviously feels that it is worth taking the risk in order to continue to run his gang from behind bars. Though he has been caught, he has never been charged with the unlawful possession of a phone whilst in prison.

Rattigan spends his long days behind bars working out religiously. His day consists of getting up, eating breakfast before going to work out in the gym on the E1 landing. He lifts weights for two hours having other prisoners 'spot' for him. He then has some lunch, and goes to the exercise yard, where he is allowed to have two hours of exercise each day and mix with the other prisoners. There are extensive educational courses on offer in the prison, as well as practical classes, such as woodwork and metalwork, but Rattigan has never bothered to better himself in jail and the only interest he shows is in weightlifting. Apart from exercising, the remainder of his day is spent in his cell watching television.

Because Portlaoise predominantly held 'political prisoners', the regime there was and is different to every other jail in the country. IRA prisoners refused to be treated like criminals, because, as far as they were concerned, they were in jail for their political beliefs. This meant that they received special privileges. Even with the ending of the Troubles, the regime stayed the same. When all of the IRA prisoners were released, under the terms of the Good Friday Agreement, to be replaced with around 50 renegade republicans, the regime and special privileges stayed in place and they were given their own landings.

The breakaway republicans control four landings in Portlaoise, and have been allowed to paint large paramilitary murals of gunmen on the walls. They take part in military drills each day and the custom has developed whereby staff have to withdraw from the landings while these drills take place. Staff in Portlaoise claim that the security cameras on the landings have 'flaps' around them, so as not to be able to capture what goes on. It has also been claimed that the cells of the 50 or so prisoners are not searched, and that people visiting them do not have to undergo searches, unlike all staff and visitors of other inmates. According to the Prison Officers' Association, this has led to the dissident groups supplying the major criminals on the E1 landing with drugs, phones and other contraband. However, the Irish Prison Service denies many of the claims.

Whatever the reasons, things had been far too easy for too long. It took a controversial phone call from a Portlaoise jail cell to ensure that the daily routines for the likes of Brian Rattigan and John Gilligan, who were effectively running their own affairs on the E1 landing, were over forever.

On May 1 2007, a journalist from the *Sunday World* was taking part in a discussion on the Joe Duffy radio programme, *Liveline*, about his linking of republicans to organised crime. Sinn Féin councillor Christy Burke was his opponent on the show, when a well-known criminal a well known criminal from the northside of Dublin, came on air. He took issue with the article the journalist had written the previous week, saying that he was involved in a dispute with a serious criminal and armed robber from Finglas called John Daly.

John Daly happened to be listening to *Liveline* in Portlaoise. He was incensed by what the journalist had to say, so he went to his cell and used his mobile to phone RTÉ to have his say. This was despite the fact that Portlaoise is the country's most highly secured prison.

John Daly hung up the phone because several prison officers had forcibly entered his cell to end the call, which would prove to be a major embarrassment to the Irish Prison Service and to the embattled Justice Minister, Michael McDowell. McDowell was predictably furious about John Daly's brazen jailhouse phone call, and immediately ordered the Director General of the prison service, Brian Purcell, to begin a top-level inquiry into how Daly had managed to pull off the stunt. McDowell said that he was deeply concerned about what he called a 'brazen and deliberate breach of security,' and said that somebody within the prison service would have to be accountable and take responsibility. If he was angry about the *Liveline* phone call, he was furious about what happened next. In a series of searches in the immediate aftermath of the controversial call, every cell on the E1 landing was turned upside down and searched with a fine-tooth comb. Illegal items were found in toilet U-bends, beds and hollowed-out chairs. The public could scarcely believe the results: seventeen mobile phones, five SIM cards, eleven chargers, eight phone batteries, one hundred and fifty ecstasy tablets, traces of cocaine powder and a large quantity of homemade alcohol. Unbelievably, three flatscreen plasma televisions were also removed from cells, and the two prison budgies, including Brian Rattigan's beloved Shrek, were also found. It was pure gold for the media, as well as the opposition. Fine Gael's Charlie Flanagan said: 'Portlaoise prison is supposed to be our Alcatraz, but with plasma TVs, pet budgies, rampant drug taking and money for tuck, it is more like a holiday camp.' If anybody needed proof that Ireland's most serious criminals were still running their empires from behind bars, then this was the definitive evidence. Michael McDowell said there was never a blind eye turned at an official level to the practice of allowing contraband and even plasma TVs into Portlaoise. However, according to the Prison Officers' Association, this was not the case. It claimed that the televisions were bought by the prisoners with the full consent of the governor of the jail. The prison service confirmed this and said a system existed in the prison, whereby inmates were allowed to purchase electrical goods. This 'tuck-shop' system had been brought in in the 1970s. Prisoners were allowed to order goods through the prison officers, which were then paid for in cash when they arrived at the jail. Prisoners are paid a small daily 'salary' for working in the jail, and relatives can also lodge money into an inmate's prison account. The system operates in all jails, but Portlaoise is the only prison that allows electrical goods to be bought. Most other jails only permit chocolate, cigarettes and newspapers to be bought from the prison tuck shop.

It would later emerge that nine plasma televisions had been bought by inmates on the E1 landing. The internal inquiry did not lead to anybody losing their jobs but several staff members were transferred to other jails and the system of buying TVs ended, much to the fury of everyone on E1, including Brian Rattigan. John Daly was a marked man after that. He was immediately transferred to Cork prison, and lost his privileges. After Daly's call put an end to the old regime in Portlaoise, there were reports that several criminals had clubbed together and put a €50,000 contract on his head. The 27-year-old was released in August 2007, and it was not long before jailhouse justice caught up with him. He was a free man for just two months, when a gunman shot him five times in a taxi, as he returned to his home in Finglas. Gardaí had warned him that his life was in danger and had given him personal security advice. He was effectively a dead man walking after the *Liveline* fiasco. Daly was murdered by a 33-year-old criminal, who took over the running of the gang once led by Martin 'Marlo' Hyland in Finglas. His murder was not directly linked to the Portlaoise incident, but there was a queue of people lining up to take him out.

Although Daly was dead, his legacy lives on in Portlaoise. As a result, sniffer dogs have been brought in to screen all staff and visitors for drugs. This crackdown has not gone down well with the inmates. A dozen prisoners, including Christy Keane and Brian Rattigan, staged a 'dirty litter' protest and gathered all their rubbish and threw it all over the landing. The dirty dozen were all sent to solitary confinement and the security measures remained in place. No security system is perfect, however, and even after the crackdown some prisoners still managed to hold onto their contraband. Brian Rattigan has been caught with a phone on three separate occasions since Daly's murder. In 2008, one cell search showed how much money the drug dealers were making. A search was carried out of Brian Meehan's cell, where a Franck Muller watch worth over €20,000 and a Briteling Bentley special edition gold watch valued at €5,850 were found. These watches were seized and subsequently sold by CAB. Meehan had long been on their radar, and CAB had previously seized €800,000, which had been hidden in his Austrian bank account. Meehan was in business long before the advent of the Celtic Tiger, so the drug dealers must have been making vast sums before the recession. In the same year, five phones, four SIM cards and chargers were also found during a search. Six criminals were implicated, including John Gilligan. Gardaí moved him to an isolation cell, and he was charged with illegally having a phone. Karl Breen was also found with a phone. Breen was something of a repeat offender, much like Brian Rattigan. He had caused the Irish Prison Service a major headache, when it emerged that he was maintaining an active Bebo page from his jail cell. Using the pseudonym 'InfamousD22', Breen posted videos of himself joking outside Garda stations and even had a demonstration video on how to use a Glock handgun.

Brian Rattigan, like all other prisoners, is only allowed to exercise outside for two hours each day and apart from that he rarely sees sunlight. He was given a rare trip to Dublin in April 2005, but the journey was not one that he would enjoy. He was going to Dublin Circuit Court to face his punishment over a vicious assault on a taxi driver on 2 April 2000. Rattigan and Natasha McEnroe were on a night out with Shay O'Byrne and Sharon Rattigan, as well as Rattigan's uncle, 37-year-old Patrick Dunphy from Galtymore Road. The group were on James's Street at around 2.00am and were trying to hail a taxi. A taxi pulled up just past them and another couple jumped in. A row developed because Rattigan and the others felt that the taxi should have picked them up and not the other couple. The taxi driver refused to throw his fare out and told Rattigan that another car would surely be along in a minute. Rattigan violently attacked the innocent cabbie, and he attempted to drive away. He jumped into the moving car. He pulled the driver's head back by the hair, and rained blows down on him and put him in a headlock. The driver managed to hit the brakes and then escaped. Two other taxi drivers drove past the scene and saw their colleague being attacked and went to assist him. They were also assaulted. Rattigan was found guilty of assault causing serious harm, violent disorder and attempted seizure of a taxi. Judge Barry White called Rattigan a 'very dangerous young man', and imposed a consecutive three-year jail sentence for each offence, to take effect when he completed his drugs sentence and term for shooting at Gardaí. He said he was concerned with the 'huge, unprovoked violence used', which resembled a 'full-blown riot'. Brian Rattigan was not impressed with the punishment handed down to him. He had expected that his sentence would run concurrent to the other two sentences he was already serving, but the judge was not playing ball. Even with good behaviour – if he could manage to behave – Rattigan would be behind bars for at least an extra two years. It was not just Rattigan who was charged and convicted over the taxi driver assault. Shay O'Byrne was fined €200 for violent disorder, and the judge accepted that he had been on the periphery of the incident. Sharon Rattigan was fined €200 for the same offence, and Natasha McEnroe received a €175 fine, also for violent disorder. The three had all pleaded guilty. Patrick Dunphy was handed a two-year suspended sentence, and ordered to carry out 240 hours community service, after pleading guilty to reckless endangerment.

Having seized the mobile phone in Rattigan's cell with photos from crime scenes, Gardaí knew that the criminal was continuing to lead his gang from the inside. An incident occurred in November 2005, which highlighted the lengths that Rattigan was prepared to go to to get revenge on the Gardaí he blamed for putting him behind bars.

Rattigan had a deep hatred for a detective involved with Declan Gavin's murder investigation. Threats against Gardaí are very rare but are taken extremely seriously by the top brass. Ireland is not like Italy, where the mafia see the police as being fair game for murder. Any threat against a Garda officer is given absolute priority, so the message is sent out that threats and intimidation will never be accepted and will result in the full rigour of the law being used against those who make threats. On 1 August 2005, a person picked up the public telephone at the junction of Old County Road and Clonard Road in Crumlin, and dialled 999. The caller informed the operator that a prisoner in Portlaoise Prison named Brian Rattigan had offered to pay €15,000 to anybody who was willing to shoot the named detective. Gardaí were immediately informed and rushed to the phone box, but the caller had left. The phone box was examined by a Scenes of

Crime Unit, but nothing of any evidential value was gleaned. A copy of the 999 call was received, and Gardaí estimate that the 15-second phone call was made by a male caller aged between 40 and 50. A full investigation was launched, but it could not be determined who had made the call. Gardaí pursued various lines of inquiry. The first was that Rattigan had taken out the contract in revenge for being charged with the Gavin murder and another was that a local crime family, who lived close to the telephone box, were responsible. It was never definitively determined if Brian Rattigan was responsible, but Gardaí had little doubt that the threat was a real and credible one. All necessary precautions were put in place, in case somebody was crazy enough to take up the contract. With junkies prepared to murder people for less than €2,000, it could not be dismissed that somebody would look at the €15,000 on the table and feel that the offer was too good to refuse. A few months later, a shotgun cartridge was placed on the windscreen wiper of the detective's car, which was parked on the road outside his house. He immediately reported the incident to his superiors and a major inquiry was launched. It was determined that the cartridge was a Brennox Deerhunting variety, which is a common type of shotgun ammunition. Detective Inspector Brian Sutton was called into the investigation because he was leading the probe into the contract placed on the detective's head two months previously. There was little doubt that the two incidents were linked. The person who left the cartridge on the car was alert enough to wear gloves, because no DNA evidence was recovered from it.

The threat on the detective's life was very worrying. The 'G' district is among the toughest areas in the country to police. It is in many ways a thankless job, dealing with criminals who have no respect for the Gardaí and who are not afraid to make threats.

To some people in Crumlin and Drimnagh, Brian

Rattigan was somewhat of a folk hero. They believed that he had been unfairly targeted by the Gardaí and stitched up for Declan Gavin's murder. He was seen as a bit of a Robin Hood type figure, who would pay for headstones on the graves of the recently deceased, if their families could not afford one. He was remembered as a young lad who worked hard and earned his wages, not like some of the other criminals. That was the perception that some people had, even if it wasn't always accurate. However, an incident occurred in December 2006 that would permanently see Brian Rattigan lose any remaining respect he had in the wider community.

ELEVEN

Sinking to a new low

There are rarely innocent victims in gangland culture. You can count on one hand the people who have been caught up in violence that had nothing to do with them and died as a result. Latvian mother of two, Baiba Saulite was one. Limerick rugby player, Shane Geoghegan was another. Apprentice plumber Anthony Campbell was murdered for being in the wrong place at the wrong time as was mechanic Eddie Ward, who was gunned down with 'Mr Fixit' car dealer Brian Downes.

Twenty-one-year old Eddie McCabe was an innocent victim of the Crumlin-Drimnagh feud, although he was no innocent and had been in prison for most of his life, since the day he turned 13. Eddie McCabe could be described as being a victim of circumstance: of being propelled into a situation over which he had no control.

For the first 12 years of his life, things looked good for Eddie McCabe. He was born into a good family who loved him dearly. He lived with his mother, Linda, and father, Eddie Snr, in Brookfield in Tallaght. Eddie was the eldest of four boys. His youngest brother was six years his junior and the twins were in the middle, just three years younger than Eddie. From an early age, McCabe showed promise and was always at the top of his class in primary school, so much so that his teacher wanted to move him to a more advanced class, because he was very intelligent for his age. He was a loveable, friendly and popular boy who was devoted to his dad. He was creative, showed great ability as an artist, was good at working with his hands and regularly wrote poems. Maybe he would have followed his father into carpentry, but like most boys at that age he didn't yet know what he wanted to do when he grew up. Something happened in November 1995 that made Eddie McCabe grow up overnight. It was a devastating event that turned Eddie's happy and secure world upside down.

On the evening of 24 November, Eddie McCabe Snr drove his wife to a friend's house in a nearby estate in her new Nissan Micra. The couple planned to enjoy a few drinks after getting a babysitter to look after the kids. Linda and Eddie had broken up a few times over the years, but had got back together six months previously, and for the first time in years were getting on really well. Eddie's mother was as happy as she had ever been, and the future seemed bright. At about 12.15am Linda decided to go home. Eddie Snr dropped her to their house. He got out of the car and kissed his wife like they were teenagers. The 35-year-old told his wife that he was just going to have a few more drinks and would be home later. The last thing Linda said to him was, 'Please be careful, that's my little baby', in a joking reference to her new car. She went to bed oblivious that that was the last time that she would ever see he husband alive. Eddie Snr went back to his friends' house and had a few more drinks, before deciding to head to a nightclub in Blessington. When they arrived the bouncers wouldn't let them in, so they sat in Linda's car for a while and listened to music. They eventually saw two women who they knew from Tallaght. One of them was a single mother of two called Catherine Brennan. McCabe, Brennan and their two friends headed back to Catherine's house in Kiltalawn. They drank more alcohol and somebody pulled out some hash for them to smoke. Nobody had any cigarette papers, so Eddie and Catherine drove to a nearby 24-hour garage. After picking up the messages, Eddie was driving back to the house party when something caused him to stop the car. He undid his seatbelt and walked to the boot of the Micra. He was approached by a gunman who shot him in the head and chest, killing him instantly. Catherine Brennan was sitting in the front passenger seat and was oblivious to what was going on. She did not seem to be panicked, because her seatbelt was still on. Whoever murdered Eddie McCabe walked up to her window and callously shot her in the face, from just inches away. Catherine Brennan died instantly.

At 4.45am, Linda was awoken by a knock on her door. It was the Gardaí asking if she owned a Nissan Micra, if her husband was at home and if he had a goatee beard. Linda instantly knew that something was wrong and feared the worst. Eddie McCabe and Catherine Brennan had been murdered literally a hundred yards away from the McCabe home, across a small field. Eddie Jnr and his brothers were also woken by the commotion. Eddie Jnr, who was only 12, jumped out of his bedroom window and ran across the field. Gardaí had not been at the murder scene long and did not have time to cover the two bodies. The youngster ran across the police line and ducked past the Garda who was on duty preserving the scene. He grabbed his dead father in his arms and held him tightly, while crying hysterically. He had to be pulled away. The ever increasing crowd, who had gathered to look at the carnage, were struck by Eddie's brothers, the young twins, praying aloud for Jesus to save their daddy. Back in 1995 murders were rare, especially double murders, and the killings attracted a lot of attention. Neither McCabe nor Brennan were involved in crime. A definitive motive for the murders has never been established. Linda issued a statement through her solicitor at the time, denying that her husband was a drug dealer or was murdered over drugs. She said that her family was greatly offended by the innuendo that suggested McCabe and Brennan were having an affair. Gardaí believe that Eddie McCabe was shot dead because two of his close associates were involved in drug dealing, but there is absolutely no evidence that McCabe himself was a drug dealer or involved in any sort of criminality. The murderer was never found, and the case remains open and unsolved to this day. The few days following the murder were a blur to the McCabe family. Eddie Jnr read the following poem out at his father's funeral, which left the congregation in floods of tears. It read:

> *To my dad*
> *You are my dad, the one and only*
> *Now you are gone we feel so lonely*
> *Dad, I will always be thinking of you*
> *When I look after Mum for you*
> *I wish we could be together*
> *But still I will love you forever and ever*
>
> *Love Edward*
> *I will miss you Daddy*

Eddie Jnr's problems began shortly after his father's murder. He found it impossible to sleep at night and lay awake thinking of what had happened to his dad. When he went to school, he invariably used to fall asleep at the back of the class and the lad that had been at the top of his class, well ahead of his other classmates, soon fell behind. He lost his will to learn and soon started bunking off school and eventually dropped out completely. Linda always brought him back, but Eddie was stubborn and always mitched off as soon as her back was turned. Eddie then started hanging around with a bad crowd and was often present when his mates were stealing cars to go joyriding. He started to attract the attention of the local Gardaí and soon developed the reputation as a truant and a general troublemaker, and was also a frequent runaway. When he was just 13, Eddie McCabe featured in a newspaper article after he ran away from home. His mother was interviewed and appealed for him to return home, saying that he had gone wild since the death of his father and was causing trouble and was not going to school. Linda McCabe said it was the tenth time that year that Eddie had left home. She was then quoted as saying: 'Last week he told me, "I don't care if I live or die." He hates everybody.'

Eddie first appeared before the Children's Court when he was just 14. He was charged with missing school and being a passenger in a stolen car. Linda accompanied him. The judge remarked that he was so small that he would need a box to be seen. The kindly judge said that he had the face of an angel, and let him off with a rap on the knuckles. It would not be the last time that he was before the courts. Just a few months later, he was back and was sent to the Oberstown young offenders' institute, for missing school and stealing a car. He spent a few weeks there before escaping in his bare feet. He told his mother that he didn't like being locked up because it gave him too much time to think. When he completed his sentence, Eddie began to run away from home regularly and effectively left the care of his mother, staying in friends' houses and also being looked after by relations. Linda McCabe could not bear to live in Tallaght any more, passing by the site of her husband's murder each day. So the family moved to a house in Rafter's Lane in Drimnagh. Eddie spent a few weeks there but kept on running away, even staying in a tent in a field near their old house in Tallaght for a week, before being tracked down by his distraught mother. On another occasion, his grandmother found Eddie unconscious, lying on top of his father's grave. She had gone to pay her respects to her dead son. An empty bottle of vodka lay by her grandson's side and his face was stained with tears. He had spent the night asleep next to his father. After running away again, Eddie was found in the shed of the old family home in Tallaght. Eddie Snr was a skilled carpenter and had built the shed. When Eddie was found, he said that he went there because it reminded him of his dad.

Linda was herself struggling to accept the loss of her husband, and life was very tough, trying to come to terms with her grief and pull her troubled son back from the brink, as well as look after his three younger brothers. But much as she tried, Eddie did not allow himself to be helped. He was in and out of detention centres, and when he was just 13, somebody gave him a painkiller to help him sleep. He said that he liked the way it made him feel and started to heavily abuse pills from then on, mixed with large amounts of cannabis and alcohol. He used to regularly steal cars while high on drink and drugs. He often crashed and was arrested by Gardaí. He would then be sent away to detention centres again. Every time he was taken into state care, he quickly escaped. Once he even managed to flee the Children's Court in Garda handcuffs, after being arrested in Blessington for stealing a car. On another occasion, he stole a horse and rode off into the countryside to escape the pressures of life and to think about his father.

Eddie once told his mother: 'I will be lucky if I live to see my 21st birthday.' His father's death had pushed him to the edge and he always imagined that he would be killed in a high-speed car crash. Although Eddie did not live at home, he was still very close to his mother and brothers. Linda met him every week. She used to take him to Joel's restaurant for a hearty meal and give him money for clothes. She was at least comforted by the fact that he was not sleeping rough and was with friends and family who understood him and understood the trauma that he had been through. Linda once asked Edward (she called her husband Eddie and son Edward) why he wouldn't come home. He answered that when he saw her, he didn't think it was right that she should be alone and without her husband by her side.

When he was 17, Eddie was old enough to be dealt with

by the law as an adult. He was sent to St Patrick's Institution for the first time. For the next three years, he was regularly sent to prison for a few months, before being released for a few months and then sent back again, mainly to Mountjoy. He was never a free man for a full year, and he managed to accumulate nearly 50 criminal convictions. The vast majority were for stealing cars and his most serious conviction was for ramming a Garda car. His addiction to tablets had gotten very serious – some days he was taking up to two dozen Valium.

Eddie McCabe was a tiny scrap of a lad, but was an accomplished boxer and fought at a high level with his friend, Joey O'Brien, who was a member of the Rattigan gang. When Eddie used to go to town, his friends always joked that he was their bodyguard because he had the ability to knock people out with one punch, although he was gentle and wouldn't fight for the sake of it. He was more likely to be seen with a smile on his face than an aggressive scowl. Eddie would never have been involved with drug dealing or gangland activity though, and was a relatively harmless sort who posed no danger to ordinary members of society, except if he took a fancy to their cars. When you are sent to prison, you have to adapt to your surroundings and do what it takes to get by. McCabe had the gift of the gab and got on with people. He was able to survive in jail by himself and didn't mess around with gangs or try to get involved with 'Mr Big' types to protect himself. This made him a vulnerable target. In 2003, McCabe was sentenced to three years imprisonment for stealing a car in Tallaght and ramming a patrol car. He served two and a half years, and when he was coming to the end of his sentence, he owned up to the fact that he had a mobile phone in his cell and handed it over to the prison authorities. It was by far the longest sentence he had ever served and he didn't want to put his release date in jeopardy by being caught with an illegal phone. This led to him being branded as a rat and he was attacked in his cell with a knife. A close associate of Brian Rattigan sliced him on the leg and face and gave him a severe beating. Almost overnight Eddie fell out with his friends who were members of the Rattigan gang. Linda McCabe knew that there was something wrong with her son, but he was never one to open up and burden her with his problems. Eddie McCabe was released from prison in December 2005. He was only out a short time when he met a local girl, Donna Mills. The couple fell in love and after they were together a couple of months, Donna became pregnant. This was the happiest that Eddie had been in a long time. He moved back in with his mother and seemed to be at peace with himself. His relationship was going strong and he spent most of his time with Donna and was looking forward to being a dad.

Unfortunately, Eddie McCabe had been messed up for so long that it was hard to break out of the dangerous cycle. He was lured back to his old ways, and was arrested for stealing a car and sentenced to four months in prison in August 2006. While he was in jail, his son, Eddie McCabe III, was born. Linda went to visit him in Mountjoy and showed him a photograph of his healthy baby. He broke down and said that he didn't want his child to grow up without a father and vowed that he was going to turn his life around and break away from the old temptations. However, Linda noticed that something had changed in her lad. His happy smile had faded, and for the last four months of his life a change came over him. It looked like he was doing heavy drugs and was worried about something. Something was wrong, but Linda couldn't put her finger on it. It didn't help that he was back in Mountjoy, where he had been attacked a few months before. He had to go into protective custody for his own sake to make sure that he wasn't attacked again. He was released from jail in November 2006, when his son was six weeks old. He then mostly stayed with Donna and her family so he could look after Eddie III. He got up for all the night feeds and never let his son out of his arms. One of Linda's most treasured possessions is a photo of the two Eddies asleep, holding hands. On 1 December 2006, Eddie had been out of jail for only three weeks. He was in Donna's house with the baby when a navy car pulled up outside. It was about 7.50pm when Eddie gave her a kiss and said that he was going out for a message and wouldn't be long. A witness described the driver of the car as being a big, heavy-set man. Eddie had been in the middle of cooking a chicken, and at 8.25pm, Donna rang him. He told her that the chicken would be ready now, but not to put the chips on, because he was on his way home and would do it then. Mobile phone cell site analysis later determined that McCabe was in the Dolphin's Barn area when he received this call. When there was no sign of him, Donna rang his mobile at 8.50pm, but it was turned off. Around the same time that Donna was trying to get Eddie on the phone, a car ground to a halt and the back seat passenger grabbed the unconscious Eddie McCabe and threw him out onto the hard concrete. The driver quickly left the area, leaving the 21-year-old for dead in a laneway just off Tyrconnell Road in Inchicore.

At 9.15pm a local resident was parking his car, when he stumbled upon the lifeless body. Gardaí described the beating that Eddie McCabe suffered as the worst they have ever seen. The torture that was inflicted on him was as needless as it was savage. One of his eyes was gouged out and was found beside his body. His second eye was loosely hanging from its socket. A sewer rod had been jammed into the back of his head and pushed through his skull in an attempt to push his eyes out. He had received multiple injuries to the back of the head and suffered 17 fractures to the skull. It was an act of sustained and savage torture that was inflicted to send out a message. When Gardaí arrived at the scene, the person lying injured on the ground had no identification. He was rushed to St James's Hospital and was put on a life support machine, but with the extent of his injuries, it didn't look good.

The following day an officer who arrived at the hospital saw the tattoo on Eddie's arm – a cross with his father's name on it – and recognised the victim as being young McCabe. Gardaí called to Linda's house and asked if Eddie was there. She immediately broke-down screaming and shouting that she didn't want to know what had happened. It was almost a carbon copy of the call that Gardaí made enquiring about her husband nearly 12 years previously. Her mother's instinct told her that something terrible had happened to Eddie. She locked herself in the bathroom and began banging her head off the wall with the grief. When she recovered, she was asked to go to St James's to see if the victim was indeed Eddie. She went with her sister, and immediately knew that it was her son lying in a vegetative state. A large bandage went around his head, covering what once had been his eyes and hiding the shocking injuries to the back of his head. His face had no cuts or bruises, and apart from the bandages, Eddie was as handsome as ever. Doctors told a heartbroken Linda that the prognosis was not good. If Eddie did survive, he would be blind in both eyes and would suffer the effects of severe brain damage, such had been the ferocity of the torture.

Six months before Eddie died, Linda McCabe became a born again Christian. She worshipped at a church in Gardiner Street. She had put herself through college and was volunteering in the Drimnagh community. Was it not for her faith, she would never have survived the ordeal of losing a second loved one. Even with her strong faith in God, Linda found it very difficult and could not easily visit her gravely ill son. Members of her church used to drive her to the hospital every night, where she would sing 'You Are My Sunshine' to Eddie. Linda knew in her heart of hearts that Eddie would not want to live without being able to see his beautiful son, and knew deep down that he would prefer to die than not be able to live a full and independent life. On 8 December, his brother George was in the hospital ward and was holding Eddie's hand when he felt a squeeze. George rushed to the doctor, who told Eddie that if he could hear them, he should squeeze George's hand. With that he squeezed, and did the same thing to a nurse who also went to examine him. It was clear Eddie had feeling in the right-side of his body and his family were initially ecstatic. However, the faint trace of life just reinforced in Linda's mind how unfulfilling a life Eddie would lead if he recovered. The chances of a full recovery were very slim indeed. Linda did what no mother ever should have to do. She leaned into her son and whispered into his ear, telling him what had happened and the extent of the injuries he had suffered. She told him that if he wanted to pass on, not to be afraid to do it. She prayed to the Lord to take her son from his living nightmare and end his pain. Six hours after whispering in Eddie's ear, neurological experts from Beaumount Hospital examined him and declared that he was brain dead. It was almost as if Eddie was waiting for his mother to tell him that everything would be okay, and that he would soon be back with his father forever. Either way, after a lengthy discussion, his family decided that they should turn the life support machine off. Linda didn't go back into the room after telling Eddie that it was okay to die and that God would look after him now. She couldn't bear to say a final goodbye to her son. She wanted her last memories of him to be happy ones, memories of him with his own son, not in the terrible state that he now found himself in.

Doctors turned the machines that had been keeping him alive off and after 15 minutes his heart stopped naturally, and Eddie died peacefully in his sleep. The following day was the McCabe twins' 18th birthday party. Eddie had donated €50 to his brothers, George and Wayne, to put towards renting a stretched Hummer, so they could celebrate in style.

The party never went ahead. In many ways a large part of Eddie McCabe died the day that his father was murdered. Although he was still alive, it was almost as if he was in a living coma and never really lived in the real world after his dad was taken from him. In many ways the person who murdered Eddie McCabe Snr and Catherine Brennan also killed a third person that night.

Because of the injuries to his face and head area, it was impossible for the McCabe family to have an open coffin so that his many friends could say goodbye to Eddie. The funeral took place at Our Lady of Good Counsel church in Drimnagh. Eddie was a massive fan of folk music, Christy Moore in particular, and loved 'The Lonesome Boatman' by the Fury Brothers. One of the people at Linda's church was a talented flautist, and touched the crowd with a moving rendition of the much loved song. It was a fitting tribute to send Eddie to his final resting place. Eddie had previously told his mother that if he died he wanted the song played at his funeral. He had first heard it at his father's funeral and had grown to love the song and took great comfort from its haunting melody. Linda had 'You'll Never Walk Alone' played at communion during the funeral. It was as a reminder to herself and Eddie's friends and family that they would always have each other and be there to support each other.

Linda McCabe is a brave and courageous woman who has somehow managed to go on despite all the pain she has suffered in her life. She is now preoccupied with helping others and trying to save a community that has been torn apart by the Rattigan and Thompson feud. She is the first to admit that she is not a rich woman. She had a dream about having a horse and carriage to transport Eddie's remains. When she woke up, she decided that that was what she must do. The funeral was an expensive one, and her loyal family chipped in, but there were still bills to be paid. The story of Linda and her double loss spread around the Christian community. People were asked to pray for her and her family and keep them in their thoughts. Out of the blue, a strange thing started to happen. Unsolicited cheques from around the world started to arrive at her church and were passed on to Linda. People from as far away as France, the US and the Netherlands were all touched by her story, and started to send her money to help with the burial costs: over €3,000 was donated to Linda and every cent went to pay for Eddie's funeral expenses. Although she had lost her first son in the most horrible way imaginable, these gestures of kindness reminded Linda that there was still good in the world.

The murder investigation was launched at Kilmainham Garda Station, and, as with so many other feud related murders, it fell to Detective Inspector Gabriel O'Gara to take care of the day-to-day running of the investigation. Superintendent Thady Muldoon, who was in overall charge of the murder probe, issued an appeal to the public for help in solving the murder. He said the victim had suffered 'a severe and brutal assault' and said his injuries had been 'absolutely horrendous', before adding: 'He would appear from our investigations to have been dumped in that laneway. There are people who have information; we are fully aware of that. There are people who know what happened to Eddie, and we are appealing to them to come forward.'

Superintendent Muldoon didn't want to add fuel to the media fire about the extent of the injuries or what weapons were used, saying: 'At the moment we don't know what implements or weapons were used. We assume there may have been more than one person involved, but that's something that will become clear as the enquiry moves on. At this stage our investigators are following several lines of inquiry but we wouldn't be able to say yet what contributed to this.' He did confirm that McCabe had completely lost the sight in one eye and that the other had been seriously damaged, but didn't want to go into too much detail.

Gardaí believe they know the identity of Eddie McCabe's killer. There is little doubt that more than one person was involved, but the actual torture is thought to have been inflicted by one of Brian Rattigan's top men, who cannot be named for legal reasons. He is regarded as being a total psychopath who takes great pleasure in inflicting pain on others, and would have thought nothing of pushing McCabe's eyes out of his head and mutilating him. It is not known whether McCabe went to meet his killers and a row developed, or if the sadistic beating was inflicted as a warning or act of revenge. Gardaí did receive one promising lead. An informant told them that McCabe might have been tortured in an empty house in Drimnagh before being dumped in the laneway. The council owned the premises and the tenants had only just moved out, so it was empty while the new tenants were preparing to move in. A Garda forensics team combed the building and removed floorboards from each room, in an attempt to find the remnants of blood, but the search drew a blank. Information received by Gardaí has suggested that Eddie went into the house thinking he would be safe. But that the Rattigan gang member was hiding in a wardrobe, then came out suddenly and attacked the unsuspecting McCabe, knocking him to the ground before commencing with the terrible torture. The extent of Brian Rattigan's involvement in the murder is unclear. Eddie McCabe served time with Brian Rattigan in Mountjoy but was never really known to associate with him all that much although he would have been friendlier with other members of the gang. Rattigan does not have a history of ordering murders to be carried out in such a brutal and heinous fashion; murders that were linked to him usually went the traditional route – a gun to the back of the head. Media reports at the time claimed that a 'jailed crime boss' had ordered that McCabe's eyes be taken out of their sockets and that the assault be filmed on a mobile phone, but there is no hard evidence of this. One newspaper quoted a 'Garda source' as saying: 'McCabe was tortured in the most horrific way just hours after the gangster issued the order. The ganglord allegedly told his henchmen, "I want his eyes. I want you to take them out of his head and film it." The plan was to circulate the footage to other criminals in the city as a warning.' The 'ganglord' referred to was Brian Rattigan, but he couldn't be named because he had been charged with Declan Gavin's murder and was awaiting trial. Gardaí do not know if Rattigan had ordered the murder to be filmed, but what is clear is that members of his gang would not have been able to go around murdering people without their boss's knowledge and permission, so it can be assumed that Rattigan was aware of the plot to kill McCabe and had given it his blessing. Gardaí know who murdered Eddie McCabe but they are still uncertain about the motive. They know that he was not involved in gang activity, but it has been speculated that he may have become involved in running small amounts of drugs for the gang to earn some money for his new son and might have been blamed for some product going missing. Detectives simply do not know, and the case is still very much open. The brutal injuries inflicted to McCabe's eyes might be symbolic. Some officers believe that the torture could mean that he saw something that he shouldn't have, or that he saw something and went to Gardaí with the information. McCabe was no rat though, and it is possible that his murder was connected to the prison stabbing and beating he received, although it is almost unprecedented for jailhouse disputes to continue like that on the streets, especially over a mobile phone, which at the time would have been easily available in Mountjoy. Gardaí say that they will keep trying to find Eddie McCabe's killers. All investigating officers are united in saying that Eddie did not deserve it, and his murder was savage and totally excessive.

Even if Brian Rattigan did not know that Eddie McCabe was going to be murdered in the fashion that he was, he was the head of his gang and he was blamed on the streets. The general public and even other criminals could not believe the savagery that had been used to kill McCabe. It was a fatal blow to Rattigan's reputation.

TWELVE

From bad to worse

After Eddie McCabe's murder, Brian Rattigan got a lot of negative publicity on the street. Things then went from bad to worse for Rattigan when he lost yet another trusted associate just weeks later. On 30 December, 24-year-old Trevor Brunton from Broombridge Road in Cabra was spotted with a gun. He was seen by a bouncer in the toilets of a nightclub at the Spawell leisure complex in Templeogue with a 9mm semi-automatic handgun sticking out of the back of his trousers when he was walking into a cubicle. Other bouncers came to the scene. Brunton came out of the cubicle voluntarily and was restrained. A number of bouncers then frogmarched Brunton through the nightclub to hold him until Gardaí arrived. When Brunton attempted to take the gun from his trousers into his hand, a bouncer slapped his wrist causing the weapon to fall to the ground. One of the security men picked up the gun and placed it into a money bag and later gave it to Gardaí. There were eight rounds in the magazine, ready to be fired.

Brunton was a big man and a keen GAA player, and was well able to handle himself, but was eventually restrained. Two of his friends were also detained but were later released without charge. When Brunton was taken into custody, it was discovered that he was renting an apartment in Castleknock.

The apartment, at Candlewood on the Castleknock Road, was searched, and 30 bags containing €159,361 worth of heroin and 78 rounds of ammunition for the gun he had in the nightclub were found. Detectives also searched Brunton's address at Broombridge Road and recovered two silencers and more ammunition. The apartment in Castleknock had been rented with the sole intention of preparing the heroin to sell for the Rattigan gang. Not only was it dangerous, but it was also careless and ridiculous to bring a loaded gun into a crowded nightclub, especially as he didn't even hide it properly when he went to use the toilet. Gardaí could not believe their luck. Brunton had served himself up on a platter. He had long been a target. He was regarded as being a middle ranking member of the Rattigan gang. Brunton's job was to be a 'minder' of the product, which was a job with a high degree of trust. Brunton later pleaded guilty to the possession of heroin for sale and supply and possession of the firearm and ammunition.

Detective Sergeant Joe Molloy told the court that Brunton possibly had the gun in the nightclub for three reasons. He could have brought it as an act of 'bravado to impress girls', to give it to somebody else or to simply have it for his own protection. DS Molloy said that Brunton never gave a 'satisfactory explanation' about why he brought the gun out with him that night. Sources say that Brunton was acting as a minder for a senior member of the Rattigan gang, who had left the nightclub before the incident but he has never told the full story.

Brunton was jailed for eight years for the drugs possession charge and handed a consecutive five-year term for possession of the firearm. The last four years of the sentence were suspended on condition that he keep the peace for four years after his release from prison. Brunton only had one previous conviction for a minor road traffic offence, but a lengthy jail sentence was another blow to Rattigan – who was seeing his gang slowly fall apart.

Things didn't get any better in early 2007 with Rattigan

receiving another setback when his close friend, Karl Kavanagh, whose house he had been in after Declan Gavin's murder, was caught with a gun. Then Wayne McNally narrowly survived a murder attempt.

On 13 February, members of the Crime Task Force attached to Crumlin Garda Station, led by Detective Inspector Brian Sutton, received intelligence that Kavanagh was in possession of a firearm in his family home on Cooley Road. A search of the attic of the house, conducted by Sergeant Dave Lynch resulted in a 9mm Smith and Wesson handgun being recovered. Kavanagh immediately took full responsibility for the firearm. He told Gardaí he didn't know whether or not it was loaded. He said he had taken it into the house two days previously, and his mother did not know that he had it there. He said that he was holding the gun for somebody, but would not name names because he feared for his and his family's safety. Kavanagh was 24 at the time of the incident. He was one of Joey Rattigan's best friends, and had taken Joey's murder, which had occurred five years previously, badly. He had amassed six criminal convictions for traffic and public order offences since his friend's killing. He was not really involved in the feuding and was not a player in the Rattigan gang, but was, nevertheless, close to the extended Rattigan family because his sister was Ritchie Rattigan's partner. Karl Kavanagh had been with Brian Rattigan before and after the murder of Declan Gavin. He had been arrested in relation to the killing, and told Gardaí that he was afraid his house would be burnt down if he cooperated with them. Gardaí believed that Kavanagh was only holding the gun for somebody as a favour and he pleaded guilty to possession of the gun. Judge Tony Hunt also had sympathy for Kavanagh, and said that he accepted that Kavanagh did not have a serious criminal record and was a 'small cog in a big wheel'. The judge added that because of his early guilty plea it would be 'unjust' to impose the minimum mandatory sentence of five years, although he added that 'this is not a marker for other firearms cases. This sentence is based on these specific circumstances.' Detective Garda Gerard Fahy told the court that Kavanagh would not be considered a 'hard man', and he would be surprised if he had ever actually fired the gun. Kavanagh was jailed for three years.

Karl Kavanagh might have been a 'small cog in a big wheel', but Wayne McNally was turning into a big, big fish in the Rattigan gang. McNally, along with Anthony Cannon, was now one of the most senior members of the Rattigan crew. Wayne McNally had been with Rattigan in the car in Bluebell in February 2003, when Rattigan shot at the Gardaí. McNally had pleaded guilty to his involvement. While Cannon and McNally were becoming more senior members of the gang, Shay O'Byrne was being actively pursued by the other side. O'Bryne had received several warnings that his life was in danger, and was given advice about his personal security.

McNally was born on 19 December 1984 and grew up in Drimnagh. He had several different addresses, and seemed to live between them. He lived in Rosemount Court in Kilmainham, Loreto Court in Dublin 8 and Baltinglass in Co. Wicklow. McNally was known as a loose cannon, and like Anthony Cannon, petty drug dealers were also terrified of him. He had a casual ambivalence towards violence and was happy to dish out beatings whenever the occasion called for it. The extent of McNally's violent tendencies was illustrated in a court appearance in July 2004, when he pleaded guilty to assault causing harm to a female motorist and unlawfully seizing her car on 2 January 2003, outside an apartment in Mount Argos in Harold's Cross. Detective Garda Jonathan Kelly told Dublin Circuit Criminal Court that two men approached a woman as she left an apartment with a friend at around 9.30pm. Wayne McNally cut the woman's throat for absolutely no reason, and then hijacked her car and drove away. The victim was taken to hospital, fortunately her injuries were minor. Although her physical injuries were not too bad, the woman's mental injuries were serious and she was left unable to go out at night for fear of falling victim to a similar attack. The judge described the victim as an 'innocent young woman' and the incident as 'serious, inexcusable and unjustified' before warning McNally that he was lucky that he had not been charged with a more serious offence. While McNally was on bail for the stabbing and hijacking incident, he committed the crime with Brian Rattigan in Bluebell. He was given an 18-month sentence for being in the stolen car with Rattigan and Wayne Zambra. He was handed two three-year sentences for the stabbing and theft of the woman's car, which were to run concurrently – meaning he received a sentence of just four and a half years. To rub salt into the wounds, the final six months were suspended. The judge said he hoped McNally would use his time in custody to tackle his drug problem. However, he did not serve even close to his full sentence. He was back on the streets in late 2006 – just months before Eddie McCabe was murdered.

On 20 February 2007 at about 9.00pm, McNally was with his girlfriend and a male friend at a house in Gray's Square in the Liberties, when there was a knock on the door. McNally was greeted by a lone gunman who shot him at point blank range with a sawn-off shotgun, hitting him in the face and head. McNally managed to run upstairs and barricade himself into a bedroom, while the gunman escaped in a getaway car that was found nearby.

McNally had been using the address as a 'safe house' and knew that his life was in serious danger, having been warned on numerous occasions by DI Gabriel O'Gara and Superintendent. Tom Mulligan. Half of his nose was blown off during the attack, and he also had injuries to his legs,

arms and shoulders. He was rushed to St James's Hospital in
a serious but stable condition. He later made a full recovery,
although he required plastic surgery to fix his nose. Two
detectives were placed on 24-hour armed guard outside his
hospital ward, so that members of the Thompson gang did
not come back to finish the job.

There was no doubt that the incident was a serious
murder attempt, and McNally was lucky to escape with
relatively minor injuries. Two well-known members of the
Thompson gang were arrested in connection with the
shooting but were never charged. Nevertheless, the shooting
meant that between his stay in hospital and keeping his head
down after he was released, McNally was out of action for
several months, just when he was needed most by the
Rattigan gang.

An incident occurred in July 2007, which illustrated just
how cheap life had become. In early 2000, a man called
Jonathan Dunne lost a consignment of heroin worth
€50,000 that belonged to the Thompson gang. Instead of
shooting Dunne or making him work to pay the money back,
he was told – Godfather style – that the day would come
when a favour would be called in. That day duly arrived and
the favour was, predictably, a big one. A 20-year-old,
nicknamed 'Mad Dog', who occasionally worked as a driver
for Freddie Thompson, was involved in a bitter dispute with
a 21-year-old called Ian Kenny, from Monasterboice Road in
Crumlin. There was an allegation that Kenny was a Garda
informant, and word began to spread around Crumlin that he
was a 'rat'. The row between the pair was becoming
increasingly violent, and, on 27 September 2006, shots were
fired into the Kenny family home in a drive-by attack. Ian
Kenny gave a description of the car to Gardaí. Then three
uniformed officers took up duty outside the house to make
sure that the gang did not come back for seconds. Ian Kenny
was not happy that Sergeant Mark Clarke from Crumlin

Garda Station and two of his female colleagues were trying to ensure his safety. So he went outside his house and started giving abuse to the officers for doing their job. Suddenly, the car that had shot up the house earlier returned. Ian Kenny threw a beer bottle he was carrying at the car. The bottle smashed the front seat passenger window. A sawn-off shotgun appeared from out of the broken window and pointed towards Kenny. Sergeant Clarke realised the danger Kenny was in, and jumped on top of him, pushing him to the ground to safety. However, Sergeant Clarke was struck with the full force of the blast and was hit in the chest and arm. He fell to the ground thinking that he was going to die. Assistance was immediately summoned to the scene. As the brave Garda lay on the concrete, Ian Kenny, who was drunk, leaned over the critically ill officer, who had taken bullets meant for him and shouted: 'Die, you bastard, die.' An unmarked patrol car drove by and Detective Garda Willie Ryan was on the scene in seconds. Ryan manhandled his injured colleague into the back of the car and rushed to St James's Hospital. Fortunately, Mark Clarke didn't die and made a full recovery from his injuries. But still has 11 of the shotgun pellets in his body, as the medics could not remove them. He is now back at work, although he has transferred out of the 'G' district.

Three people would later be convicted for their roles in the shooting. Even with the shooting of a member of An Garda Síochána, Mad Dog still vowed to make Kenny pay for touting. He was doing more and more work for Freddie Thompson and his men, and was accepted into the gang. Mad Dog explained the history of his row with Ian Kenny and told members of the gang that he wanted to have him shot. They didn't object and said they knew just the man for the job – Jonathan Dunne. The only problem was that Jonathan Dunne and Ian Kenny were lifelong friends. However, you do not turn down an order from the

Thompson gang if you value your legs, and Dunne had no choice but to plan the shooting. Ian Kenny, who was a father of two, was no innocent and was involved in criminality at a low level. He had already served a sentence in Mountjoy in 2005, and had survived a vicious prison beating ordered by his sworn enemy. On 4 July 2007, Jonathan Dunne told Kenny that he was going out to buy a quantity of herbal cannabis in south Dublin with another man and invited his friend to join him. The trio drove to a shopping complex in Stillorgan. Johnny Dunne parked the car and said that he had to get something from the boot. He had hidden a sawn-off shotgun earlier in the day and took it out of the boot. Dunne then walked to the window of his own car and fired at Kenny at point blank range. The first shot struck him in the shoulder and Kenny stared, frozen, not believing that one of his best mates was trying to kill him. Dunne fired again, aiming for the shoulder, but he had no experience of using a gun and hit Kenny in the head. The 22-year-old threw his victim from the car then drove to a nearby wooded area, where he made an unsuccessful attempt to burn the car. Dunne panicked and began running up the Lakelands Road, where he was observed by a passing patrol car from Tallaght Garda Station. He was covered in Ian Kenny's blood and brain matter. Dunne swiftly put his hands up and admitted that he was responsible for the attempted murder. Gardaí were puzzled about what had happened. It was one of the most botched and amateur murder attempts in a long time. No criminal with an iota of experience uses their own private car to carry out a murder, and certainly doesn't run away from the scene into the hands of investigators and admit to the crime. Dunne had no previous convictions and wasn't known to Gardaí. Maybe the fact that he was ordered to kill one of his best friends made him blow the whole job. The pieces of the jigsaw started to come together when Dunne told detectives from Crumlin that he owed a favour to two men 'who run things' in the local area. Although he was too scared to name names, it soon became clear that he was talking about Thompson gang members. Gardaí soon learned about the lost drugs and that Dunne had been told that he and his family would be murdered if he didn't carry out the shooting. Jonathan Dunne told Gardaí that the incident was the 'most horrible moment of my life'. 'If I could take it back I would. I am sorry for what was done. Ian was my friend. I was told to put two shots in his head but hadn't got the bottle. I am not a killer.' He was charged with the attempted murder and pleaded guilty. He was handed a 12-year sentence, which the Kenny family called a 'disgrace'. After he was shot in the head and shoulder, Kenny immediately lost consciousness and never woke up. He was fed through a tube in St Vincent's Hospital, and had no control over his bodily functions. His family finally took the decision to turn off his life support machine in July 2009, just over two years after he was shot. Because Jonathan Dunne had already been convicted of Kenny's attempted murder, he could not be re-charged with his killing.

Under the law, a person cannot be charged with murder if their victim stays alive for more than one year and one day after the initial attack. Although Jonathan Dunne was a relative innocent when he was sent to jail, it did not take long for prison life to get the better of him, and whatever remorse he had soon disappeared. Ian Kenny's father, Jon claims that Dunne has constantly mocked his other son over the murder. 'When he sees my other son, he makes jokes about what he did. "Is it vegetable soup we're having today?" he shouted, in reference to Ian's condition, before he finally passed away. He also tells [him] that our family should expect his car valeting bill because of all of my son's blood that was spilt in his car', continues his father, anger in his voice. 'Are those the words of a remorseful man?'

Jon Kenny does not believe that Freddie Thompson was

behind the murder. 'Jonathan Dunne told a story to the judge and the judge believed it. Dunne killed my son; why did the court believe the story of a killer? I know who was responsible for my son's murder and he wasn't killed because Dunne owed a drug dealer money. I don't care what the Gardaí have been saying, I can tell you without any doubt in my mind that Freddie Thompson was not behind my son's killing. I know Crumlin and everyone in it. It was not Thompson who gave the order.'

After Ian Kenny's death in hospital, his girlfriend's mother placed a cross and chain around his neck, but the cross fell to the ground. Jon Kenny said: 'She said, "The heavy cross that he's been carrying around has been lifted off him". Truer words about my son have never been spoken.'

THIRTEEN

War on unexpected fronts

Times were good for Freddie Thompson. With Wayne McNally out of the picture after being shot, and the Rattigan gang in its weakest ever position, the way was theoretically clear for Thompson and his gang to take over and assume near total control of drug dealing in the south of the city without much impediment. However, it wasn't to be, and instead of enjoying the fruits of the murder and mayhem that they had created, the Thompson gang found itself confronted by an unlikely enemy – the Irish National Liberation Army (INLA). In February 2007, one of the leading figures in the INLA, 35-year-old Declan 'Whacker' Duffy was released from Portlaoise Prison after completing a nine-year sentence for his role in the 'Ballymount Bloodbath' in 1999. During the infamous incident, an INLA active service unit took six men hostage when they went to a factory in the Ballymount industrial estate to demand money from the owner. The men were viciously tortured. Then 12 of their friends arrived. A mass brawl ensued and INLA volunteer Patrick 'Bo' Campbell died after being struck with a machete. The INLA man in charge of the operation was Declan Duffy. He was convicted on the strength of a note to the INLA leadership that was discovered in his possession, detailing exactly what happened at the warehouse. The Northern leadership had been horrified at the unwanted publicity surrounding the brawl and was conducting an internal investigation. The fact that Duffy was caught with his statement on him showed that although he was big on brawn, he was rather less well endowed when it came to brains.

Whacker Duffy was involved in a long-term relationship with a Dublin woman and had two children with her. When he was released, he moved to an apartment on Dean Street in Dublin 8, to be close to his family. His apartment was a mere stone's throw away from Freddie Thompson's family home. Duffy started drinking with his INLA cronies in various pubs around the south-inner city, and surveyed the state of the drugs scene there. He decided that he would become the INLA's Dublin commander. So he set about reinvigorating an organisation that had been in almost terminal decline. There were only an estimated 20 core members, mainly from Tallaght, Blanchardstown and Finglas. Duffy was a believer in quality, not quantity and set his merry band of men to work to earn some serious money. He liked what he saw in Dublin 8. There were dozens of pubs where his men could be put to work as bouncers on the door, a trade which was often little more than a protection racket to get cash from the establishments' owners in some areas of the city. The Provisional IRA was already supplying bouncers to several pub doors, but Duffy simply stated that he was now in charge and if anybody refused to pay, there would be consequences. Of course, frightened publicans had to cough up, and Duffy did not care what the Provos thought. He went about establishing himself and stepped on a lot of toes in the process.

The INLA traditionally 'taxes' drug dealers to allow them to continue in business. Duffy was only in Dublin a matter of weeks when he paid a visit to three medium sized dealers who were being supplied by the Thompson gang. He told them that he expected a weekly retainer or they would be driven out of the area. The dealers didn't know what to think. Duffy had acquired a fearsome reputation since the Ballymount

Bloodbath. It was also common knowledge that he acted as the 'Border Fox', Dessie O'Hare's, bodyguard, one of the most feared terrorists in the history of the Troubles, while he was in jail. The dealers went to Freddie Thompson for advice, and a meeting was set up between the two men. Declan Duffy explained the situation and said that he was in the area to stay and that everybody – including Thompson himself – would be expected to share the proceeds of dealing. Thompson told him to f*** off, and that he wouldn't see a single penny either from him or any dealers around the south-inner city who were supplied by him. Fat Freddie wasn't afraid of Duffy and told him that if he wanted a war he could have one. The meeting ended amicably, but both men left in little doubt that if one of them didn't back down then there was potential for serious bloodshed. Over the next few weeks and months, a series of threats was issued by both sides, and there were stories circulating that each man was taking out a contract on the other. Freddie and the people he was sub-contracting his drugs to were nervous because of the threats – as a result business pretty much ground to a halt, while people waited to see what Whacker's next move would be. While Thompson should have been cleaning up because of the weakness of the Rattigan gang, the money just simply wasn't coming in. Freddie was not a happy camper. Gardaí were forced to warn both Duffy and Thompson that their lives were in danger and gave them the usual security advice. Duffy didn't react well to the news. He had always been a fan of talking to the media, and in June 2007, after reports that Thompson had taken a contract out on him because of how his drug dealing operations had been disrupted, Duffy gave an interview to a newspaper. He vowed that the INLA would kill anyone who threatened him or hurt his family. 'If any member of the INLA or our political wing is harmed, the INLA will wipe them out. If they think they can run off to Spain and live happy ever after, they should think again.

They will be hunted down and executed', he said. Duffy did the interview a day after being warned that his life was in danger. He went on to say about the feud with Thompson: 'I did not start any feud with them and I haven't carried out any attacks. I am aware that they are trying to hire a gunman to kill me. They have approached criminals in Spain to do their dirty work but no-one will get involved.'

Duffy's move to Dublin seriously put out the Provisonal IRA. The Provos had traditionally been strong in the area, and although the movement was on a permanent ceasefire, its leaders had moved to criminality and extorting money for allowing drug dealers to operate in the area. Several medium sized dealers, who would have been supplied by the Thompson gang, were making weekly payments to the Provos. So Duffy decided that the IRA would have to be put in its place. In early July 2007, he held a meeting with the head of the IRA in a crowded pub in the Coombe. Duffy informed the Provos that he would be taking over its territory. The IRA leader laughed in Duffy's face and threatened to have him shot – a brawl ensued between around a dozen INLA and IRA members. One of the IRA men received serious stab wounds. Declan Duffy beat up the Provo boss. As a result, Duffy effectively took over after that night and started to make very good money from its protection rackets. The IRA did not respond to the beating of its boss, because it was unable to retaliate with extreme violence because of political considerations.

Senior Gardaí were alarmed by how quickly Duffy's control was growing, and members of the Special Detective Unit started to take a keen interest in him. The Branch men didn't have to wait long to meet him face-to-face. In August, Gardaí received a tip-off that a man had been kidnapped and was being held hostage at a house on in Tallaght.

When armed ERU officers, led by Inspector Mike Larkin, raided the house, they discovered a 21-year-old man bound and gagged lying naked in the bath upstairs. He was in agony and covered in blood, having been attacked with a wheel-brace and a broom handle. The torture went on for a number of hours. The victim was a son of a small West Dublin businessman, who the gang was trying to extort money from. Nine people were arrested in a downstairs room and Duffy was among them. Gardaí believe that those in the house constituted an active INLA service unit, and say that the victim could easily have been murdered had they not arrived in time. The man was so scared of the gang that he refused to make a complaint.

Duffy was a man who revelled in violence and causing people needless pain and suffering. He had previously bragged that he enjoyed kneecapping people and hearing them scream. Duffy was from Armagh, so you would assume that he would head back to his roots in Northern Ireland. However, he couldn't go anywhere near the six counties, because he was wanted for questioning over the murder of Sergeant Michael Newman, who was shot dead by the INLA outside an army recruitment office in Derby in 1992. Duffy joined the INLA when he was just 13, after his older brother was shot dead by the British army in 1987. Duffy has previously served a five-year sentence for escaping from custody at gunpoint.

Because of its experience fighting the British forces, the INLA had experts in bomb making. When he was freed from jail, Declan Duffy saw the potential to make some easy money by selling pipe bombs that its members had either made themselves or imported during the Troubles. In June 2007 Duffy became involved in a petty dispute with a small-time criminal in Dublin 8. He threw a hand grenade at his home but nobody was injured. Weeks later another frag-mentation grenade attack occurred at a house on Slane Road in Crumlin, following the death of an inmate in Mountjoy prison. Garda forensic experts linked these two incidents. An investigation determined that the INLA sold a South-Dublin criminal gang the device for around €2,500. The two grenades were part of a batch smuggled by the INLA from the former Yugoslavia. It appears that the Dublin INLA were only too happy to sell them in a lucrative sideline. In the summer of 2007, the army bomb disposal unit was called out on 16 separate occasions, in just six weeks, because of pipe bomb and granade attacks, many originating from the INLA. It got to the stage where the INLA was selling crude devices for just €350 each, because they had so many and it became easier to source a pipe bomb in Dublin than a gun. People were throwing pipe bombs at each other over even the most minor of squabbles. Before Duffy's release from jail, pipe bombs and fragmentation grenades had never been seen on the streets, so Duffy became the Gardaí's public enemy number one.

Garda Commissioner Fachtna Murphy ordered that a special unit be established to investigate and limit the number of pipe bombs. It was led by Detective Superintendent Padraig Kennedy from Store Street Garda Station. It gradually managed to put a dent in the number of bombs available on the streets. In September 2007, a car that was used by Freddie Thompson was found with a pipe bomb underneath it, although Thompson wasn't in Dublin at the time. Nevertheless, it was a serious escalation by Duffy, and Freddie took out a fresh contract on his life. Duffy again ran to the papers, after Gardaí, told him that a €10,000 price had been placed on his head. Duffy warned that anyone who threatened him would face the consequences, and he put off would be assassins by saying: 'Anyone who even considers taking up the contract will be held as accountable as those taking it out'. He then added: 'The Gardaí told a relative of mine that someone is offering €10,000 to kill me. Others are saying that I am out to kill members of that gang. It is also said that I am in hiding and I am in fear of my life.' He was obviously concerned enough to take precaution to avoid assassination though: 'Even if I am out for a drink with my family, I have people looking after my back. They might not be as obvious as the men here today, but they will be a couple of tables away.' Duffy said that he had taken to wearing full body armour and had bodyguards protecting him in case of an attack. The previous six months had been a bit of a phoney war between Duffy and Freddie, but things then started to get really serious between them in November 2007, with Fat Freddie being told that he would be shot on sight if he was seen by INLA members. On 22 November, a passing patrol car spotted a young INLA volunteer, Denis Dwyer from Jobstown, walking briskly up Camden Street. The apprentice plumber was carrying a sports bag and what looked like the barrel of a gun was sticking out of it. He was stopped and searched and found to be carrying an AK-47. It was 8.45pm, and, when he was searched, two magazines were also found, one of them fully loaded with 21 rounds of 7.62mm ammunition. Investigations by Gardaí in Harcourt Terrace, assisted by the Organised Crime Unit, revealed that this AK-47 had just been transported from Limerick on behalf of Duffy, who had organised for Freddie Thompson to be shot. Dwyer was arrested and claimed that he didn't know what was in the bag and had picked it up for somebody else and was only going to drop it off. Dwyer would later be jailed for four years. Gardaí believe that he was on his way to deliver the gun to another INLA member, who was going to shoot Fat Freddie. Freddie was again warned that his life was in danger. He knew that he had a lucky escape and decided to leave the country while he was still able to.

The obvious place for Thompson to go to regroup was the Spanish Costas, where Paddy Doyle had headed after the three murders in November 2005. Doyle was by now well established in Spain, and had built up a reliable network of contacts who made sure that the drugs kept on arriving into

Ireland. Doyle was comfortable in Spain because the Costa del Sol was like Little Ireland with many of the country's biggest villains calling the region home. Spain had taken over from the Netherlands as the main place where the Thompson gang was sourcing its drugs from. There are several reasons why the Spanish Costas are so attractive for Irish drug dealers.

There is a perception that the Spanish police are particularly lax and simply do not have the will to crack down on the drug importers and exporters that give the country such a bad name. It doesn't help that the country's coastline measures a massive 4,900 kilometres, which means that drugs can be smuggled in from South America via countries like Morocco and Algeria without much fear of getting seized, because it is impossible to police that amount of coastline. From there the drugs are broken up and then smuggled to other European countries. So southern Spain is the European clearing house for organising large scale drug importation.

The Costa del Sol is not known as the 'Costa del Crime' for nothing. In the early 1980s it developed its reputation with the exodus of major criminals from Britain to Spain because of the complicated extradition laws. The British criminals set up their drugs businesses in Spain and were soon followed by their Irish counterparts.

But in recent years, political pressure from abroad has led the Spaniards to tighten up their act and do more to prevent the drug barons from doing their business with virtual impunity. Since 2006, the Spanish authorities have increased the volume of correspondence through the European police agency, Europol, by nearly 40%, which is a sign that at least things are starting to get better. With the introduction of European arrest warrants, which are enforceable throughout the EU, non-accession countries, such as Turkey and Latvia, are now emerging as the countries of choice, but Spain is still very much a gangster's paradise. There are so many Irish criminals operating out of the country, creating so much work for Gardaí that a Detective Sergeant is permanently based in Madrid to act as a liaison between the two police forces.

In February 2008, Michael Colgan, the director of Customs and Excise Drug Enforcement Intelligence Unit, explained why Spain attracts drug dealers: 'If you look at the products that we traditionally import from Spain, such as fresh fruit and vegetables, consignments of these are ideal for hiding drugs. It is also cheaper to purchase large quantities of drugs in Spain than anywhere else. If you take all these factors into consideration it is easy to see why criminals moved out there. They could organise their business more efficiently.'

Christy Kinihan and John Cunningham are the two undisputed godfathers of Irish crime based in Peurto Banus. The Thompson gang sourced their drugs from them.

John 'The Colonel' Cunningham was one of the main members of 'The General' Martin Cahill's gang. Cunningham infamously burnt his right hand after torching the van that was used in the £2m raid on O'Connor's jewellery warehouse in 1983. He still has a scar today. The 59-year-old really came to public attention in Ireland when he was handed a 17-year jail term in 1986, for one of the most high-profile kidnappings ever carried out here. Guinness heiress Jennifer Guinness was snatched from her home in Howth, Co. Dublin, in April 1986, by a gang led by Cunningham. A ransom of £2.5m was demanded, and for five days Gardaí around the country combed empty barns and houses in search of the hostage. Officers eventually tracked the gang down to a house on Waterloo Road in Dublin 4. After a brief exchange of gunfire and protracted negotiations, the kidnappers surrendered. In 1996 Cunningham walked out of Shelton Abbey open prison, after almost completing his sentence, and fled the country, moving to Amsterdam. It is believed that John Gilligan arranged a false passport for him and set him up with contacts in Amsterdam when he arrived. He quickly took advantage of Gilligan's hospitality and developed into a major player in the drugs importation business. However, Dutch Police had learned of his growing reputation. So, they had him under constant surveillance, which eventually paid off big time. In February 2001, Cunningham was jailed for nine years by a court in Amsterdam for his role in a multi-million-euro drugs and guns smuggling ring between Ireland and the Netherlands. Dutch Police and Gardaí were involved in the lengthy operation that had gone on for several years. Cunningham was arrested at a house near Schipol Airport in March 2000, with a fully loaded pistol in his possession. Follow-up searches recovered nearly €10m worth of cannabis, ecstasy, machine guns and other weapons. Some of the items were found hidden in a swimming pool at an apartment used by Cunningham and his wife Mary.

Cunningham had been under surveillance for months as part of 'Operation Clover', which also involved senior Gardaí cooperating with their Dutch and Belgian counterparts. The high-tech surveillance operation involved phone-taps, photographs and videos, and proved that Cunningham was the main figure in a gang that smuggled several shipments of drugs and guns into Ireland. He was careful about how he operated. In telephone conversations with his criminal associates, he only spoke in code. 'Wallpaper' was code for money, 'computers' was cocaine and 'jokes' was weapons, while 'nuts' was a code for ecstasy. When he was specifying the amount of drugs involved in a transaction he used house numbers, and mobile phone numbers were given in SOUTHRIDGE code. Dutch military experts later cracked the code. S was one, O was two, U was three and so on, up until E, which was code for ten. Suddenly, and much to the annoyance and confusion of Cunningham, various police forces started to seize his shipments. He was filmed meeting a truck driver who was heading to Ireland at a motorway stop in Antwerp, Belgium. Cunningham handed him an assault rifle and semi-automatic handgun to bring with him. Cunningham was later recorded on the phone describing how the driver was worried because the handgun was too bulky to fit in his pocket. The driver was arrested before he left Belgium. On another occasion, he sought to set up a new supply route because too many of his shipments were being intercepted. He met an English man in Blackpool and was given a diamond ring as a gift that was worth €7,500. It had been stolen in a robbery in Manchester, and Cunningham later gave it to his wife as a Christmas present. The Police recorded Mary Cunningham, oblivious as to the origin of the ring, bragging to her friends in Ireland over the phone about her swanky Christmas gift.

The court heard how one shipment organised by Cunningham in December 1998 was hidden in pallets of Pitta bread. It was only discovered when a forklift operator accidentally opened up one of the pallets at a warehouse in Castleblaney in Co. Monaghan. Cunningham was so paranoid that he did not trust anybody to do deals on his behalf and that is why he was so hands-on. Police believe that from his Amsterdam base, Cunningham shipped as much as €25m worth of drugs into Ireland in just a few years. He was buying ecstasy tablets for £1 from his supplier, and was making a 700% profit, after all his expenses were paid, when the drugs were sent to Ireland. In November 2004, after completing his Dutch sentence, Cunningham was extradited back to Ireland and sent back to prison to serve the remainder of his term for the Guinness kidnap. He was released after a matter of months and moved to Puerto Banus, where he re-established himself as a major drug importer, using all his old contacts.

Christy Kinahan is 52 and originally hails from the Oliver Bond flats complex in Dublin's city centre. He is a former

heroin addict who got his first criminal conviction back in
1979. In 1987 he was jailed for six years after being caught in
possession of heroin worth over £100,000. Soon after his
release, he was caught with £16,000 worth of stolen cheques
that had been taken in an armed robbery at a North Dublin
bank in 1993. He fled to England, but returned home four
years later and was given a four-year jail term. After being in
prison for 11 out of 15 years, he decided to educate himself,
leave Ireland for the continent and go into the large scale
drugs business. He fancied himself as a bit of a gentleman and
used his time locked up to educate himself. He learned several
European languages, as well as earning a degree in sociology.
Kinahan was so determined to get his degree that he even
turned down the chance of early release to leave Portlaoise
Prison in the late 1990s in order to finish his degree. For the
best part of ten years Kinahan has built himself into one of the
biggest drug importers in all of Europe. He lives in San Pedro,
close to Marbella, and counts John Cunningham as one of his
best friends and one of his most trusted business associates.
Kinahan has been nicknamed the 'Dapper Don' because he
has shed his working-class Dublin accent for a more cultured
European brogue, and is always seen in the best of clothes
made by top tailors. One of his favourite outfits is a white silk
suit with a Panama hat. Kinahan is actively targeted by police
forces in Ireland, Britain, Belgium, the Netherlands, France
and Portugal. He features in intelligence reports by the US
Drug Enforcement Administration. He is also one of Europol's
top targets. He has cultivated drug-dealing associates in the
Russian mafia, with Israeli drugs gangs, as well as Colombian
drug cartels. The vast majority of drugs that end up on Irish
streets have originated through Kinihan and his contacts.

Paddy Doyle and Freddie Thompson were supplied by
him. Doyle would have done business directly with the
Dapper Don. The sheer size of Kinahan's business empire is
illustrated by the fact that since 2002, various police agencies

throughout continental Europe, and including An Garda Síochána – have seized in excess of €50m worth of drugs that originated from Kinahan. After being caught handling drugs in both Ireland and the Netherlands, he learned his lesson. He now refuses to directly touch any drugs, and plays a hands-off role. He now operates in the background – leaving his minions to take all the risk, while he pockets the rewards.

Not far below the two dons is Peter 'Fatso' Mitchell, a 40-year-old who is originally from Summerhill in Dublin's north-inner city, and who was a key member of John Gilligan's drug gang. He had fled Ireland and permanently moved to Spain in 1996, allegedly after helping to organise the murder of Veronica Guerin. Mitchell didn't waste much time in establishing links with international smuggling syndicates in Britain, Spain and the Netherlands. Mitchell lived in a €1.5m villa in the millionaires' playground of Puerto Banus. He owned the Paparazzi bar, which was popular with other Irish drug dealers, including Paddy Doyle and Freddie Thompson. In November 2004, Dutch police arrested him along with his cousin Paddy, while they were in the process of organising a shipment of drugs and guns to be sent home. The two men received 20-month jail sentences. Fatso went by the name 'Anthony Swanson'. His true identity was only confirmed after CAB detectives paid a visit to the mystery man and realised who he actually was. After his release, Mitchell vowed that he would never again directly touch drugs or guns, so now leaves it to his employees. However, Mitchell obviously rubbed somebody up the wrong way – he was lucky to escape a murder attempt in April 2008, when he was shot twice in the shoulder outside a bar in Puerto Banus. He is a close friend of Christy Kinihan's son Daniel.

Both John Cunningham and Christy Kinihan are consummate businessmen who use diplomacy to operate alongside their international counterparts in harmony, without drawing the attention of the local police or

government. The main players on the Spanish Costa are the
Russian and Turkish mafias, who operate below the radar,
live in private gated communities and do not flaunt their
wealth. Discretion is the only way to have a long and safe
career in Spain.

If Irish criminals operate with professionalism and
respect, and adhere to the long established ways of doing
business, they are usually okay. Many haven't though, and
have ended up dead or missing, the likelihood of their bodies
ever being found being remote. In September 2005, Sean
Dunne from Donaghmede in North Dublin, who was
involved in large-scale drug importation, disappeared
without a trace. His own family believe that he was chopped
up and buried in an unmarked grave. In January 2004,
members of the Russian mob lured Stephen Sugg and Shane
Coates to a meeting. The two leaders of the feared 'Westies'
group from Blanchardstown in West Dublin, met the
Russian mob and disappeared. It was not until July 2006 that
their bodies were found in a concrete grave next to a
warehouse in Catral, near Alicante. Both had been shot in
the head. It is thought that they had tried to double cross the
Russian mob during a drug deal, and paid the ultimate price.
In January 2007, John 'The Mexican' McKeown, from
Finglas, vanished in Torrevieja near Alicante. McKeown
organised drugs shipments on behalf of Martin 'Marlo'
Hyland – he is also presumed to have been murdered. In
January 2009, drug dealer Richard Keogh, from Cabra, was
shot dead outside a casino in Belamadena. There was
suspected Venezualan involvement in his murder. The
following month, armed robber and heroin addict
Christopher Gilroy, from Dublin's north-inner city, was
spirited out of Ireland after carrying out a double murder for
a Finglas gang. It was feared that he couldn't be trusted to
keep quiet. He vanished and is also thought to have been
murdered.

*   *   *

Spain suited Paddy Doyle and Freddie Thompson and they grew to enjoy it. Their lifestyle in Spain is not one that ordinary working people can relate to – they can only dream of it. Doyle had a luxury three-bedroom apartment in Cancelada, in a gated community close to a golf course. His days revolved around waking up late, going to the gym and working out for up to two hours. This was followed by a long lunch in nearby Puerto Banus or Marbella, washed down with several bottles of good wine. Business was conducted at lunch and in the early afternoon. This could involve meeting other criminals to arrange drugs shipments or going to pay people money that was owed or collect cash that was owed to his gang. In the evenings Doyle would drive the 15-minute journey down to Puerto Banus and meet up with the likes of Fatso Mitchell and Gary Hutch (a 27-year-old from the north-inner city). Hutch had a villa in the Vista Golf luxury resort in Estepona. They would spend the night drinking in Mitchell's bar, and, invariably, ended up in the popular Linekers English bar and nightclub in New Town. There they would drink for half the night – with many taking cocaine – before going back to bed and doing it all again the next day. Doyle and the other well-heeled Irish criminals forked out €20,000 each per year to enjoy private parking at the upmarket Puerto Banus port, which is not accessible to ordinary members of the public. While down at the port, Doyle and his cronies would rub shoulders with multi-millionaires from around the world, who probably had no idea just who these young Irish people were, or of the reputations they had acquired at home. Doyle's friends and family frequently went to visit him in Spain because he was exiled from Ireland. Apparently, his tan never faded in the near year-round sunshine.

When Freddie Thompson started to go to Spain to supervise Doyle, he initially stayed with his mate, but the gang is believed to have purchased several apartments in the heart of Puerto Banus, and Thompson subsequently relocated there. With Doyle permanently in Spain and Thompson spending frequent periods there because of the Whacker Duffy situation, Thompson was eager to ingratiate himself to Christy Kinihan, his main supplier. So much so, that in January 2008, he arranged for one of his main mentors, the notorious Martin 'The Viper' Foley, to be shot and killed. Gardaí regarded 55-year-old Foley as a serious criminal. Foley is involved in protection rackets and general criminality. He is from Cashel Avenue in Crumlin. Brian Rattigan and Freddie Thompson and their respective gangs would have looked up to Foley when they were growing up, and they regarded him as a father figure to many members of both sides of the feud. When Declan Gavin started his criminal career, he worked for The Viper. Foley was clever and managed to stay in with both feuding gangs. He rose to prominence as one of 'The General', Martin Cahill's, most trusted lieutenants in the 1980s, and has been a controversial figure ever since. In 2006, he went to the High Court to stop the *Sunday World* newspaper from running stories about him, which he claimed endangered his life. He said his safety was being put in danger by claims in the newspaper that he was a Garda informant. His solicitor described a four-page article by journalist Paul Williams headlined: 'Foley's a dead man walking' as being 'among the most profoundly irresponsible journalism and editorship of a widely circulating national newspaper that I could conceive of'. Foley conveniently forgot to tell the court that it was his associates who masterminded a campaign of terror against the high-profile journalist – even leaving a pipe bomb under his car, which led to the journalist needing permanent armed Garda security.

A number of years ago, Foley was threatened with murder by the IRA if he did not pay them a percentage of the money he received from drug dealing. It is believed that he does pay the Provisionals, although he has always denied this. Martin

Foley is a great survivor. Brian Meehan, who was jailed over Veronica Guerin's murder, tried to kill Foley twice. In 1995, Meehan entered a pub and shot him in the arm and stomach, but Foley survived. Three months later, he made a second attempt. As Foley reversed out of his home, Meehan ambushed him and fired five shots from a machine gun, before Foley escaped through back gardens. In an interview in 2003, Foley spoke about Meehan's second assassination attempt. 'I had read a lot of books about survival. Well, techniques to avoid being assassinated. I had the door unlocked in the car; I kept it open. It would be a bad mistake for anybody to stay in the car, because if the car is put out of action, you're still stuck in the car. I jumped over a nearby back wall, into a house and up the stairs. The back door had been open. I could hear crackling. I later learned that one of the guns had jammed. As I was going up the stairs, I was shot in the back. I had the entry of a .45 bullet in the back and the exit in the stomach, through the lung and so on. I kept going, yes. You're inclined to run a little bit fast when somebody is firing at you. I jumped feet first through a window.' He also spoke of the trauma that being shot had had on him. 'When you are shot on three different occasions and you have 11 holes in your body, psychologically the thing is never going to leave you and you would react to certain situations where anything bad might happen.'

In September 2000, Foley was shot in the legs, when two men approached him as he left the swimming pool at Terenure College. One of the gunman walked over, as he lay on the ground, and prepared to shoot him in the head, only for the gun to misfire.

In March 1984, he was abducted by an IRA death squad, following a row with the IRA and Foley's boss, Martin Cahill. Foley was snatched by four men who burst into the house where he was staying and beat him with a baton and

sawn off shotgun, before bundling him into a van. A
neighbour quickly phoned 999, and the Provisionals shot at
unarmed Garda Tony Tighe as he gave chase. A gunfight
then ensued, and all the gang were detained and eventually
convicted. Foley has been in the news over the last couple of
years because of his debt collecting business: 'Viper Debt
Collection Agency'. He has been accused of sending heavies
to people who allegedly owe money, and of intimidating
people and threatening violence if he wasn't paid in full.
Foley has amassed 42 criminal convictions in the course of
his long career in crime.

Christy Kinihan and Foley fell out in the late 1990s after
Kinihan accused the Viper of scamming him out of
€100,000. Kinihan despised Martin Foley, but he never tried
to reclaim the money or exact revenge on Foley for the
alleged con job. However, Kinihan was eager to return to
Ireland but knew that he couldn't show his face in Dublin
and hold his head high if he did not seek revenge for the
missing money. So, he asked Thompson to take out the Viper
as a personal favour to him. It is not believed that money
exchanged hands, but Kinihan cancelled a debt that
Thompson owed him for a drug shipment that Gardaí had
recovered.

On Saturday 26 January 2008, Foley was driving out of
the Carlisle Health and Fitness gym, on the Kimmage Road,
at around 3.00pm. As he stopped at a junction, a gunman
walked up to Foley's Audi A6 and opened fire with a Glock
9mm pistol, firing a total of seven shots at the Viper from
close range. Four bullets hit their target striking Foley in the
lower chest, shoulder, leg and one grazed his head. Being an
expert in survival, Foley crouched under the steering wheel
and managed to continue driving the car until it hit a wall
across the road. This act of quick thinking would turn out to
save his life. Nevertheless, thinking that he was going to die,
Foley shouted out the name of the man who shot him. The

name he mentioned was a 24-year-old key member of the Thompson gang. Ironically, the alleged gunman was close to Foley, but once Thompson had given the order he was happy to carry it out. Foley was rushed to St James's Hospital, but miraculously was not seriously injured and was out of hospital after a couple of weeks. He has now been directly hit with a total of 15 bullets. Gardaí put his remarkable survival down to the fact that he is a fitness fanatic who works out every day and is seriously fit and strong.

Christy Kinihan is said not to have been pleased at all that the hit was botched. To make matters worse, the gunman failed to burn out the getaway car, so Gardaí were able to get a number of DNA samples from it. However, Foley refused to make a statement and has not named the gunman since, although Gardaí are hopeful that they will eventually get charges. The 24-year-old and his brother were both detained for questioning. The men's father is a well-known hitman from west Dublin. Four other men were also arrested and questioned. However, their DNA was not found at the scene, nor was the brothers'. Some sources say that Foley didn't actually see the gunman and named the person most likely to have been responsible, in his eyes anyway. Foley has been around for so long that some Gardaí believe that it could have been any number of suspects, as the list of possibilities is endless, a bit like the famous *Simpsons* episode, 'Who shot Mr Burns?'. It is believed that a peace deal between Foley and Kinihan has since been brokered, although Thompson and the Viper have permanently fallen out. Although Thompson was concerned that there would be retribution for the Foley hit, he soon had other things to worry about.

On 4 February 2008, Paddy Doyle, Gary Hutch and Freddie Thompson were in Cancelada, sitting in Doyle's BMW jeep. Paddy Doyle was in the front passenger's seat of the luxury BMW X5, Gary Hutch was driving and Freddie was in the back seat. It was Doyle's jeep and he had recently paid an estimated €70,000 for it and was letting Hutch take a spin to see how it drove. Hutch was a nephew of 'The Monk', Gerry Hutch, the infamous criminal. Gary travelled a lot between Ireland and Spain. The three amigos had just finished working out in the gym in Cancelada, near Doyle's home. They were heading towards Marbella, when another BMW jeep pulled up alongside theirs. It was about 2.00pm and Paddy Doyle turned his head to the right and looked out his window just in time to see a machine pistol being raised by a passenger in the other car. Shots started to rain out with four flying through the windscreen on the passenger side of the jeep and a fifth piercing the door where Doyle was sitting. In an attempt to escape, Gary Hutch smashed the car into a lamppost, around 30 metres from where the rival jeep initially approached them, and his jeep ground to a halt. He and Thompson hopped out of the car and started to run away in blind panic, in an attempt to get away from whoever was shooting at them. They fled into an apartment complex close to where the BMW had crashed, and luckily for the two men, the gunmen were obviously not after them and made no attempt to pursue them. Paddy Doyle was the man they wanted, and as he lay wounded in the jeep, the shooter came up and shot him twice in the head from point-blank range, killing him instantly. The killer hadn't even bothered to wear a mask. He must have been confident that the Spanish police would never bring him to justice.

As usual, Freddie was totally unscathed and didn't have as much as a mark on him. Gary Hutch was taken to hospital and given treatment for an arm injury he had sustained in the crash. It was not until an hour after the shooting that both men returned to the scene and presented themselves to Spanish police for questioning, although no charges were ever brought against either man.

The day of the Doyle murder, Spanish police found a

consignment of €8m worth of cocaine in Estepona, but the seizure had nothing to do with Doyle's shooting.

Although it was initially reported that Doyle had been murdered after falling foul of the Russian mafia, it is actually Turkish criminals that are suspected of killing him. In October 2007, Gardaí began to receive information from Spanish police that a dispute had arisen between Patrick Doyle and a Turkish crime syndicate. The gang had been introduced to a major Turkish crime family in London in early 2005 and had been supplied with cheap heroin, which was being imported from Afghanistan, since then. Paddy Doyle was the point man in Spain, and initially things had gone very smoothly, with both sides being very satisfied with their business arrangement. The dispute with Whacker Duffy had meant that business had to take a back seat to staying alive, so there hadn't been a whole lot of revenue coming in for the previous six months or so, so paying suppliers wasn't Freddie's main priority. Gardaí had also been increasingly successful in intercepting shipments and several seizures had cost the gang millions of euro in profits and hundreds of thousands of euro that was their original investment. The Turks organised a €2.4m heroin seizure in Dublin Port in late August 2007, on behalf of the Thompson gang. The drugs were smuggled from Rotterdam to Dublin in a truck that was supposedly carrying 'Antique style wood burning ranges'. Customs officials examined the ranges. Lulu, a Revenue drug detection dog, smelled drugs in the ranges. Two ranges revealed 12 kilos of heroin, with a street value of €2.4m, along with cocaine worth €175,000. At the time it was the biggest ever seizure in Dublin Port. It was a serious blow to the gang, because the majority of the drugs had been given on credit, which meant that Thompson and Doyle were seriously out of pocket. Because they were short on cash, Thompson and Doyle had been putting off paying the Turks. Because Freddie Thompson was back and forth between Ireland and Spain the whole time, he also became involved in the growing dispute. Spanish police told Gardaí that Doyle and Thompson had been told that they would both be murdered if they did not pay outstanding bills for a number of sizeable heroin shipments that the Turks had supplied to them. When a messenger was sent to warn the pair, Thompson is said to have given him the two fingers, while Doyle laughed at them. Although the two gangsters put on brave faces, things were not going well for them at all, but they didn't believe that the threats would amount to anything. Two weeks before his murder, Doyle was given a final warning that if he did not settle his bill, action would be taken. Again, it seems he underestimated the sheer ruthlessness of the Turks.

It seems that Paddy Doyle didn't learn the lessons of some of the younger gangsters before him. Doyle tried to use his brawn, instead of using diplomacy like John Cunningham or Christy Kinihan did. Because he was a big fish in a small pond in Ireland, he thought he could go to Spain and push people around. Although he was feared in Dublin, he was considered a nobody in Spain. In reality, Doyle and Thompson were way out of their depth, swimming with the international sharks and operating on the Costa del Sol.

Paddy Doyle's family were not happy with the Irish media's coverage of his murder. His father Donal complained to the Broadcasting Complaints Commission that a report on RTÉ's *Six One News* and *Nine O'Clock News* bulletins had breached regulations by causing undue distress or offence to his family. Donal Doyle complained that the news item showed the bullet-ridden car his son had been shot in, and also showed a private family photo of his son. He said that he didn't know how RTÉ had obtained the photo and that RTÉ had not asked permission to use it. Doyle claimed that the family's personal grief had not been considered. The complaint was rejected. Donal Doyle was a prominent anti-drugs campaigner in the north-inner city, and his sister is a respected youth worker. The Doyles rushed out to Spain, as soon as the news of Paddy's murder reached them, and went to the scene of his murder, where they laid flowers and other mementos. Doyle was a father of two boys with his partner Melanie Thompson, Fat Freddie's cousin. Although Paddy Doyle was a ruthless criminal with 42 convictions, he still left behind him a loving family who will obviously miss him dearly.

Freddie Thompson was rattled after Paddy Doyle's murder. As well as losing a close friend and his international fixer, he had also lost his main enforcer, which meant that he was now very vulnerable. Freddie didn't know if the Turks would come back and look for him, so he decided to leave Spain, head back to Ireland and try to resolve the Declan Duffy row. It didn't help things that the day after the Doyle killing, a Toyota Avensis taxi was stopped by the Crumlin Garda Drugs Unit on Davitt Road in Drimnagh, and the passenger was searched. Gary Johnston a 28-year-old from Monasterboice Road in Crumlin, was found in possession of €198,000 worth of heroin that he was holding for the Thompson gang. Johnston was a former heroin addict who owed a significant amount of money to the Thompson mob, so he was used by the gang to ferry drugs around for them. His arrest and the seizure of the drugs was another bitter blow to Thompson. But double trouble was also coming for Thompson. Declan Duffy soon learned of Freddie's return, and went all-out to try to eliminate him and move in on his turf. He is said to have upped the contract on Freddie's head. Gardaí warned Thompson on three occasions that there was a contract out on his life, and Gardaí who spoke to him at the time say that he was incredibly rattled. There was also the Rattigan gang to be concerned about. They had also taken a keen interest in Thompson's change of circumstances and realised that if they could collect themselves a scalp or two, they could redress their recent losses and even out the feud again. So, it really was trouble on two fronts for Thompson.

At lunchtime on 13 March 2008, Freddie Thompson was drinking in a pub on Parnell Street, when members of the Emergency Response Unit swooped on a car as it crossed from the south-side of the city across O'Connell Bridge. The two men in the car, aged 32 and 45, were both from Ballyfermot. They had been under surveillance for several days, after information was received that they had agreed to shoot Freddie. The 32-year-old is regarded as being a hitman, and is the suspect in at least five unsolved gangland murders. He has links to the Rattigan side of the feud, but is very much a gun for hire, so Gardaí did not know whether the contract was being carried out for Duffy or Rattigan, although sources believe that Rattigan was the more likely candidate. The pair of would-be assassins were followed after they left an address in Crumlin and drove towards the city centre. They were in a stolen car that had been fitted with false number plates. Gardaí believe that they were supposed to meet a motorbike on Parnell Street to pick up a handgun, but detectives decided to stop their vehicle before the rendezvous – in order to ensure that the safety of members of the public was not compromised.

Four unmarked Garda cars boxed the vehicle in as it crossed O'Connell Bridge, as dozens of shocked onlookers watched in horror. The driver of the motorbike on Parnell Street became concerned when the hitman didn't show and drove away. The suspects were taken away to Store Street Garda Station. Freddie Thompson got into a car minutes later and drove away from the city, unaware of what happened. He was soon informed of what had occurred, and Gardaí believe that he boarded a flight back to Spain to regroup until the heat died down. Gardaí did not even know that Thompson was in the country at the time of the incident, so there were major suspicions that one of his own side set him up to be murdered. The two men were released without charge because they had not been arrested in possession of a firearm and there was no concrete evidence that they were planning to shoot Thompson. It was frustrating to Gardaí, but they took the attitude that they had probably prevented an assassination attempt, so they were happy with that and would just have to try to bring charges against the hitman and his driver again.

With the two feuding gangs and the INLA all operating furiously, because of the vacuum created after Doyle's murder, Gardaí from the Organised Crime Unit started to make some notable successes against the three groups. On 18 March, Paul Dunphy, a 45-year-old Rattigan ally from Allenton Drive in Tallaght, was stopped on the Walkinstown Road and searched. Two hand grenades and a Glock 9mm pistol were recovered from down his trousers. Gardaí had received a tip-off that the devices were being stored at an empty premises in Walkinstown. Dunphy was subsequently jailed for five years. As part of the same operation, the following day detectives searched the back garden of a house on Rutland Avenue in Crumlin, and recovered €2m worth of cocaine and heroin that was being stored in a hole in the ground. Three men were detained – the drugs also belonged to the Rattigan gang.

On 7 April, Gardaí from Roxboro Road Station in Limerick, stopped a car on the Loughmore Link Road, and arrested two men after finding €200,000 worth of heroin in the boot. One of those detained was a 27-year-old key ally of Brian Rattigan – the arrest just illustrated the links between Dublin and Limerick criminals. The man was charged with possession of drugs with intent to supply, and is currently before the courts. On 23 April, a pipe bomb exploded in the front garden of a house on Monasterboice Road in Crumlin. Gary Johnston was the target; the 28-year-old had been arrested in the taxi with €198,000 worth of heroin, the previous February. There was a small amount of damage to the front of the house but nobody was injured. It is thought that the INLA was behind the attack. It was one of four pipe bomb attacks in the capital in less than a week. In April 2009 Johnston was jailed for ten years after pleading guilty to having the drugs in his possession. Just days after being sentenced, two Thompson associates viciously assaulted Johnston in Mountjoy as punishment for losing the drugs. He suffered a punctured lung, ruptured spleen and broken jaw. In mid May, Freddie Thompson returned from Spain, and it was not long before he was appearing on the Gardaí's radar.

In early June, an attempt was made by a local drug boss who was being supplied by Thompson to run over Declan Duffy. The drug dealer was driving his Alfa Romeo car close to Duffy's partner's home on Hanover Street when he saw the INLA leader and mounted the footpath in a bid to mow him down. Duffy managed to cower in a doorway and escaped. Because of the huge increase in incidents involving the Thompson gang and the INLA, senior Garda management, in an unprecedented move, ordered uniformed Gardaí to request armed back-up if they had any suspicions about emergency calls they were responding to. Senior Gardaí were so concerned that the simmering feud was going to escalate into all-out war that they told armed detectives to back-up their uniformed colleagues before dealing with any callouts that could be linked to Freddie, Duffy or Rattigan. A series of bogus 999 calls were made to both Crumlin and Kevin Street Garda Stations, claiming that an incident was happening in one area of the division. While Gardaí directed their resources to that area, criminal activity was taking place somewhere else. The calls were designed to divert Gardaí,so that the criminals could go about their business in peace. Detective Superintendent Denis Donegan directed that not all resources would react to calls, as he felt response times to incidents was being monitored by the feuding criminals. So while some units responded to calls, others patrolled the general division and headed in the opposite direction. The decision came after a spate of gang related incidents in the space of a couple of weeks. On 15 June, Gardaí were called to a popular pub in Dublin 8, after two masked men walked in in the middle of the afternoon and asked where Freddie Thompson was. The pair had been seen loitering outside the pub in a white van. When they realised that Thompson was not on the premises, they got back into their vehicle and drove off. The following day, two armed and masked men burst into a bookmaker's in the south-inner city, where Thompson had been seen placing bets earlier in the day. When there was no sign of him, they again left without any serious incident. Freddie was on high alert at this stage and knew that his life was in serious danger. Duffy stabbed one of Thompson's close associates in the arm in an incident on Dean Street. Duffy was arrested and at 4.00pm the same day, Gardaí received a call that shots had been fired outside shops on Galtymore Road in Drimnagh. The reports Gardaí received stated that a black Volkswagen Golf GTI had been involved in a hit-and-run accident. Witnesses said that after the incident, a lone male with his hood pulled up had run from the victim towards the Volkswagen with a handgun in his possession. CCTV footage later led Gardaí to believe that the man with the gun was Freddie Thompson. This was backed up when Aidan Gavin walked into Sundrive Road Garda Station that same day to report that his car had been damaged in a hit-and-run incident.

What happened was that Freddie Thompson was cruising around Crumlin, Drimnagh and Dublin 8; he was hyper and trying to avoid being shot. By coincidence, he happened upon a car, a Volkswagen GTI, that was being driven by a relation of the man that had been arrested on O'Connell Bridge, the previous March, on his way to murder Thompson. As luck would have it, the hitman for hire was also in the car, along with Mr X, one of Rattigan's top dogs. When Aidan Gavin saw the car, he drove towards it; Thompson pulled out a handgun and jumped out of the car. He was prepared to open fire and get instant sweet revenge. The driver of the Golf GTI saw what was happening and slammed his car into reverse and struck the wing mirrors of several parked cars as well as hitting Aidan Gavin's rear taillight. Passersby mistook the sound of the wing mirrors being hit as gunshots, but CCTV later showed a person who looked uncannily like Freddie Thompson getting out of a car brandishing a handgun. The GTI fled the area but armed Gardaí from the Organised Crime Unit stopped it at around 4.00pm near Dolphin Road. All the occupants were searched and Mr X was arrested after being found in possession of a knife. Freddie Thompson and Aidan Gavin were both arrested, but the gun was well gone by that stage. The CCTV footage was not of good enough quality to bring a prosecution against Thompson. Despite it being an almost unprecedented 24 hours, Fat Freddie again managed to survive unscathed and lived to fight another battle. Because of the sheer number of threats to his life and those of other gang members, Thompson then routinely started travelling in convoys of at least three vehicles, with between six and ten gang members accompanying him at all times. A number of 'spotters' also travelled around Crumlin, Drimnagh and the south-inner city on motorbikes on the lookout for Duffy and his mob. The spotters were armed and ready to rush to Thompson's gang at short notice, to provide them with weapons to be used in opportunistic attacks on the INLA and the Rattigan gang. So well-disciplined was Thompson's gang that they had an appointed 'nobody', who would act as a 'runner' if the convoy was stopped by the Gardaí. This runner would literally run or speed away and hope that the Gardaí would chase him, while the main gang got away. The runner would never carry any drugs or weapons.

A spur of the moment attack happened on 21 June at the Planet Love music festival in Fairyhouse, Co. Meath. Freddie Thompson's cousin, 24-year-old Eoin O'Connor, was involved in an altercation with an associate of Brian Rattigan, Gerard Eglington. Elington, who was 21 and from Fatima Mansions in Dublin 8, was a passenger in the stolen sports car that struck and killed Garda Tony Tighe and Garda Michael Padden on the Stillorgan dual carriageway in April 2002. Eglington was only 15 at the time of the incident, and was handed a four-year jail term in St Patrick's young offenders' institute. He got to know Brian Rattigan in prison, and was at the music festival with Rattigan's most senior enforcer, Anthony Cannon, when they happened upon O'Connor. O'Connor and Eglington became involved in a fight and were both detained. While O'Connor was in handcuffs, Cannon managed to slip away, and he brutally slashed O'Connor from one cheek to the other, causing him horrific and permanent facial scars. O'Connor was found to be in possession of a flick-knife and was taken to Connolly Hospital for treatment under arrest. Cannon was also detained but was ultimately not charged. Freddie Thompson is said to have gone absolutely ballistic when he heard about the vicious assault.

On 24 June 2008, Freddie Thompson's grandparents were preparing to go to bed in their home in the Coombe, when gunmen fired three shots at the house. The couple, who were both in their eighties, were lucky to escape injury during the shooting, which took place just after 10.00pm. A car was heard screeching away from the scene after the shots were fired. Anthony Cannon is thought to have been the man who fired the shots. Thompson was furious when he heard how his innocent and elderly grandparents had been dragged into a feud that had absolutely nothing to do with them. However, the incident did not happen out of the blue, and it was meant to send out a message to Thompson. Earlier that day an eight-month old baby had a close escape when his 50-year-old grandmother was shot in the shoulder in another drive-by attack. The victim was carrying her baby grandson when six shots were fired at her house on Knocknarea Road in Drimnagh. Three men in a silver-coloured BMW car pulled up outside the house shortly before 1.00pm, after chasing a man. The man running away managed to gain entry to the victim's house and barricade himself inside. Two men jumped out of the car and fired three shots from a handgun into the glass panels of the front door and another into the letterbox before trying to kick it in. They failed, so one of the men ran to the front window and fired another two shots, one of which hit the victim in the left shoulder, and missed her little grandson by a matter of inches. The quick thinking woman threw the baby to the safety of a couch. Had the youngster been hit by the stray bullet he would surely have been killed. The woman's 84-year-old grandmother and two other adults were in the house at the time of the broad-daylight attack, which took place just 20 metres away from Our Lady of Good Counsel primary school on the Mourne Road. The gunmen escaped and the BMW was later found partially burnt out at the back of Superquinn in Walkinstown. It had been stolen and fitted with false number plates. The woman whose house had been shot at was not the intended target, and the attack was a case of mistaken identity. She was rushed to St James's Hospital and luckily made a full recovery. Freddie Thompson's gang are thought to have been behind the shooting.

It was a case of grandparent for a grandparent. The woman who had been attacked was an innocent grandparent and so were Freddie Thompson's grandparents. Gardaí were very concerned that both sides were starting to target innocent people who had nothing to with the feud, especially when children were being dragged into the hostilities. Gardaí got a great boost when Declan Duffy was arrested on 25 June on suspicion of membership of the INLA. He was remanded into custody to Portlaoise Prison, just metres away from Brian Rattigan, although the two men were on different landings. Gardaí had put a lot of resources into collating evidence to use against Duffy, and once he was off the streets, the threat of the INLA against Thompson was effectively lifted. This meant that all of the Gardaí's resources could be put into keeping a watchful eye on Freddie's escalating feud with the Rattigan gang.

On 28 June 2008, innocent people were again targeted in a horrendous grenade attack. Madeleine Frazer, mother of former Freddie Thompson associate Michael Frazer, had her home attacked with a hand grenade. At 2.30am a red Fiat Punto pulled up outside the Frazer home, and somebody used a rock to smash a glass panel on the front door, before lobbing a Czech fragmentation grenade into the house. The grenade exploded, causing a considerable amount of damage to the downstairs rooms, the ceilings of an upstairs bedroom, the upstairs toilet area and as high up as the attic. The grenade was designed to kill anyone within a 6 metre radius. It was the most serious fragmentation grenade incident in the history of the state. Gardaí say that the house looked like 'a bomb site in Beirut', such was the amount of damage caused. Sources said it was a miracle that nobody inside the house had as much as a scratch on them, especially considering that six people were in the house, including a six year-old boy.

Paul Dunphy, who was arrested on the Walkinstown Road in possession of two grenades and a handgun, less than four months previously, was arrested for questioning about the incident, but was never charged, as there wasn't enough evidence to charge him. After the Frazer grenade attack and the shooting of the innocent grandmother, tensions in Drimnagh were at an all-time high, because of the tit-for-tat incidents that had resulted in innocent grandmothers being injured. Detective Superintendent Denis Donegan and

Detective Inspector Brian Sutton made direct
representations to senior figures on both sides, and with the
assistance of the local clergy, brokered an agreement whereby
family members would not be targeted in the future. Both
sides agreed and things settled down. Just days later, Freddie
caught a flight bound for Spain. His mother was quoted in
the *Sunday Times* as saying: 'He doesn't want to talk to
anyone. The Gardaí told him he was under threat. He hasn't
done anything, but he's being blamed for everything that's
happening.' Freddie spent several weeks in Spain, and the
sort of ceasefire agreed by Gardaí seemed to be holding for
the moment.

As for Declan Duffy, his arrest meant the beginning of the
end for both him and the INLA. He was held in Portlaoise
until 8 May 2009, when he appeared at the Special Criminal
Court to face trial for his membership charge. Surprisingly,
he pleaded guilty when he took to the witness box to address
the judge. His counsel, Michael O'Higgins, asked him: 'You
are disassociating yourself from the group, the INLA, to
which you have pleaded guilty to membership?' 'Yes, that's
right,' Duffy replied, before adding that he had applied to
the Governor of Portlaoise Prison to be moved away from the
INLA landing. Because of his guilty plea, he was granted bail
on condition that he lodge his own bond of €100 with the
court, as well as two independent sureties of €10,000 each.
And with that he walked out of the court a free man – much
to the annoyance of Gardaí, who did not trust Duffy's
renouncement of the INLA one little bit. The INLA top-
brass in Belfast went ballistic when he learned of Duffy's
public denouncement and issued a statement criticising him.
On 17 May 2009, Duffy granted an interview to the *Irish
Daily Star on Sunday*, in which he claimed that he had
abandoned a life of crime in favour of learning to play the
piano and becoming a guidance counsellor. The criminal said
that he wanted to lead a 'normal life' away from crime. 'I

have had enough of violence and that is basically it. I would hope to lead some sort of relatively normal life now and I would hope to leave the violence behind. I'm learning to play the piano now. I'm doing OK; it's very slow. The only song I can play is Raglan Road. I'm also starting a BA postgraduate course in guidance counselling.' Duffy was wearing a bullet proof vest when he spoke to the *Star* reporter, Cathal McMahon, and talked about deciding to turn his back on the INLA and crime, after lengthy discussions with family and friends. 'I have been a member of the INLA all my life, so it was not an easy decision to take. After speaking with a number of former members who left, as well as my own family, I decided to leave it.' It is thought that Duffy was about to be expelled from the organisation, after an internal inquiry was ordered by the Northern leadership into the negative publicity that Duffy's feud with Freddie Thompson had brought. 'The investigation is a load of crap as far as I'm concerned. It is my opinion that the organisation wasn't able to handle the negative media coverage that is attached to me. They need to grow a thicker skin.' Duffy did not mention Freddie Thompson by name during the interview, but was asked if it was true that his group demands protection money from drug dealers. He answered: 'It doesn't work like that. If a drug dealer has money you go and take it. You don't ask questions.' It was probably an attitude like that which got Duffy into the bother that he now found himself in. Operating in Dublin is very different from working up north where paramilitary groups control each area. In Dublin it is criminal gangs that rule and they don't take kindly to 'Northies' coming down and stepping on their toes. Nevertheless, Duffy claimed that his peace had been made with Freddie Thompson and that all the previous tension between the gang and the INLA had been resolved. 'I have no enemies. The feuds with drug dealers are over and no one is out to get me, but that could change over night.' Gardaí were very suspicious, especially as they knew that Duffy's almost biblical transformation from criminal to pacifist was made to curry favour with the judge who would be sentencing him for membership of an illegal organisation. If Duffy thought that he would be free for long to enjoy his newfound status as a peace lover, without any enemies, then he was in for a shock. On 21 May, he was arrested on foot of a European arrest warrant and taken to the High Court. The British authorities had requested his extradition for questioning about the murder of army recruitment officer Michael Newman in 1992.

Sergeant Newman had never even served in Northern Ireland and was not wearing his uniform when he was shot in the head as he left his office in Derby city centre. The 34-year-old, who was engaged to be married, was so badly injured that his life support machine had to be turned off the following morning. A three-man INLA cell carried out the murder. Declan Duffy was involved along with Joseph Magee and Anthony 'Fanta' Gorman. Magee was jailed for 25 years in 2004, after pleading guilty to the murder on the understanding that he would be released under the terms of the Good Friday Agreement after just two years. Anthony Gorman was arrested in the same month as Duffy, and was also being sought for extradition. The case against Duffy was adjourned, and he was remanded back into custody pending a later court appearance.

Just eight days later, he appeared before the Special Criminal Court, where details of his arrest the previous June were heard. Detective Superintendent Diarmaid O'Sullivan from the Garda Special Detective Unit gave evidence that officers had received confidential information in August 2007 that the INLA had planned to extort money from Co. Cork businessman Denis Maguire by kidnapping him. A massive Garda surveillance operation got underway. On 18 October, Duffy and another man were seen driving to Cork, where they booked into the Silver Springs hotel using false names and addresses. The next day Duffy and his pal drove to Maguire's home in Montenotte, but used anti-surveillance techniques along the way to make sure that they weren't being followed. Little did Duffy know that there were a number of Garda teams assigned to watch him at various locations. Duffy was obviously doing a dry run, and returned to the Silver Springs hotel. On November 6, Duffy and the same man again travelled to Cork and booked into the same hotel, using the same false names and addresses. Three other men from the INLA booked into Jury's Inn in Cork City. They all travelled to Maguire's house. Three of the men went into the premises but Duffy stayed outside. After a few minutes the men came out and all drove back to the city centre. The following morning, Duffy was again spotted outside the Maguire home. When Maguire's wife got into her car and drove to the city centre, Duffy followed her. However, Dermot Maguire then made an unexpected trip to Spain, which threw the kidnap plan into jeopardy. Duffy and the four other men then shook hands and parted. The four men and a fifth man were later arrested and charged with attempted extortion of the businessman and of INLA membership. Evidence was heard that when Duffy was detained on 22 June 2007, his house was searched, and books of evidence relating to three of the men charged in connection with the Cork extortion plot were found. Gardaí interviewed Duffy a total of 12 times; Detective Superintendent O'Sullivan said he 'generally was evasive in relation to the answers'. O'Sullivan agreed with Duffy's defence counsel that he had since disassociated with the INLA and this was a 'significant factor'.

Paul Hogan, a school principal and member of the Castlerea Prison visiting committee, also gave evidence and said that he had a 'degree of contact' with Duffy while he was previously in jail. He told the court that he believed the 'penny has finally dropped' for Duffy. Hogan said: 'He has kids – eight and ten years old – who are at a critical point. They need a dad. His partner told me she put it up to him if he doesn't disassociate with all forms of subversive activity, she'll part ways with him. I honestly believe Declan is not going to re-offend. I think Declan is ready to move on with his life, if he's given a chance.'

Because Duffy was being tried in the non-jury Special Criminal Court, three judges decided his fate. The presiding Judge, Ms Justice Elizabeth Dunne, said the offence was a 'serious one'. She said a 'significant factor' in her mind was Duffy's previous conviction 'arising out of the so-called Ballymount incident'. However, she said that he had pleaded guilty to the charge and added that the court 'places significant weight on the public disassociation from the INLA'. She jailed him for four years and backdated the sentence to 2 July 2007. In June 2009 the 35-year-old was in touch with the media again to talk about his proposed extradition to the UK over the Sergeant Newman murder case. He said, in an interview with the *Derby Telegraph* before his court appearance, 'The police have wanted to speak to me about this killing for a very long time and I'm ready to meet them. I won't gain anything by remaining silent during the interview, so I'm going to tell them everything I know. I would never have spoken to the police in the past, but my war is over and there are things I have to get off my chest.' He even claimed that he was prepared to write an apology letter to the dead soldier's family. 'This man was a family man and it is regrettable that he was killed. I would be happy to meet with any member of his family to explain to them the circumstances of why soldiers at that time were targeted. The war is over now and I acknowledge the hurt caused to Irish and English people. I just want to put my past behind me.' Elizabeth Robinson, who was Michael Newman's fiancée, blasted Duffy's apology, saying: 'Writing a letter would devastate his mum and dad. What could he say to his parents? How could he apologise for taking their only son? They [the INLA] wrote to them at the time, explaining that he was just another cog in the wheel. I don't know what he is hoping to achieve by writing to me or his parents. Is he wanting forgiveness for murder? He can say what he likes but he will never get that from me. I became a completely different person after the man I loved was taken away. This is a political war but we are not part of it. I was only 28 when he died and I did not know much about the situation. I am more worldly now and understand they have a political war. I understand they think they have their reasons, but what reason is there for killing anybody?' In October 2009, the INLA issued a statement saying that the time had now come for it to lay down its arms permanently. Although we may have seen the last of the INLA, there is little chance that Declan 'Whacker' Duffy will fade into oblivion once he is finally freed.

FOURTEEN

The emergence of the next generation

Life was becoming very eventful for Wayne McNally, now a senior member of the Rattigan gang. Ever since being shot in the face in February 2007, in what was a very up-close-and-personal encounter with death, Wayne McNally was on a path of self destruction. His self-destructive path would inevitably lead to a lengthy spell behind bars or a violent end. After recuperating for a few months, he came back into the feud with a vengeance and was involved in several incidents. Getting McNally off the streets had been high on the Gardaí's list of priorities. On 10 February 2008, the 23-year-old attempted to gain entry into the Hush Nightclub at the popular Red Cow Inn complex, just off the M50. After getting into the queue, the bouncers decided that they did not want McNally on the premises and turned him away. McNally was angry at the perceived slight. He then got into a row with another man who was also in the queue. One of the bouncers, David Gilsenan, stepped in between the two men to stop the fight. McNally and his opponent walked away, which seemed like the end of the incident. However, McNally returned a while later and asked to go into the club to talk to his girlfriend, who had been allowed in. Mr Gilsenan refused him entry because the club was closing in half an hour. McNally said nothing and walked away, but a few minutes later somebody shouted, 'Watch your back', and the bouncer turned around to see the flash of a gun muzzle and heard a gunshot. The bullet hit Gilsenan between his nose and upper ear and exited behind the same ear. He suffered extensive injuries and was rushed to hospital, while McNally fled in an Audi A4 car. The car had been stolen earlier that night from outside The Square shopping centre in Tallaght. News of the shooting was quickly broadcast on the Garda radio system and officers across the city were on the lookout for a male, his identity not being known at that time. Witnesses described the gunman as 'having the gaunt look of a junkie' and being seemingly 'out of it'. A couple of hours after the shooting, Detective Gardaí Tim O'Keefe and Kieran O'Sullivan from Kevin Street Garda Station were on patrol around the Dolphin's Barn flats complex when they saw Wayne McNally walking towards them. McNally's reputation for violence made him instantly recognisable to the Gardaí. When McNally saw the two officers he dropped a screwdriver from his hand. The Gardaí searched him. They found a second screwdriver and a flashlight. Detective Garda O'Keefe told McNally to put his hands behind his back to be handcuffed. McNally refused, so the Garda grabbed his arm to forcibly cuff him. However, McNally got free and ran through several gardens trying to escape. He had to duck under several clothes lines to avoid knocking himself on his ear. With Detective Garda O'Keefe in hot pursuit, McNally grabbed a wooden pole from a clothesline and pulled it down as he ran past it, hitting the detective on the hand and breaking a bone. The brave Garda kept up the pursuit and tackled McNally, who punched him in the face. The two detectives then managed to restrain and arrest McNally. Unknown to them, McNally was attempting to get back to the stolen Audi and get his hands on the Glock pistol that was sitting on the front passenger's seat. When he was taken back to Kevin Street for questioning, McNally denied any knowledge of the gun or the stolen car, but later confessed when he was shown the firearm. It was fully loaded with six rounds ready to fire. The serial number of the gun had been filed off to make it untraceable. McNally eventually opened up about the shooting of the bouncer and claimed that he had meant to shoot over his head. CCTV footage captured the incident – a young boy had been standing less than 200 yards away from where Gilsenan was shot. McNally told Gardaí: 'I was walking away and something clicked, so I turned around and let a shot off.' McNally was on heroin at the time of the incident and later pleaded guilty to possessing a handgun with intent to endanger life, attempting to cause serious harm to David Gilsenan, possessing a stolen car, assaulting the two Gardaí and having two screwdrivers with intent to commit a crime. He was remanded in custody from the day he was arrested. He was held in prison until he was sentenced in October 2009, when he was jailed for 13 years. It meant that he was now out of the feud permanently, which was a massive blow to the Rattigan mob and a great victory for Gardaí. McNally is considered a violent psychopath, who let his drug addiction get the better of him. He is suspected of being involved in planning the Wayne Zambra murder. His prison term really meant that a violent and dangerous man was off the streets, which had the effect of quelling the feud for a time, because he was a central player and one of Rattigan's major lieutenants.

With Freddie Thompson moving back and forth between Ireland and Spain, because of the various threats to his life, Declan Duffy in prison, and now Wayne McNally locked up, a vacuum developed in Crumlin and Drimagh with new opportunities to move in on territory that Thompson and Rattigan once controlled with iron fists. Much like the way that Declan Gavin and Brian Rattigan had seen an opportunity with the break-up of the Gilligan gang ten years previously – six young upstarts from the local area also saw their chance to make a name for themselves and began to get involved in the feud. Rattigan and Thompson were inclined to turn a blind eye to this next generation of drug dealers, because the youngsters aligned themselves with the two gangs. The six youngsters didn't go out on their own and take on Thompson and Rattigan, because in many cases they were either related to or close associates of some of the main players. Three of the new generation took Thompson's side and the other three joined Rattigan's mob. The new generation, while effectively working for the two gang bosses, pretty much did what they wanted to do, and started to target each other with gusto, much as their bosses did when Declan Gavin's gang split after the Holiday Inn seizure. However, due to legal reasons their identities cannot be relieved. They are all in their late teens or early twenties. The leader of the three that were aligned to the Thompson side is known as 'Mad Dog', from Crumlin. He was the individual who had been Freddie Thompson's driver and who had convinced Thompson to have Jonathan Dunne murder Ian Kenny in July 2007, because he had been involved in a bitter feud with Kenny. The second man is also from Crumlin. He is the son of one of Martin 'The Viper' Foley's closest friends. The third is a relation of one of Freddie Thompson's close associates. On the Rattigan side two of the young men are from Drimnagh, one of which is distantly related to John and Noel Roche, who were both murdered in the feud. The third young member is from Crumlin.

The six men also have their own followers and junior gang members and there are a total of 20 individuals in the second-generation of Crumlin-Drimnagh criminals. Unlike the Thompson and Rattigan gangs who preferred drug dealing to carrying out actual physical crime, the youngsters saw big potential in robbing jewellery stores. There was a spate of armed robberies on jewellers from Dublin to Galway, with members of both sides being arrested and charged with armed robberies. From the summer of 2008 onwards, these next generation of criminals really came into their own and went on the rampage, making sure that Gardaí did not get a second's respite investigating a feud that really should have been coming to a natural end, because most of the main players were either in prison or dead. In July 2008, it seemed – for at least a day – that the youngsters would get their chance to take over one side of the gang completely, when a rumour started to circulate that Freddie Thompson had been murdered in Spain. Several informers contacted their Garda handlers with the news, and Gardaí made informal contact with Police in Spain, but there was no truth to the stories. It is believed that Thompson himself spread the rumour as some sort of tactical ploy to see what the reaction would be back in Dublin to his death. The youngsters would just have to bide their time before taking over completely.

In August 2008, the Gardaí suffered a very public humiliation when a top secret and highly sensitive intelligence document containing the names, addresses, photographs and car registrations of 20 feuding criminals was stolen from the back of a Garda squad car that was parked at Blackrock Garda Station in South Dublin. The highly restricted Criminal Intelligence Bulletin was stolen from the car when it was parked in the private car park at the station. Gardaí in the Organised Crime Unit had compiled the confidential dossier, after learning that both sides of the feud had being renting houses in some of the most salubrious areas of Dublin, including Stepaside, Blackrock, Leopardstown and Dún Laoghaire. The houses were being used as 'safe' accommodation, and the criminals had no idea that Gardaí knew where they were. The list was compiled so that local Gardaí would not be surprised if any of the safe houses were attacked. Garda management was also concerned that innocent people living in houses next to the ones being rented by gang members – or new tenants in houses previously occupied by the criminals – could also inadvertently get caught up in the feuding if their home was pipe bombed or shot at in error. The intelligence report was circulated to detectives around South Dublin stations with a warning that it should not be left where members of the public could access it. The car was left unattended while a detective went into Blackrock station to do some work, and by sheer coincidence, the younger brother of one of the next generation of criminals saw the empty squad car and decided to break into it. As luck would have it, he happened upon the list, which was a veritable treasure trove of information on both the Thompson gang and the Rattigan gang. The names and updated addresses would be highly valuable to the opposite side and they would pay thousands of euro to know the location of their rivals. Gardaí have little doubt that the list was photocopied and distributed to the Thompson gang to be acted on, but once the story of the break-in appeared in the *Sunday Tribune*, the criminals knew their addresses had been compromised, and, nearly without exception, moved away from the addresses. The following week Ken Foy, Crime Correspondent of the *Irish Daily Star Sunday*, received a copy of the dossier in the post. The sender said he was from an organisation called 'Black Watch'. Gardaí have no doubt that the document was sent to Foy so it would be published and the Gardaí embarrassed. Foy printed non-sensitive extracts of the report, and his newspaper received a sizeable circulation boost in the process. In a statement to the *Sunday Tribune* when the story broke, the then Garda Press Officer said: 'The Gardaí are aware that a criminal intelligence document is in the possession of a member of the public. The document was compiled for Garda use only and contains aspects of criminal intelligence, including some personal information. Gardaí are endeavouring to contact those named in the document, and appropriate advice will be given. The circumstances in which this document ended up outside of the Garda organisation are being actively investigated.' Nothing ever came of the investigation though.

During this period Freddie was frequently travelling between Ireland and Spain. He even grew a full beard in a futile effort to avoid recognition. On 19 August, he was stopped in a car, along with his brother Ritchie, on Dolphin Road in Drimnagh. He was wearing a bulletproof vest and joked with Gardaí about his new look. With not a hair on his head and a massive beard, his attempt to go incognito backfired, and he was more recognisable than ever. He soon shaved the beard off and went back to his tried and tested wig.

* * *

On 9 September 2008, Christopher 'Git' McDonagh was watching TV in the bedroom of his home at Woodavens Estate in Ronanstown, West Dublin, when he was startled by the sound of the front door being kicked in. It was just before midnight and by the time the 27-year-old realised what was happening, he was confronted by two gunmen who opened fire on him, with one bullet hitting him in the chest. McDonagh's girlfriend was lying in bed next to him. She ran for her life into the next bedroom. The father of one desperately tried to escape and stumbled across the room to the window, where he jumped onto the porch of the front door before leaping onto the bonnet of a car parked in the driveway. When the two shooters saw him flee they took the sensible option and ran down the stairs into the front garden. Because he had been badly injured after he was shot, McDonagh could only manage to crawl away on his knees and hadn't even made it past the front gate. One of the gunmen ran over to him and fired four shots into his head from close range. He died just minutes later, and the two gunmen escaped in a waiting car, which was driven by a third man. The car had been fitted with a taxi plate so as to not attract people's attention while it was casing the area to check if McDonagh was home. The shooting took place just metres from Ronanstown Garda Station, but by the time officers arrived at the scene, the car was gone, in the direction of Lucan. McDonagh's girlfriend was obviously extremely traumatised by seeing her partner murdered in front of her and she was comforted by friends and relations. The day after the murder, McDonagh's mother left a floral tribute of red and pink roses in the front garden with a note saying: 'All my love my son... I love you, Mam. XXX'

Git McDonagh was a second-hand car dealer and owned a company that operated out of a premises on the Naas Road. McDonagh was involved in criminality and was suspected of laundering drugs money through his company. He was also suspected of associating with several well-known criminal gangs, including Freddie Thompson and Karl Breen. McDonagh was originally from Raphoe Road in Crumlin, and had only moved to Ronanstown four months before his murder. He was well known to Gardaí. In 2006, he handed over €60,000 to the CAB, after he could not account for €40,000 in cash that was found in his possession when Gardaí stopped him in Crumlin in 2004. In 2005, he was given a three-year suspended sentence for possession of a firearm. Both Gardaí and McDonagh knew that his life was in danger, and he had been told that he was being targeted on several occasions before his death. McDonagh obviously took these warnings very seriously and had installed an expensive, high-quality CCTV system in his home, and was paranoid about his personal safety.

Christopher McDonagh's fate might have been sealed on 31 July 2006, when members of the OCU, led by Detective Superintendent Dominic Hayes, stopped two cars at Browns Barn near Tallaght. One of the vehicles contained 350 kg of cannabis resin – the haul had a street value of €2.7m. Four men were detained at the scene and Git McDonagh was arrested later in Terenure. As is commonplace, several criminal gangs had clubbed together to buy the cannabis shipment. Among those involved in the deal was the Thompson gang, the mob led by Karl Breen and the gang that had once been led by Marlo Hyland in Finglas. McDonagh was told to drive out to Dublin 22 to act as a scout around the area and to make sure that no Gardaí were around carrying out surveillance. The drugs run was so secretive that McDonagh was only told a short time before where the drop was going to take place. Twenty minutes after he was told, the Gardaí moved in and arrested the five men. Luckily – or unluckily – for McDonagh, he was not near the location of the drugs bust when he was lifted, so he was released without charge. The fact that McDonagh escaped prosecution, when three of the other four men were charged, coupled with the fact that the arrests had taken place just minutes after he had been told where the drugs delivery was taking place, obviously led the criminals behind the shipment to put two and two together and declare that he was a Garda informant. McDonagh swore that he was not a tout but his pleas fell on deaf ears. The drugs syndicate would obviously want a scapegoat for the Browns Barn seizure and he was going to be it. After the seizure, McDonagh told several Gardaí that he knew he was being blamed for the captured haul and would be shot because of it. McDonagh was never a Garda informant and was not in fact the source of the information received by officers on the day of the bust. Following the seizure, McDonagh concentrated on his used car business and stayed away from dealing drugs. Because he knew his life was under threat, he was ducking and diving and making sure that he did all he could to remain alive. He stopped associating with gangs and probably thought that he had escaped vengeance, as over two years had passed since the Browns Barn seizure. However, two years later his past caught up with him, and revenge, when it came, was ice cold.

Despite not being an informant, Git McDonagh had been a marked man since the day he avoided the drugs rap. The fact that he had only received a suspended sentence after he was found guilty of possession of a firearm didn't help his reputation as a supposed tout. The fact is that several people wanted him dead and there were several gangs in the frame for the murder. McDonagh had been close enough to Freddie Thompson, but detectives favoured the gang that had been led by Karl Breen prior to his jailing as the most likely to have taken McDonagh out. One of the members of the Breen gang, 36-year-old Michael Hendrick, was arrested by Gardaí on suspicion of withholding information in relation to McDonagh's murder but was released without charge. Then Michael Hendrick was murdered in February 2009, as part of an internal gang dispute.

Superintendent Pat Clavin led the investigation into McDonagh's murder, assisted by DI Richard McDonnell and his staff at Ronanstown Garda Station. The officers received a break when the CCTV camera installed at McDonagh's home captured images of the two gunmen. Because the shooting took place at night, the pictures were not very clear, but when officers studied the evidence, they were all in agreement that the stills looked incredibly like Freddie Thompson, although the shooter had been wearing a balaclava. A man who was the same height and weight as Thompson was identifiable, although the images were not strong enough to bring any charges. Gardaí from Crumlin called to Ronanstown Garda Station to offer a second opinion, and they too were in agreement that the stills looked uncannily like Thompson. Detectives in the 'G' District had initially been very skeptical when Freddie Thompson's gang had been mentioned as being possibly involved in the murder. Thompson had been involved in the group purchase of the seized drugs, but his exposure had been less than other criminals, so it was thought that he just simply moved on and got over it. The Browns Barn incident was hardly the first time that his drugs had been seized by Gardaí. Touts were then leaned on for information and several people came back to say that the Thompson gang – although maybe not Freddie himself – may have in fact carried out the murder because they owed money to another gang because of another Garda seizure.

Murdering McDonagh was a way of significantly reducing the debt. The investigation into McDonagh's murder is very much open, and Gardaí have called in the technical experts to help them catch his killer. They are using a UK firm to try to enhance the CCTV images. The system used by this company is tried and tested by British police forces, and has proved successful in UK court cases, but at the beginning of 2010 had yet to be tested before the Irish judiciary. The system can measure the facial features of the killer, the length of his nose and ears, for example, or the distance from his nose to his chin. This information can then be cross-referenced against any suspects in the case, and if it does not confirm the identity of the person caught on camera, it will at least eliminate possible suspects and could even clear Freddie Thompson.

Gardaí policing the day-to-day feud made a very interesting discovery on 29 September 2008, when they raided a luxury apartment in Foxrock after receiving a tip-off that it was being used to store drugs. The detectives from Crumlin and Sundrive Road Garda Stations found a quantity of cocaine, cannabis, weighing scales, as well as document-ation about a property that was being rented in the Castleknock area. The registered renter of the apartment in Foxrock was a 29-year-old from Rathfarnham, who went by three different aliases. He was a known member of the Thompson gang, and Gardaí believed that he was the front man used to rent properties on behalf of the gang. The apartment in Foxrock cost €2,800 a month to rent, and investigations led Gardaí to discover that this individual had rented, using three different aliases and false documentation, at least 16 apartments throughout South Dublin. It was in these apartments that the criminals, whose names had been accidentally leaked in the Garda intelligence bulletin, had stayed in. A number of properties were raided, but all Gardaí found were empty spaces with no personal belongings, except, in almost every case, two bin liners full of top of the range Gucci, Ralph Lauren and Tommy Hilfiger clothes. The criminals were obviously well prepared if they had to make a quick getaway for any reason. They would simply abandon the apartments after spending a few weeks there and walk away. This was despite the fact that six months rent had often been paid in cash to the landlord up front. The only thing that would even have given a hint that they had ever been occupied was the mountains of takeaway cartons and empty pizza boxes stacked in the kitchens. After searching the address in Castleknock, Gardaí found two kilos of cocaine worth about €100,000, as well as weighing scales. The only other item found on the premises was a pair of size four shoes, the size worn by the front man. He was an elusive, dapper sort. Although he had tiny feet, his mouth was big and his silver tongue was well able to fool landlords into thinking he was a businessman and not a gangster. The man was subsequently charged with possession of the cocaine. He is currently before the courts, so cannot be named for legal reasons.

On 9 October, a 25-year-old received serious stab injuries to his face, hand, head and stomach in an alleyway off Ave Maria Avenue in Maryland, after being attacked by Thompson. The victim was singled out by Thompson and his mob, because he was frustrated that Gardaí had been seizing too many drugs belonging to his gang. The man was associating with senior members of the Thompson gang, including David Byrne, Freddie Thompson's cousin. The man is believed to have owed Freddie a sum of money. He was rushed to hospital but refused to cooperate with Gardaí and would not make a statement. He suffered scarring as a result of the attack. Freddie Thompson was arrested close to the scene, along with Liam Brannigan and another man, but they were released without charge. Six days later, Gardaí from the OCU searched a house on Windmill Crescent in Crumlin after securing a search warrant and located a Glock 9mm handgun concealed in an air vent and a further 250 rounds of ammunition for the gun, that was found hidden in the attic. Three members of the Rattigan gang, aged 26, 19 and 17 were arrested, but nobody was charged because the gun was not actually in their possession. The 26-year-old was caught a few weeks later by the Crumlin Drugs Unit, with a large quantity of drugs, and is currently before the courts. The rest of 2008 was relatively quiet and the feud settled down until St Stephen's Day, when Gardaí were called to the Marble Arch Pub on Davitt Road in Drimnagh. When they arrived they saw a man lying unconscious in a side storage area of the pub. The 21-year-old had suffered serious stab wounds, and a trail of blood led from the pub's smoking area to the storage room. The victim had suffered a stab wound to his upper left thigh. He had been attacked for no reason at all. One of the next generation of criminals, who has links to Freddy Thompson was responsible but, the injured party knew the type of individual he was dealing with, and decided not to make a complaint to Gardaí.

On 4 January 2009, Joey O'Brien, who had a habit of getting into trouble with the Thompson gang, walked into Charlie's Chinese fast food shop on Dame Street. He was followed in by five of the main young players in the Thompson mob. 'Mad Dog' started to abuse O'Brien, who was a very handy boxer. Words were exchanged and a 19-year-old from Crumlin walked over and caught O'Brien with a sucker punch to the side of the head, knocking him unconscious. While O'Brien lay helpless on the ground, 'Mad Dog' started to repeatedly jump on his head. He had to be physically pulled off the injured man. Another 19-year-old from Crumlin then hopped on O'Brien's head before the five left the restaurant. Somebody immediately called 999, and Gardaí from nearby Pearse Street rushed to the scene. They observed three men running from the restaurant in the direction of the Lord Edward pub, near Dublin Castle. The Gardaí who arrived at the scene recognised the men, because of their growing notoriety across the city, and were able to give a description, so Gardaí operating the CCTV cameras at Pearse Street were able to follow their every move. Two of the men got into a taxi, which was stopped on Dame Street. A bloodstained hammer was recovered on one of them. A file has been sent to the DPP in relation to the incident and charges are expected to be filed soon.

On the same night, a member of the public rang Gardaí and said that he had observed a man getting out of a jeep, near the Halfway House pub in Walkinstown, and fire three or four shots at a black BMW. The BMW did a u-turn at high speed and drove towards the Walkinstown roundabout. The gunman jumped back into the jeep and turned left onto the Longmile Road. The witness saw four men in the jeep, and the gunman was described as wearing a baseball cap and grey tracksuit. No broken glass or bullet shells were found at the scene. Gardaí believe that a pellet gun may have been used. A 27-year-old from Walkinstown, who is a close associate of Freddie Thompson, was detained nearby along with a 22-year-old. Gardaí were forced to release the two men due to a lack of evidence.

In early 2009, a series of bomb warnings were phoned in to Gardaí, which necessitated the deployment of the army bomb squad to Crumlin and Drimnagh, to deal with the suspect devices. In the first four months of the year, 32 calls were received. Only two devices were found to be viable.

Gardaí believe that the gangs were trying to tie up as much Garda resources as possible, so that they could operate with fewer restrictions. The first hoax call came on 16 January 2009, when Fat Freddie and his cronies were dining at Tiffany's café on the Crumlin Road. Gardaí received a 999 call that a bomb had been placed at the café. Sure enough it was searched and nothing was found. Thompson and his men waved at Gardaí who came to investigate and were obviously aware of the fake call. The criminals had seen how seriously Gardaí took bomb warnings and thought it was hilarious that so much time and resources were being given to every little false warning, so they kept on phoning false reports in. The feuding thugs had also heard that Pringles tubes were often used to hold pipe bombs, so as part of their sick humour, they would get an empty Pringles tube and stick wires out of it. Then they would watch while army bomb disposal experts examined the device, often using robots to check for explosives. At one stage an 11-year-old was arrested for carrying a fake Pringles pipe bomb. The youth was dealt with under the youth cautioning system. Several high-profile members of the feuding gangs were targeted in pipe bomb attacks. On 18 February, a bomb was found under a car belonging to the innocent mother of Freddie Thompson's cousin and key ally, David Byrne. Luckily it didn't explode.

One of the most serious pipe bomb incidents took place on 27 January 2009, when a viable device was placed under the car belonging to Christina Dempsey, mother of Thompson's partner, Vicky, outside the family home on Stanaway Road in Crumlin.

The army bomb disposal unit was called to the scene and carried out a controlled explosion on the pipe bomb. The incident did not go down at all well with Thompson, who was obviously furious that the unwritten rule about leaving family and friends out of the feud had been broken.

Thompson and Vicky Dempsey have been going out since

they were teenagers and have a seven year-old son. They have broken up on numerous occasions only to get back together.

People who know 28-year-old Vicky Dempsey say she is a decent sort who has absolutely no involvement in crime.

The same cannot be said of Vicky's brother, 31-year-old Karl, who was jailed for seven years in July 2000, after being caught with over €60,000 worth of heroin in October 1998, when he was just 21 years old. Detective Garda Frank O'Neill from the Garda National Drugs Unit – and one of the founding members of the Crumlin Drugs Unit – lifted him in The Mill shopping centre in Clondalkin. Dempsey had taken a black plastic bag out of his pocket and thrown it on the floor and attempted to run away. The bag contained five ounces of heroin. In March 2002, CAB went to court and secured a judgment of €424,987 against Dempsey for failing to declare income tax. It was a serious hit to the pocket of the dealer, who had large amounts of property and cars throughout the city.

Karl Dempsey had started using his own product and became an addict, although he cleaned up his act when he was in prison and is now involved in the used car business. Karl Dempsey is regarded as being quite close to Freddie Thompson.

The Dempsey family is very close-knit. They were hit by a terrible tragedy on 18 August 2008, when 26-year-old Lesley Dempsey committed suicide at his apartment in Clondalkin.

Lesley was not involved in crime and was a sensitive young man. His tragic suicide was a massive blow to the whole Dempsey family. Freddie Thompson flew home from Spain to attend the massive funeral. On his first anniversary a big 'do' took place in Lesley Dempsey's honour at the Green Isle hotel in Newlands Cross. It was attended by major gangland figures from across the city and whole country, who were all there to pay their respects. Gardaí kept a discreet eye on the party to see if Freddie Thompson would come back from Spain for it. He didn't but is believed to have donated a sizeable sum towards Suicide Awareness. €100,000 is thought to have been raised that night. Gardaí kept a close eye on the party but it passed off peacefully.

Probably the most successful year that Gardaí have had in taking the feuding gangsters off the streets to serve long stretches behind bars was 2009. Eric Wansboro was a case in point. Born on 13 February 1988, Wansboro was a gifted boxer who represented Ireland and had been national amateur champion in his weight division. He was perhaps talented enough to progress to professional level. However, he suffered a hand injury when he turned 18, which put an end to his promising career and he started to go off the rails. He quickly slipped into a life of cocaine and alcohol abuse. Although Wansboro became a parent, this wasn't enough to keep him on the straight and narrow. He joined the army as a private after his injury, but the disciplined life of a soldier didn't suit him. Wansboro was constantly in trouble with the Gardaí, and was often absent without leave from the army. Wansboro was brought up in Crumlin and although he lived in Rivervalley in Swords, he socialised in Crumlin. He was a member of the Rattigan gang, though he was really only used to do the gang's dirty work, and was never really a trusted lieutenant. Wansboro really began to feature in the feud in 2008. On 13 March that year, he was arrested on Balfe Road in Walkinstown, after a member of the public reported that two cars were involved in a high-speed chase, and that shots had been fired by the occupants of one vehicle. The witness subsequently found two spent shotgun cartridges, which they handed into Crumlin Garda Station. It is not known who the intended target was. Wansboro was released without charge. Military Police officials arrested him on 25 March. He was taken into custody at McKee Barracks after being absent without leave for two months. Three days after his arrest, he appeared before a court martial and was fined 59 days' pay. He was then ordered to remain in soldiers' accommodation in the barracks for ten days. He didn't waste much time sneaking out of his room though, and scaled the wall of the barracks to freedom. Gardaí were immediately alerted. Quick thinking detectives in Crumlin combed Wansboro's known haunts, and arrested him a day after his bid for freedom. He was returned to the custody of the Military Police. In early April 2008, Wansboro paid €300 to buy himself out of his army contract, and there is little doubt that the army was glad to see the back of him, especially considering the public embarrassment he had caused them. Gardaí had serious concerns that army intelligence had failed to note that Wansboro's name was regularly materialising in intelligence reports as being heavily involved in the Crumlin-Drimnagh feud. Wansboro was not the only soldier who was involved in gangland activity. Gardaí and the Defence Forces are aware of at least five incidents over the last few years, where serving soldiers had been approached by organised crime gangs looking for help in carrying out armed robberies and other criminal acts. The high levels of training in firearms and other military techniques make soldiers particularly attractive for criminals, and Wansboro was a good example. He was only out of the army a matter of days when he was again arrested by Gardaí. On 9 April, he was questioned on suspicion of firing two blasts from a shotgun into a house in Crumlin. Four days later, he was also arrested after allegedly firing shots through the window of an associate of Freddie Thompson, after words were exchanged in a pub in Dublin 8. Nobody was injured in either incident, but because he had become such a key player in the feud, Gardaí began to place him under constant surveillance. This paid off on 19 August when Detective Inspector Peter O'Boyle, who had been a Detective Sergeant in Crumlin at the time of Declan Gavin's murder but had since been promoted and transferred to Ballyfermot, received confidential information about Eric Wansboro and the proposed delivery of a gun.

Garda Padraig O'Meara stopped a taxi at Ruby Finnegan's pub on Sarsfield Road in Ballyfermot. Wansboro was searched and a 9mm revolver was found hidden in his sock and four rounds of ammunition were found in his jacket pocket. The revolver had originally been a starting gun but had been reconstructed so that it could be fired as a conventional gun. Wansboro had only been holding the gun for the Rattigan mob and was due to hand it over to another gang member when he was nabbed by Gardaí. Gardaí arrested gang member Mr X close to the pub at the same time as Wansboro, but detectives swooped before the handover took place. Mr X was arrested and questioned, but was subsequently released without charge. Wansboro was immediately charged, and because of the seriousness of the offence, was remanded in custody, which was a major boost for Gardaí, because he has been causing them so much trouble over the past few months. In October 2009, Wansboro appeared before Dublin Circuit Criminal Court and was handed a four-year sentence for possession of the firearm after he pleaded guilty. He was also charged with a serious assault that took place on O'Connell Street in May 2007, in which the victim suffered serious facial injuries. Wansboro had used his boxing skills to knock a man to the ground, after words were exchanged between two groups, and proceeded to kick him while he lay helpless. He was jailed for two years for that assault, but the sentence was to run concurrently with his firearms sentence. It was his 21st criminal conviction.

In July 2009, the Rattigan gang was dealt yet another hammer blow when Shane Maloney, a close friend of Rattigan, was jailed for ten years, after being arrested with €1.2m worth of heroin at the Palmerstown Shopping Centre on 13 August 2008. Maloney, from Drimnagh Road, had driven to Abrakebabra in his own car on the night that Declan Gavin was murdered. Maloney pleaded guilty to the possession of the drugs for sale or supply. He had been caught on the hop by Gardaí, carrying the product, after the person who was meant to pick up the drugs pulled out at the last minute. Members of the Organised Crime Unit, led by former Crumlin Detective Garda Ronan Lafferty, had received a tip-off that drugs were being moved and watched from a discreet distance as Maloney parked his car outside the shopping centre and took a bag from the back seat of a car that was parked nearby. Gardaí swooped when Maloney returned to his own car. The officers saw two brown packages in the passenger seat of his car and more packages in the back. Resigned to his fate, he said: 'It's only brown,' meaning heroin. When he was arrested the 27-year-old refused to comment during a series of interviews. At his court appearance his barrister said that Maloney came from a decent family and regretted his involvement. The barrister added that Maloney was making the best of a bad situation and had started studying in prison. The conviction was his 85th.

Although Gardaí were getting some notable collars, they were still fighting an almost impossible battle, because the new generation of criminals were so prolific in causing mayhem. On 24 February, 'Mad Dog' and one of his minions were arrested after one of them got out of a car on Sperrin Road in Drimnagh, and fired five shotgun rounds through the front window. Young members of the Rattigan gang were in the house and managed to run out to the back garden and flee without anybody being injured. On the same day, the house that had once belonged to the young relation of Noel and John Roche had windows damaged. The members of the Thompson gang didn't realise that their target hadn't lived in the house for years. Three days later, there was retaliation from the Rattigan side, when the family home of 'Mad Dog' had windows damaged and a car parked in the front garden was also vandalised. The tit-for-tat petty attacks continued. Later the same day, the house on Sperrin Road that had been shot at a few days before had windows damaged by the Thompson mob, while the home of a Thompson member was attacked causing damage to the windows. On 28 February, the same house was shot up and five shotgun cartridges were recovered. 'Mad Dog' was detained, along with three of his junior cronies, but the homeowner refused to make a statement to Gardaí. There were dozens of petty attacks like this throughout the first three months of 2009. The young criminals were causing a nuisance to Gardaí more than anything else, but nevertheless, they were regularly discharging firearms, which was obviously potentially very dangerous and a massive challenge to Gardaí trying to police Crumlin and Drimnagh.

The older feuding criminals had long since stopped smashing windows – when they struck they meant business and went armed with firearms. The youngsters hadn't been educated to this extent yet. On 7 March, four or five young men from the Rattigan gang tried to break into Graham Whelan's home on Clonard Road in Crumlin. They shouted from outside the front door that they were there to kill the drug dealer. Armed with lump hammers, they smashed glass in the front door and windows, but couldn't force their way into the house – luckily for Whelan. They escaped in a silver Renault Megane. On the same day, a silver Megane pulled up outside a house on Dolphin Road in Drimnagh, and a number of men got out armed with lump hammers. The men proceeded to smash up three cars that were parked in one front garden. They obviously took the fact that they couldn't get to Graham Whelan out on the cars. Over the next two days, the same Renault Megane was seen ferrying young men around the area. Several more vehicles were damaged and four more houses were shot up. Again, it was the next generation of criminals trying to make their mark.

Although Gardaí had their hands full trying to investigate these dozens of relatively minor incidents, detectives would soon have much bigger problems on their hands. Not as big as Brian Rattigan though. By July 2009, his gang would effectively be permanently broken up. Rattigan would be finally facing his day of reckoning over Declan Gavin's murder, over eight years previously. Rattigan's fate was in the hands of a jury of 12 who had the power to decide his future. If they believed that he was responsible for Declan Gavin's murder, he would be facing life in prison. If they didn't, then he would be a free man in just a few short years. It was a prospect that Gardaí in Crumlin didn't even want to contemplate.

FIFTEEN

The demise of the
Rattigan gang

In January 2009, Brian Rattigan's murder trial for the stabbing to death of Declan Gavin in August 2001 finally got under way at Dublin's Central Criminal Court. Rattigan had done everything possible to stop the trial ever going ahead. He was in and out of the High Court and Supreme Court, on dozens of occasions, filing applications to have the charges dismissed because of negative media coverage or the fact that several of the witnesses that he had planned to call had died. It was all to no avail though, and on 13 January, he arrived at the court to face a jury of 12 of his peers who would decide whether or not he was going to spend the rest of his life behind bars.

From the beginning, Gardaí had severe trouble in trying to get witnesses, who had given statements in 2001, to go to court and repeat in public what they had seen. A lot of the reluctance stemmed from the fact that many witnesses were very young when Declan Gavin was murdered; they had since moved on with their lives and didn't want the past dragged up again. However, in a lot of cases there was a more sinister explanation. There is no doubt that many people scheduled to give evidence were intimidated and threatened that if they turned up in court, there would be repercussions. Several people went to Gardaí and informally told them that they had been approached by associates of Rattigan, but everyone was too scared to make statements. As a result, the long list of good witnesses that Gardaí had – the number of people that could actually be counted on to speak out in open court – started to shrink. The Crime Task Force at Crumlin Garda Station was tasked with delivering the 37 civilian witness orders. It was a nightmare job with many of the witnesses ducking and diving from the Gardaí and refusing to take possession of the subpoenas. By the first day of the trial, 31 orders had been served and six were outstanding. The case was to be heard in front of experienced trial judge Barry White. One of the first things the judge did was to issue six bench warrants for the arrests of the no-show witnesses. In most cases, those arrest warrants still haven't been executed because Gardaí haven't been able to track down the half-dozen witnesses who are in contempt of court.

Opening the case for the prosecution, senior counsel Edward Comyn called the incident outside Abrakebabra a 'targeted attack'. He went on to say that a lot of young people had been gathered outside the restaurant and 'a body of credible evidence will emerge from their descriptions'. He went into detail about Shane Maloney's Nissan Micra pulling up outside with three or four young men inside.

'A passenger got out of the car. He had a sort of balaclava on his head, had a large knife in one of his hands. It appears that people in the car were shouting "Get him, get the rat," Comyn said, before adding that the shouting 'seems to show there was some malice toward somebody outside Abrakebabra. It is the prosecution's case that that person was Declan Gavin.' Comyn said that Brian Rattigan 'ran at Mr Gavin and attacked him. The evidence will show you that the first blow was to the arm and that the second blow struck the chest, deep enough to reach into his heart, which ultimately proved fatal.' The barrister said that blood found on the front window of Abrakebabra and to the left of the front door would be of 'particular significance' in the trial.

During the first few days of the trial, several witnesses were called and spoke about their memories of the night in question. Brian Rattigan was present in court and listened intently to the evidence, as did a large number of journalists. Dinah Rattigan attended the trial every day along with her sister. Mark Skerrit, who had hit the person who stabbed Gavin with a golf club, took to the stand on the second day of the trial. He spoke of the original row outside the chipper and said, 'There was a lot of tension going on.' He then described how a Nissan Micra pulled up outside Abrakebabra. 'It looked like there was a few in it. It pulled in like a taxi pulling in to pick someone up.' He then 'heard a scream' from the Micra, 'they screamed "rat"', he added. 'All of a sudden there was a fella running with a balaclava on... He had a knife... It was big. When he got out of the car, everybody scattered. He was running with a knife in his hand. He was running for someone. He was running around like he was looking for someone. He found the fella he was looking for and Declan Gavin was on the ground, stabbed like.' Skerritt continued that the man in the balaclava 'ran towards him and stabbed him. I don't know where, in the chest I think.'

Skerritt then described how he 'grabbed a golf club off one of the young fellas and chased the guy. I hit him a couple of times in the shoulders and head as he was getting into the car.' After the Nissan Micra pulled away, Declan Gavin was on the ground, 'He was pale white, blood all over him.'

A young woman gave evidence about meeting Declan Gavin in the queue in the chipper. 'I hadn't seen him in a few years. We talked for about 10 minutes. He was in grand form; he was real relaxed.' She added: 'Declan said he'd pay for the food.'

Another woman, who had gone to the assistance of Gavin in the kitchen of the chipper, swore under oath that she 'can't remember a thing about that night'. 'It's all a blur to me', she said. She said that she knew about what happened to Declan

Gavin 'from the newspapers'. She did manage to get over her amnesia for a time though, and said that she saw Gavin go into Abrakebabra and that people were 'screaming his name'. She heard that he was hurt and she and a friend assisted him by putting toilet roll on his chest wound. Other witnesses gave evidence about not remembering anything of the events which took place on the night of the murder.

After this, the trial went into legal argument in the absence of the jury for four days. Senior Counsel for the defence, Brendan Grehan, had made an application to have the case dismissed after claiming that there was not enough evidence to sustain the murder charge. This meant that all the evidence in the case had to be heard by the judge before it could be put before the jury. In any event, Judge White agreed that the trial should proceed, but during this legal argument, the Achilles heel of the state's case against Rattigan came out. This was the decision by Gardaí from the Technical Bureau not to take a sample of blood from the fingerprint left by Rattigan on the exterior door of Abrakebabra, instead taking a sample of blood splatter four inches below. With hindsight it was a serious mistake, and left the defence an angle to argue that nobody knew for sure if it was Declan Gavin's blood in the middle of Rattigan's fingermark.

After the trial resumed, Detective Sergeant Joe O'Hara spoke about arresting Brian Rattigan for the murder and of Rattigan saying that he had 'the wrong person' and that he had, done nothing wrong. I am a nobody.' O'Hara also told of how a doctor had examined Rattigan and had found 'no physical injury of note,' which was at odds with what Mark Skerritt had said about hitting the person who stabbed Gavin with a golf club about the shoulders and head. Detective Superintendent Dominic Hayes told of how Rattigan had claimed he was with a married woman whose 'fella was away' on the night of the murder. When Hayes asked Rattigan who the woman was, so she could give him an alibi, Rattigan

responded: 'No f***ing way, you can find her for yourself.'
Dominic Hayes also spoke about putting it to Rattigan that a
lot of people witnessed the stabbing that night and said
Rattigan answered him with, 'They can say what they like,
but they will have to say it all in court.' It seems that Brian
Rattigan was prophetic in that respect. People were reluctant
to speak up when it came to the crunch. Rattigan's defence
counsel, Brendan Grehan, put it to Hayes that his client had
'no recollection' of saying that he had not been to
Abrakebabra for four months before the murder. The
Detective Superintendent responded: 'His replies were noted.
He agreed they were correct.'

The trial then moved on to the forensic evidence against
the accused. Detective Garda Christopher O'Connor told
the court that he had 14 years' experience with the
fingerprint section of the Garda Technical Bureau and
noticed 'a mark in what appeared to be blood' on the exterior
of the window to the left of the front door. He used a
developing agent of grey powder to develop an area around
the mark, which was photographed by Detective Garda
Caroline Hughes. Detective Garda O'Connor said that he
then compared the mark with a set of fingerprints taken from
Brian Rattigan on 22 November 2001, and 'formed the
opinion that the mark found on the window is the same as
the set of prints bearing the name Brian Rattigan'. He said
that he found '12 features of comparison' in both. He
continued his evidence by describing how he compared a
mark on the exterior of the door, above the door handles; he
had compared it to Brian Rattignan's fingerprints, and
formed the opinion that the prints were the same. Of the 21
prints found on the door and window that night, all except
two had been matched.

On Friday 6 February, the prosecution finished presenting
its case, leaving the way clear for the defence to present

evidence. Brendan Grehan took to his feet and announced that Brian Rattigan wasn't mounting any defence. Grehan is a master legal operator – maybe the best in the country. Grehan formulated a very unusual and bold strategy by instructing the jury that Brian Rattigan had been in custody since 15 February 2003, and was serving cumulative sentences of 13 years with one year suspended. It was a remarkable tactic. One can only assume that Grehan and his client were playing the honesty card with the jury, by admitting that Rattigan was involved in criminality, and thought that this honesty would make the jury think that if he willingly told them that he was in prison, then maybe he hadn't murdered Declan Gavin. Whatever the reason, it was almost unprecedented, and in many ways it was a masterstroke and really served to muddy the waters. This had senior Gardaí incredibly worried.

On 9 February, both sides began their summing-up evidence for the jury. Senior Counsel Pauline Walley summed up the prosecution's case. She told the jury: 'The knife-man was Mr Rattigan for very simple reasons. You can be satisfied beyond reasonable doubt because his marks were found on the window beside the door. The marks were found in places central to the movement of the injured man, bleeding, trying to get in the door of Abrakebabra.' She said that after Rattigan was interviewed by Gardaí, eleven days after the murder, he had claimed that he had not been to Abrakebabra for four months. 'You know that that is a huge and whopping great lie, because, nine days before the alleged murder, the glass of the window was changed. If Mr Rattigan was telling the truth and was not there for four months how could his palm mark be there on the window?' Walley asked.

She said that the mark was found four inches above an area from which a swab of blood was taken, which was later matched to Mr Gavin. 'Although the swab was taken below the mark, you can infer the blood at the mark was Mr Gavin's.'

Brendan Grehan, in summing up the defence's case, said that 'the most striking thing about this case... is the lack of evidence. Ms Walley omits the fact that 17 other prints were found there, never identified. When you look at the evidence in this case, be very sceptical of what has been served up to you.'

Grehan returned to the decision to inform the jury of the fact that Rattigan was currently serving a lengthy prison sentence. He said that this was necessary because Rattigan had been 'surrounded by three burly prison officers' during the trial and this fact must have 'struck' the jury. He said that Rattigan displayed 'a total lack of co-operation or respect for the Gardai' when he was interviewed about the murder, and added: 'Mr Rattigan is no angel. I don't pretend he is. Nor does he.'

Grehan also brought up the delay in bringing the case to court, saying his client 'has been available for charge since February 2003, but here you are told by Ms Walley that they have an open-shut case with the benefit of forensic science'. Grehan said that 'key evidence the prosecution sought to rely on simply collapsed in on itself – the suggestion that the swab of blood taken from the print at the scene matched to Mr Rattigan and the blood DNA-matched to Mr Gavin. The swab didn't come from the mark at all. It was taken from somewhere below the mark.' This meant the prosecution 'cannot prove it is blood'. Grehan said that it could even be 'tomato sauce' that they simply did not know. He said that this was not evidence on which the jury could be satisfied beyond reasonable doubt, and that the prosecution had failed to forensically link the print to Declan Gavin. Grehan added that this created a reasonable doubt and therefore the jury must find in favour of his client and return a not guilty verdict.'

The jury was then directed by Mr Justice White and sent to consider its verdict. After four days, there was still no verdict and the jury was obviously judiciously carrying out its function and carefully considering all the evidence. Under new legislation introduced just weeks before, the jury was allowed to go home each evening rather than being sequestered in a hotel. Some Gardaí believed that if they were forced to stay in a hotel, it might concentrate their minds and help them to reach a verdict if they knew they couldn't go home to their comfortable beds until they had done so. The jury was told after two days of deliberation that the court would accept a majority verdict but they were still deadlocked. After the fourth day, the jury of six men and six women returned and told Mr Justice White that they could not agree on a verdict. The Judge had little choice but to declare a hung jury, which was an excellent result for Rattigan. He had seen the Gardaí's case against him and would not be surprised by any evidence that would be thrown at him if and when another trial took place. Gardaí and the DPP quickly decided that they would seek a retrial, so although Rattigan had probably won the battle, he had not won the war. The new trial date was set for November 2009. Back on the streets, where the real war was happening, Rattigan was not so lucky, and over the next few months would be hit with a fatal double blow.

At 8.40pm on 13 March, Shay O'Byrne and Brian Rattigan's 26-year-old sister, Sharon, were loading a buggy into their car outside their rented house in Tymon North Park in Tallaght, when a lone gunman emerged from the shadows. The gunman calmly walked over towards O'Byrne and quickly let off three rounds from a revolver, hitting him in the back. Sharon turned around and realised what was happening. She made a beeline for the balaclava-wearing assassin and jumped at him. The last thing the shooter expected was to be tackled by the plucky female. She lunged at the gunman and pulled the balaclava partially off his head and scratched his face. The man didn't know what to do, so he pulled the trigger of his gun and shot Rattigan in the leg, but the bullet miraculously went straight through her. Even being shot didn't stop the gutsy mother, and she managed to knock the gun out of the shooter's hand and also made him drop his mobile phone. The gunman didn't wait around for round two. He ran to a getaway car that was revving its engine just metres away and managed to escape. Sharon didn't stop to think about her injury but ran over to Shay O'Byrne, who was her childhood sweetheart. O'Byrne was lying slumped on the concrete, a large pool of blood flowing from his open wounds. The emergency services were summoned to the scene but it was too late for O'Byrne, who died on the way to hospital. Sharon Rattigan was also taken to Tallaght Hospital for treatment, but she discharged herself soon after. Her 18 month-old son had been in the house when his daddy was shot outside the front garden. Sharon had to be heavily sedated. She was brought back to her mother Dinah's house, and never returned to Tymon Park North, because she couldn't deal with what happened there. She was in shock for weeks after O'Byrne's slaying.

If Sharon was in shock over the murder, then her brother Brian was in an uncontrollable rage. When he heard what happened, in his cell in Portlaoise Prison, he saw red and smashed the cell up and started screaming and crying at the top of his voice. Prison staff had to restrain him. He was put into a special straight jacket until he calmed down and was sent to solitary confinement. Shooting a female was a new low in the feud, and there was little doubt that it would lead to repercussions down the line, even if the gunman wasn't actually trying to murder Sharon Rattigan, but merely trying to get her off him so he could escape. Shay O'Byrne's murder was a personal killing carried out to send out a message to Brian Rattigan that his power base was now gone and that he was effectively defeated. O'Byrne and Rattigan were like brothers, and O'Byrne's murder was a type of genocide, with the Thompson gang wanting to kill as many of Rattigan's relatives as possible. Shay was 15 months younger than Rattigan. He had been going out with Sharon since his early teens. He was one of the founding members of the drugs gang. It is fair to say that he was far from one of the top dogs in the gang, but he was a trusted junior lieutenant and regularly acted as Rattigan's driver before he was jailed. O'Byrne worked as a runner for the gang on and off. He would pick a bit of product up in one place and drop it off at another. He had been a target for the Garda National Drugs Unit for years but had never been caught with drugs. O'Byrne was not the worst type of criminal in that he was a dedicated family man and was very much in love with Sharon. He was probably only still used by the gang because he was effectively related to Brian and was part of the Rattigan family. He lived at the family home on Cooley Road for several years, and was asleep in bed with Sharon when Freddie Thompson and Paddy Doyle burst in and shot Brian in March 2002. In November 2005, Gardaí had found 14 shotgun cartridges in a car that was used by O'Byrne, close to his old address at Lansdowne Valley in Drimnagh, but apart from that, he very much operated on the periphery of the gang, and like other victims of the feud, was an easy target. O'Byrne had not taken the proper precautions when it came to his personal safety. He had changed addresses on several occasions over the years but had lived at the same rented house in Tallaght for nearly six months prior to his murder, and his address was well known by the rival gang. Because he was not a key player in the Rattigan gang, he might have thought that he was safe enough.

A murder investigation was immediately launched at Tallaght Garda Station under the command of Detective Inspector Pat Lordan. On the face of it, Gardaí had a huge amount of evidence because although the murder had been carried out, several aspects of it had been spectacularly botched. The suspected gunman, who is 31 and from Bray, Co. Wicklow, was waiting close to O'Byrne's house for well over an hour before the actual shooting took place. The man decided that he was thirsty and went to a nearby newsagent where he bought a four pack of Red Bull energy drinks. He drank one, and naïvely threw it on the ground, obviously not realising that Gardaí would be soon combing the area for any little bit of forensic evidence. His DNA was all over the drink can. When the gunman saw Shay O'Byrne emerge from the house, he did manage to shoot him dead, but was taken by surprise by Sharon Rattigan's ferocity and determination. Instead of shrugging her off and getting away, he got involved in a tussle, where Sharon managed to partially pull his balaclava off his head. She also scratched him. This again left open the possibility that Sharon would have his DNA under her fingernails. Undoubtedly his biggest error was dropping his own gun on the ground after being struck by Rattigan. The forensic evidence that could be gleaned from the gun was immense and a huge plus for Gardaí. He also dropped his mobile phone at the scene, but, luckily for him, it was later determined that the handset had just been bought, and no numbers had been dialled from the phone, therefore there was not a lot the Gardaí could do with it. The Red Bull can would prove to be a crucial piece of evidence. Another full can was found close to the murder scene, and Gardaí were able to tie the drink to the local newsagents by the special batch number printed on the side of the can. This discovery opened up the possibility of witnesses in and around the newsagents and CCTV footage being available to identify the shooter. It was an almost comical tale of ineptitude, which was not typical of the gunman. He was hired by the Thompson gang through a well-known criminal based in Bray. The gunman came highly recommended, and is a suspect in four other gangland killings. He is the man that some Gardaí believe may have murdered Darren Geoghegan and Darren Byrne in November 2005, although most sources don't believe it. He had obviously had a bad day at the office when he went to shoot O'Byrne.

Detectives arrested three members of the Thompson gang in a car in Crumlin just an hour after the murder. Members of the Organised Crime Unit had spotted the men around Tallaght on the afternoon of the murder in a Nissan car. When witnesses described seeing a Nissan speed away from the scene, Gardaí immediately thought of the trio and took them into custody, but they were released because they had nothing to do with the shooting.

Another four people – including a 16-year-old girl – were also detained in the days after the murder, and again released without charge. After tying the mobile phone to the suspected hitman through DNA, Gardaí had enough evidence to arrest him and swooped on the afternoon of 17 March. The 31-year-old was arrested at his home in Bray and taken into custody at Tallaght Garda Station. During his four days of questioning, he refused to say a single word and would not engage with Gardaí at all. Despite him exercising his right to silence, Gardaí were very confident that the DPP would come back with directions to charge him. If they couldn't get a charge after all of the mistakes he had made and the evidence he had left behind him, then something would have been seriously wrong. But that is exactly what happened. The DPP's office reviewed the evidence in the case and decided that there was not enough to charge the suspect there and then. They ordered that he should be released and a full file be sent in for consideration. In truth, it was embarrassing for Gardaí, but sources say that once the completed file is submitted, they are very confident that directions will come back to charge the man with murder.

The gunman left Ireland in the days after the murder, because he was afraid that the Thompson gang would try to murder him to stop him from being tempted to cooperate with Gardaí. However, he came back after a couple of months.

Shay O'Byrne's murder was a big personal blow to Brian Rattigan and his extended family, but it had little impact on his ability to do business and the feud continued in earnest. Gardaí were continuing to have major success against the feuding criminals. In March, a 22-year-old was arrested in possession of a loaded Glock handgun on the Crumlin Road. A search of his house saw a stolen sawn-off shotgun seized as well as a pistol silencer. He is currently charged before the courts. In April, a member of the Rattigan gang was arrested in possession of a 9mm Luger handgun close to his home in Crumlin. The 27-year-old is also before the courts. The Limerick connection is obviously still alive and well, with the various feuding factions continuing to do business together. In April 2009, Gardaí from Mayorstone Park in Limerick, observed 'Fat' John McCarthy from Moyross in the passenger seat of a car on the Long Pavement Road being closely followed by a Dublin registered Range Rover. The Range Rover was stopped, and among its passengers were Graham Whelan and two junior members of the Thompson mob. They were doing nothing wrong and were allowed to go on their way, but it is doubtful that Whelan was down in Limerick on his holidays.

The following night, Brian Rattigan received yet another kick in the stomach when Mr X was arrested following an incident in which shots were fired at a pursuing Garda squad car. Mr X was arrested and a Walther pistol with seven rounds of ammunition was recovered. A 25-year-old is currently before the courts charged with the possession of a firearm.

The final nail in the coffin of Brian Rattigan's gang was struck on 17 July 2009. Anthony Cannon, a 26-year-old

Rattigan enforcer, was dropped off by car close to Ruby
Finnegan's pub in Ballyfermot at 3.50pm to go to a pre-
arranged meeting. The area is known locally as 'The Ranch'.
Cannon walked along the street behind the pub and turned
onto a laneway leading to the Liffey Gaels GAA pitch. He
realised that he was being followed and had been set up. So
he attempted to climb a gate onto Longmeadows Park, when
he was confronted by a man armed with a pistol. He ran
down the road to try to escape from his killer, but the
gunman pursued him, opening fire as he ran. Cannon was hit
with a bullet to the back and fell to the ground. The gunman
stepped over him and shot him twice in the head at point-
blank range, killing him. A total of 11 shots were discharged.
CCTV footage clearly captured Cannon attempting to run
away, before the gunman, who was wearing a motorbike
helmet, caught up with him, shot him and escaped on a
motorbike being driven by an accomplice. Cannon was well
aware that his life was in danger and was wearing a
bulletproof vest when he was shot. But as Freddie Thompson
once told Gardaí, there is little point in wearing a vest when
you get shot in the head. Youngsters who had been playing
on the street witnessed the murder, which took place in
broad daylight. Cannon was originally from Robert Street in
Dublin 8, and was the last remaining 'hard man' in the
Rattigan gang. His job was to get money that was owed to the
gang from addicts who hadn't paid up. Apparently, the sight
of Anthony Cannon in a van was enough to make junkies
soil themselves. He was said to have taken several people up
the mountains and handed out horrendous beatings over
small sums of money that were owed. As well as dishing out
the hidings, Cannon often acted as the middleman in drugs
deliveries. He was arrested on 21 May 2008 at a house on
Hughes Road South in Crumlin. Unbeknownst to him,
Gardaí had raided the house a few minutes before and
recovered €1m worth of heroin and €36,850 in cash. Three

members of the one family were in the process of being arrested when Cannon, using his own key, let himself into the house. Gardaí believe that he was there to collect the drugs and deliver them elsewhere. Cannon was arrested and charged under sections 3 and 15 of the Misuse of Drugs Act, but the charges were subsequently dropped because he was not in the house with the drugs when detectives first arrived. Gardaí had raided the house after receiving confidential information about Cannon's activities. An informant had told them of how he would ring a drugs courier on his mobile phone and tell him to go to a certain location. When the courier got there, a holdall would be waiting for him with a couple of kilos of heroin and another mobile phone. The courier then picked up the drugs; Cannon would ring the new phone and tell the courier to break the drugs up into a certain amount of individual deals. When the drugs were broken down, the courier would get another call from Cannon, who would tell them where to drop the holdall. When the drop took place, an envelope containing €2,000 in cash would be waiting for the courier. Cannon would then pick up the drugs and deliver them to other smaller dealers. He himself would receive in excess of €5,000 for his troubles, so it was a lucrative little business.

Cannon had a number of criminal convictions. He was fined for the possession of cannabis resin in 2006, but had a more serious charge of possession of ecstasy for sale and supply struck out in 2002. His longest prison sentence was one year for criminal damage. He was suspended from driving for ten years in February 2008, and given a suspended six-month jail sentence for careless driving and giving a false name to Gardaí. He was due in court the week after his murder on public-order and assault charges. These were subsequently struck out. Cannon, along with Wayne McNally, had become the main lynchpin for the Rattigan gang and the pair of them wreaked havoc together. Cannon was the suspect in the shooting of Freddie Thompson's grandparent's home in June 2008. He was also under investigation for an incident where the home of a 26-year-old Rattigan associate was shot at on the June Bank Holiday weekend in 2009. The man was asleep on the couch in his home on Derry Road, when three shots were fired through the front window. One of them hit him in the leg, although he was not seriously injured. He had paid €6,000 the previous week for reinforced glass. His house had been shot at the previous March, with damage being done to the front door, so he didn't want to take any chances and invested in the expensive glass, although it failed to stop the bullet anyway. A car was heard screeching away from the scene, and Cannon was nominated as having fired the shots. He had been involved in the feud for years but had only really started to get to the top rung of the ladder in the gang in the last couple of years before his death. He was arrested as part of the Paul Warren murder investigation, as far back as March 2004, although he is not regarded as having been involved in the actual killing. Loyalty means a lot to Brian Rattigan, and Cannon had earned his stripes time and time again over the years. Rattigan had trusted him enough to let him be the point man with the Keane gang in Limerick. It was Cannon who was arrested outside the pub in Crumlin in April 2007, when Liam Keane pointed a Glock at a motorist who had wolf whistled at Natasha McEnroe.

The Gardaí at Ballyfermot Garda Station were tasked with handling the investigation into Anthony Cannon's murder. The probe was led by Superintendent John Quirke with Detective Inspector Peter O'Boyle leading the plainclothes officers who would investigate the shooting on a day-to-day basis. The investigation is still ongoing and it is known that Anthony Cannon had started to encroach on the drug dealing territory in Dublin 22 that had once been controlled by Karl Breen, prior to his jail sentence.

Rattigan had seen Fat Freddie and his mob cannibalise a lot of his territory in Crumlin and Drimnagh because of the gang's sheer size and the fact that it had far more muscle than his side. Rattigan ordered his associates to broaden their horizons and to expand in order to keep making money. This was obviously a very dangerous tactic, because areas are traditionally well defined, and a gang only starts dealing in rival areas if it is prepared to fight for the privilege. The Rattigan gang simply did not have the appetite or the strength to fight anyone, so Cannon was playing a dangerous game. The man suspected of ordering the hit on Cannon is 34 years old and is a well-known figure in organised crime in Dublin. He has been responsible for at least three gangland murders over the last decade. This man has been implicated in the murder of suspected informer Keith Ennis, who was followed to Amsterdam in March 2009, dismembered and put in a suitcase before being thrown into a canal. When the 34-year-old finished a jail sentence, he took over Karl Breen's former business in Ballyfermot. He has also become embroiled in a feud in Dublin 22, in which several men have been murdered. Anthony Cannon was blamed for an assassination attempt on this man in 2006 in Tallaght, in which the crime lord was hit in the arm. Cannon owed him money and decided to murder him rather than pay the debt, but the hit did not go down as planned. Cannon always knew that revenge for that botched hit was on the cards at some point, and once he and other gang members started dealing in Ballyfermot, there was only one way things were going to go. If it wasn't the 34-year-old that got Cannon, somebody else would have. It can't have failed to have struck Thompson and his gang that he was the last remaining rock in Rattigan's crumbling foundation, especially because Cannon had shot at Fat Freddie's grandparent's house, which was like putting a red rag in front of a bull. When you live by the sword you invariably die by it, and Cannon knew that as well as anyone. He probably knew that it was inevitable that he would breathe his last breath staring down the barrel of a gun.

With McNally jailed and Cannon dead, the Rattigan gang had effectively been defeated. There were still members on the streets, but they were only concerning themselves with moving drugs around the place and had no real interest in taking up arms against the Thompson gang. According to prison officer sources, when Rattigan heard of the murder of his right-hand man, he was deeply depressed. He put on a brave face and continued to direct operations from his prison cell but he must have privately known that the game was up and that his power base was destroyed, probably forever. It might have been different if he was on the streets himself, taking the fight to the other side, but there was only so much you could do in jail. Even if he managed to get off on the Declan Gavin murder, it would be 2012 before he was a free man. Probably by then he would be forgotten, subsumed by the even more ruthless next generation of criminals who were already starting to smell blood and wanted to take over his patch for themselves.

With Gardaí quietly confident that the worst of the feud was now over and that a victory of sorts was in sights, the boys in blue got the chance to get their first ever feud-related murder conviction. This chance came when Craig White appeared before Dublin's Central Criminal Court charged with the murder of Noel Roche, on the Clontarf Road on 15 November 2005. The trial kicked off on 14 July 2009, in front of Mr Justice George Birmingham. Senior Counsel Anthony Sammon told the jury during his opening statement that they would hear that on the night of the murder, Noel Roche left the Point Depot with friends suddenly at around 9.30pm in a Ford Mondeo. A stolen Peugeot drove up alongside the Mondeo near the junction of Seafield Road and Clontarf Road, and a number of shots were fired, killing Roche. Some time later, a lady on nearby

Furry Park Road, saw two men abandon the Peugeot. The Gardaí arrived and the vehicle was forensically examined. Evidence was found linking 23-year-old Craig White to the car. Sammon continued that a brown paper bag containing a balaclava, a gun, a tea towel and gloves was found in the rear seat of the Peugeot. White's fingerprints were found on the bag and his DNA was also recovered from the handles of bag. Two gloves that were found along Furry Park Road both contained White's DNA, and fibres on the gloves could also be linked to the abandoned Peugeot. A container of petrol was found in the footwell of the car, and Sammon said that the inference could be drawn that there had been the intention to burn the car and destroy all the evidence. He said that the bullet casings found at the murder scene could also be linked to the Glock semi-automatic pistol found in the car. While there were no actual witnesses to the murder, the jury would be shown a video taken by an American tourist on a passing bus. The jury was told that Eddie Rice, who had been driving the car when it was ambushed by White, would not be giving evidence. The prosecution also made the point that White was involved in Roche's murder as part of a joint enterprise. It was not necessary to establish whether White had actually pulled the trigger or just driven the car. Sammon added that White was one of those two people, and each was as guilty of murder as the other. During the trial the elephant in the room – Paddy Doyle – was brought up in evidence. Detective Inspector Willie McKenna agreed with Defence Senior Counsel, Brendan Grehan, that Gardaí had been told by other sources that Paddy Doyle had been the one who had shot Roche, and that he was on the back of a motorbike when he pulled the trigger. The jury was told that Doyle had been murdered in Spain in 2008, and was known to Gardaí. DI McKenna also said that when Noel Roche's mother, Caroline, arrived at the scene, she named Paddy Doyle as having been responsible. McKenna added that sources, other than Mrs Roche, had given information about Doyle's alleged involvement, and that the Garda investigation could find no evidence that a motorbike had been used in the murder. He added that the driver of the Ford Mondeo in which Noel Roche was shot provided no helpful information to Gardaí. The most interesting part of the trial – and certainly the part that had the potential to cast the most doubts in the minds of jurors about Craig White's guilt – was when Detective Garda Ray Kane from the fingerprint section of the Garda Technical Bureau gave evidence. He told the prosecution that he found three fingerprints and one thumb print on the paper bag that was found in the Peugeot. He subsequently compared them to the prints taken from Craig White. Detective Garda Kane said that he had no doubts that the finger marks found on the bag matched White's prints. He himself had taken fingerprints from White at Raheny Garda Station on 5 December 2005, after White was first arrested. DG Kane matched White's right thumb, left little finger, right forefinger and right middle finger to the fingermarks that he took from the paper bag.

When Brendan Grehan took to his feet to cross examine the Garda, he said that he accepted that Kane made statements in April 2006 and May 2008, in which he said he had identified the thumb print as belonging to Craig White, but Grehan said that he was of the view that the other three prints on the bag did not reach the required standard for presentation as evidence in court. The detective replied that he was never in any doubt that the finger marks were made by White. He then said that the usual standard for print evidence to be accepted in court is if there was a minimum 12 point match. Detective Garda Kane agreed with Brendan Grehan that he had heard about the case, in which the FBI had wrongly identified a man as a suspect in the Madrid bombings based on incorrect fingerprint analysis. The Garda said that he has heard that an independent expert in that

case who had agreed with the FBI's inaccurate findings may
have been influenced by a database search that came back
with a name that had been flagged as being linked to
terrorism. Ray Kane stated that he had searched the
Automated Fingerprint Identification System (AFIS) using a
thumbprint that had been found on the paper bag found in
the car, and that Craig White's name had come back as a
match. He added that no prints had been found from the
Glock in the paper bag, and White's prints were not found
anywhere in or on the Peugeot, apart from the bag. Other
unidentified prints were found. Detective Garda Kane agreed
that while he was of the opinion that Craig White had
handled the bag, he could not tell when he had touched it.
He accepted that prints could persist for years in the right
sort of conditions and also accepted that the presence of
prints on the bag did not necessarily mean that White had
put the gun into it. Nor could he definitively say that White
had put the bag into the car and could not rule out the
possibility that other people, maybe people who wore gloves,
had handled the paper bag.

The rest of the trial was straight forwarded and
uneventful. Craig White did not offer a defence for himself.
When the jury were sent out to deliberate on 29 July, Gardaí
were quietly confident of getting a conviction, but most
agreed that the cross examination on the fingerprint
evidence could have thrown up reasonable doubt. In any
event, the jury of seven men and five women took little more
than half an hour to convict Craig White of Noel Roche's
murder. It was a major victory for the Gardaí who had
investigated the murder and proved that gangland criminals
could not simply get away with murder and would be held
accountable for their actions. Still, the swiftness with which
the jury came back with their decision shocked everybody
who had attended the court case. The worry was that it
would give White grounds for appealing the decision down

the line. Mr Justice Birmingham imposed a mandatory life sentence for the crime, which he said that all sides in the case had agreed was an 'assassination' and a 'gangland hit'. He thanked the jury for presiding over what he described as a 'sensitive trial'. It was indeed sensitive, and the jury roll call had to be held in private each morning, rather than the usual procedure of taking place in open court, because of fears that jury members could be tampered with. Craig White has also been linked to the murder of innocent Latvian mother of two, Baiba Saulite, who was shot dead outside her home in Swords in November 2006. Detectives believe that it was White who knocked at Baiba's door before she was shot, pretending to be a pizza delivery man. The unsuspecting Latvian turned him away, saying she did not order a pizza. In reality the man was making sure she was at home. A few minutes later, a gunman shot her dead as she smoked a cigarette outside her door. White is believed to have driven the getaway car. White had links to the gang run by Martin 'Marlo' Hyland, and it was Hyland who set up the murder. Saulite's estranged husband, Lebanese national Hassan Hassan, is suspected of organising the hit because of a custody dispute. The investigation remains open, and Gardaí have not ruled out the possibility that White could face charges in the future in relation to the murder.

Although Craig White will spend a long time in jail, he did gain respect in criminal circles for keeping his mouth shut and not trying to implicate Paddy Doyle in the slaying, which he could easily have done. Paddy Doyle's DNA was also found at the scene, and if he had returned to Ireland prior to his murder, he would have been arrested and charged with Noel Roche's murder. Nevertheless, White's conviction was a very welcome development.

During the trial of Craig White, Paddy Doyle's father broke his silence on his son's murder and involvement in the Crumlin-Drimnagh feud, when he gave an interview to Niall

Donald of the *Irish Daily Star Sunday*. Donal Doyle claimed
that Paddy had been trying to turn his life around and give
up his life of crime when he was murdered. 'He wished he
could start his life over, that's the hardest thing.' Donal
Doyle admitted his lad was 'no saint' but was a 'brilliant' dad
who wanted to turn his life around. 'Patrick told me he
wished he could start his life again and do it all differently.
He said, "I'd give anything to be able to go out, do a week's
work and come home and have my dinner." But he had got
in too deep and didn't know how to get out.' Donal Doyle
was a staunch anti-drugs campaigner and had fallen out with
his son because of his involvement in crime and drug dealing.
However, they made up shortly before he died. 'We had cut
our ties with Paddy and we hadn't spoken for six years. But
following a family illness, he got a message to me apologising
for the past and we both picked up the phone. I hadn't
spoken to him in a long time and it seemed we were able to
open up to each other a lot more. He told me he felt, by not
being here, he had let his two brothers down because he
wasn't around for them. Paddy had his wild years, like a lot
of young men, and now he was sitting back and taking stock.
In October, I visited him in Spain and we talked about
getting a bit of stability into his life and start moving away
from these people he had classed as friends. Five months later
he was dead.'

Donal Doyle also spoke about how Darren Geoghegan's
grandfather had contacted him to tell him that he didn't
believe that Doyle was responsible for Geoghegan's murder.
'Darren was raised by his grandfather, and after Patrick was
killed they came over and told us how much they loved our
son – the two of them were very close friends. They told us
they had never dreamed even for a second that Patrick was
involved in Darren's death. We were gobsmacked. We have
kept in touch ever since. They are lovely people and are
going through hell just like us.'

Despite his involvement in crime, Donal Doyle said that his son was a good father. 'He was always very protective of his family and he was a brilliant father to his kids. Patrick was a very thoughtful person; I think that was part of his problem – people were able to zone in on him. He was no saint; he could be as hard as nails, but, at the same time, he had a very soft side to him.'

Mr Doyle believes that his son's involvement in drugs has been exaggerated even though he has previous convictions for drugs offences and masterminded the smuggling of tens of millions of euro worth of drugs from Spain into Ireland.

'Patrick was made out to be a major drug importer, but his only conviction for drugs was when he was caught with five wraps of speed when he was 17. The fact is the Spanish police had no intelligence files on Paddy; they knew nothing about him being a drug importer. He is also made out to be a hitman and an enforcer, but it is all supposition. The Gardaí might believe this but they never arrested him for it.'

Doyle says that he learned about his son's death from the television and says the Gardaí never informed him. There are protocols to go through before Gardaí are able to inform relations about the deaths of Irish nationals abroad, but Doyle is nonetheless unhappy at how his family was treated. 'I was speaking to Patrick an hour before he was killed and we just talked about his son, just normal family talk. We got all our news from the television, but we were never officially informed by the Gardaí. We thought until we get a knock on the door we don't know for sure. The reports said there were three people in the jeep after all. We stayed up all night waiting for someone to get in touch with us. The next morning I phoned up the Department of Foreign Affairs and told them I had been informed by the media that my son was killed in Spain. I said I was a taxpayer, my wife is a taxpayer, we have no criminal convictions and we are entitled to courtesy. Eventually, later that day, after another phone call to the Department of Foreign Affairs, we finally got a call from Fitzgibbon Street station.'

During this interview, which gave a fascinating insight into how the families of criminals are affected by their crime, Donal Doyle concluded by talking about the support he had received from the community where he lives in the north-inner city.

'The odd person would avoid you, mightn't catch your eye, but on the whole, I can't say enough about the support we have received. People know what we have been through and what we've tried to do over the years. They aren't going to judge us over what has been written about Patrick in a few articles. You have to take what consolation you can. We made our peace with Patrick and he gave us beautiful grandchildren.'

CONCLUSION

By the beginning of 2010, the Crumlin-Drimnagh feud had settled down. Now, hopefully, the worst part is over, but as former Justice Minister Michael McDowell found out to his cost with his 'the sting of the dying wasp' comment, predictions can often come back to haunt you. There are several reasons why the tension has subsided, but the most important factor has arguably been the introduction of amended legislation to the Criminal Justice Bill in July 2009. Under the new laws people suspected of being members of criminal gangs can be arrested and tried in the non-jury Special Criminal Court. In this court a Chief Superintendent's belief that the suspect is a member of a gang is enough to see the person convicted. This sent shockwaves through gangs around the country, which led to senior members fleeing abroad to places like the Netherlands and Spain. The Thompson and Rattigan gang members were no different – the main figures are almost permanently out of the country. Freddie Thompson now calls Puerto Banus home, where he is usually accompanied by several of his trusted lieutenants. He only flies back to Ireland occasionally. Another rumour of his death spread in October 2009, but again it proved to be a hoax. Although by the end of 2009, nobody had been arrested under the new legislation, much less convicted, the very threat of arrest on sight has proven to be enough to keep criminals on their toes and on the run. This development is obviously warmly welcomed on the streets of Crumlin and Drimnagh.

Ironically, Rattigan gang members have also ended up in

Puerto Banus, and the two factions regularly bump into each other. Things are different there, as they don't seem to have the will to fight each other any more, and they appear to live in relative harmony. Perhaps they realise that the feud was pointless and achieved nothing except needless loss of life. Traditionally, the violence has been orchestrated by just a handful of individuals. Anthony Cannon's death and Wayne McNally's jail sentence were real turning points, because two of the most feared and violent members of the Rattigan gang were out of action permanently. With them out of the picture, there wasn't really anybody prepared to step up to the plate and replace them in doing any violent dirty work. If victory can be claimed by either side, then there is no doubt that the Thompson faction has come out of the hostilities the healthier. Freddie Thompson's cronies are now concentrating on developing their drug dealing business rather than being involved in a near permanent war.

Although Spain is still where the majority of product is sourced from, things have changed since Paddy Doyle's murder. The negative publicity that the Spanish authorities received in the aftermath of Doyle's murder led to a severe crackdown on foreign drug barons, with local police and Europol now redoubling their efforts to end the cushy lifestyles of the drugs barons. This has worked and drug seizures in Ireland in 2009 were way up, with large seizures happening on almost a weekly basis. This has resulted in a severe reduction in the amount of drugs available on the streets. This has led to customers buying so called 'legal highs' on the internet, and shunning traditional drugs, like cocaine, ecstasy and heroin, because they are increasingly hard to come by. Both gangs still manage to smuggle drugs into the country, but the seizures have really hit them in the pocket, and their profit margins have gone way down. As a result, the drugs business at the moment is not as lucrative as it was a few years ago.

Although Brian Rattigan's gang has effectively disintegrated, except for a handful of hardcore youngsters, it was remarkable that he maintained his power base for so long. Rattigan has now been in prison for nearly eight years but still managed to lead a mini-army from behind bars. It is a testament to his sheer force of character that he has brought so many people with him for such a long period of time. In December 2009, Brian Rattigan was finally convicted of the murder of Declan Gavin following a second trial. He was handed a mandatory life sentence, which means that it will be at least 2025 before he is likely to be released. It is inconceivable that, when he is eventually freed, Rattigan will be allowed to live for long. By the time he breathes air as a free man, his gang will have moved on. With Rattigan's senior people either dead or permanently out of the picture, the next generation will take over and seize control of his territory. They have little or no loyalty to Rattigan because they were so young when he was arrested. If he tries to reassert control or steps on their toes, he will be taken out, a bit like Thompson or Rattigan would take out John Gilligan when he is finally freed. That is just the way it works in the dog-eat-dog world of gangland. If you are out of sight, you are out of mind, and when you re-emerge, it does not always go down well. If the feud is to reignite, it will be the next generation of thugs waging war, but there is no evidence so far that this is going to happen.

Brian Rattigan's family have paid a high price for his involvement in criminality. His brother Joey was murdered to send out a message to him. His sister, Sharon, was shot in the leg, while she was unsuccessfully trying to stop her partner Shay O'Byrne being shot dead. Brian's older brother, Ritchie, is a virtual prisoner in his own home because there is a contract out on his life, even though he has no involvement in the feud. Again, he is seen as an easy target. Through the face of unthinkable tragedy and adversity,

Dinah Rattigan has been there trying to hold her family together. It must be very difficult for her. The events of August 2001, when Brian stabbed Declan Gavin to death, continue to have consequences today for so many people. Indeed, many of those who attended Joey Rattigan's 18th birthday party celebrations have fallen victim to what some might call a 'curse'. John Roche, who first saw Declan Gavin outside Abrakebabra and then went back to the party and told the others, was murdered as part of the feud. Joey Rattigan was also murdered, as were Darren Geoghegan and Paddy Doyle, who arrived at the restaurant just minutes after Declan Gavin was stabbed. Shay O'Byrne, who was at the party with Sharon Rattigan, was also shot dead. Shane Maloney, who drove his Nissan Micra to the scene of the murder, was handed a lengthy sentence for drug possession. Karl Kavanagh was jailed for possession of a firearm, Brian Rattigan for drugs possession and shooting at Gardaí. Andrew Murray, who was present outside Abrakebabra when the murder happened, was jailed for two years for contempt of court after refusing to give evidence during Rattigan's second murder trial. The events of the night of Joey Rattigan's 18th birthday party have had consequences for many people nine years after it took place, and the lives of dozens of people have been ruined because of what happened that night.

Freddie Thompson has come through the worst of the feud unscathed, which is remarkable considering the central role that he played. When Thompson was stopped and searched by a senior Garda in 2008, and told that his life was in danger, he responded that the police had been telling him that he was going to be shot since he was 14 years old. Although Freddie is nominally in charge of his gang and is the public face of the feud, he is not really taken seriously by his fellow gangsters. The real brains behind his operation float in the background, and shun publicity or anything that brings them to the attention of the Gardaí and media. There are probably five of these individuals, and most cannot be named for legal reasons. These men are happy for Freddie to bask in the media limelight, which he is only too happy to do, and the thoughts of their names being published horrifies them. The future for Freddie Thompson looks grim, though he has defied the odds for so long by staying alive that Gardaí would not be in the least bit surprised if he lives to a ripe old age.

The 'G' District has always been seen as one of the toughest areas to police in the county, but the dedication and skill of the brave Gardaí who work there does not go unnoticed by Garda management. Many of the senior officers who police Crumlin and Drimnagh have gone on to be promoted. Many of them must take a lot of credit for the fact that, during the feud, the murder count was not far greater. Detective Inspector Brian Sutton, who was well respected by both feuding gangs because of his tireless efforts at brokering peace, was promoted to Superintendent in June 2009. He is now based in Boyle, Co. Roscommon. Another one of the most influential officers involved in keeping a lid on hostilities is Detective Sergeant John Walsh. Walsh has a knowledge of the feud that is second to none, and this was recognised in February 2009, when he was promoted to Inspector. He is currently based in Arklow, Co. Wicklow. Detective Garda Ronan Lafferty, who worked out of Sundrive Road Garda Station, has been promoted to Detective Sergeant. He is now a senior investigator in the Organised Crime Unit.

The hard work of the Gardaí in the 'A' District of Kevin Street and Kilmainham has also not gone unnoticed. Detective Inspector Gabriel O'Gara was often awoken in the early hours of the morning to be told that the Crumlin and Drimnagh feud had spilled over into his patch, leaving him with another murder investigation on his hands. O'Gara was

promoted to Superintendent in February 2008. After a short
stretch in Kilrush, Co. Clare, he was transferred back to
Dublin, where he is now the Detective Superintendent in
charge of investigating serious crime in the Dublin
Metropolitan South Central region. He mainly works in
Pearse Street Garda Station.

In early 2010, Freddie Thompson and Brian Rattigan are
really looking like the John Gilligans of the new millennium.
Garda crackdowns and a relentless war have seen them both
fade into shadows of their former selves. Rattigan is in a
prison cell alone with his thoughts of his fading empire.
Freddie Thompson is on the run in Spain, scared to death of
coming home because there is a bullet with his name on it.
Meanwhile, the next generation of dealers jockey for
position, looking at how vulnerable the two gang bosses are
and biding their time until they take over, much like Brian
Rattigan and Declan Gavin did after Gilligan's demise.
While this goes on, the families of sixteen young men
continue to grieve for their loved ones, and a community
struggles to come to terms with the devastating feud that will
mean that Crumlin and Drimnagh will be forever associated
with death and destruction.